LETTERS
FROM YOUNG
ACTIVISTS

LETTERS
FROM YOUNG
ACTIVISTS

TODAY'S REBELS SPEAK OUT

Edited by
Dan Berger, Chesa Boudin, and Kenyon Farrow

Preface by Bernardine Dohrn

NATION
BOOKS

LETTERS FROM YOUNG ACTIVISTS
TODAY'S REBELS SPEAK OUT

Published by
Nation Books
An Imprint of Avalon Publishing Group
245 West 17th St., 11th Floor
New York, NY 10011

AVALON
publishing group incorporated

Copyright © 2005 by Chesa Boudin, Kenyon Farrow, Dan Berger
Preface copyright © 2005 by Bernardine Dohrn

Nation Books is a co-publishing venture of the Nation Institute and Avalon Publishing Group Incorporated.

Library of Congress Cataloging-in-Publication Data is available.

ISBN: 1-56025-747-4
ISBN 13: 978-1-56025-747-9

9 8 7 6 5 4 3 2 1

Book design by Maria E. Torres
Printed in the United States of America
Distributed by Publishers Group West

For people everywhere who struggle for peace, justice, and liberation; for the movements of yesterday, today, and tomorrow, that act with the promise of a better world

CONTENTS

SECTION II

ACKNOWLEDGMENTS

Much like the Movement, a book like this could not be possible without the support of wide array of people—far too many to list by name here. First and foremost we owe all of our authors a huge debt of gratitude for their hard work, seemingly endless rounds of edits, and commitment. We have lifelong activist and educator Bill Ayers to thank for guidance throughout this process, particularly his early encouragement as we developed the idea for the book and began looking for a publisher. Also a special thanks to Thane Rosenbaum for generously offering his advice at the onset of this project. Much respect and appreciation to Andrew Lavalle and Christopher Abueg, who designed the www.lettersfromyoung activists.org Web site so that we could make more letters available online. Several elder activist women—including Kai Lumumba Barrow, Bernardine Dohrn, Yuri Kochiyama, Elizabeth "Betita" Martinez, and Gwendolyn Zoharah Simmons—played key roles in advising us on the book, and we thank them for their time, energy, feedback, and for adding their names to this project. A special thanks to Michele Martin and John Oakes at Avalon Publishing Group for their support from the beginning. Ruth Baldwin and Carl Bromley, our editors at Nation Books, immediately saw the value in this project and were more than patient while working with three geographically far-flung editors over the course of countless changes in our lives, jobs, locations, and more. Their feedback on and willingness to discuss the political direction of the book or the minutiae of writing were of immeasurable help—and proved a welcome reminder of the need for independent publishing. Finally, each of us, in notably different ways, has our families to thank for leading us to politics and for giving us the space and support to dedicate ourselves to this book—and to the Movement.

PREFACE

BERNARDINE DOHRN

In my lifetime, young people have changed the world. From Little Rock to Greensboro, from Selma to Soweto, in Tien An Mien and Seattle, it was the young who dared to act in the face of the overwhelming certainty that nothing could be done. It was their direct action that educated, opened doors and minds, shattered the taken-for-granted.

It will happen again. It's happening now.

This volume, *Letters from Young Activists*, arrives at a moment of U.S. triumphalism, permanent war, global domination, and reactionary fundamentalism so deliberately intimidating, so insistent, so totalizing that we are meant *not* to see. The gritty consequences of empire at home include economic collapse, job flight, a national security state, unprecedented caging of people of color, renewed assaults against women, gays, and fundamental liberties, ecological plunder, barricaded and isolated North America as a fortress against immigrants, and the pandering of fear. Against this milieu, *Letters* is a clarion call of hope, defiance, critical analysis, humor, irony, and self-conscious insistence that the queer, the Palestinian, the immigrant, the privileged, the children of prisoners and hip-hopsters have arrived. *Young Activists* asks us to wake up from our state of amnesia and despair. They are taking over. These voices are united not in a strategic plan, nor a cult; they are not a political party or a formation. But don't overlook their unity, their networks, their umbrellas. Put your ear to the ground and read on.

For us, those parents of the mythical sixties generation (now well into our sixties), they have some generous, sobering, and sharp words. But they invite us to come along, to engage them within their terms. In their embrace, they are far too forgiving.

For we have, despite our dreams and labors, left them to inherit a planet of rampant injustice and inequality far worse than the world we once grabbed by the throat. Today, the three great dangers that Dr. Martin Luther King Jr. warned of in his last year—militarism, racism, and materialism—have re-emerged unabashed. Empire is openly the goal, U.S. military outposts, weapons, and wars multiply across the continents, old and new racial hierarchies are invented and promoted, neoliberal capitalism is imposed, the North is glutted with stuff and sporting perfect teeth but feeling poor, while the global South is fighting for survival, for life, for land and humanity. Here, in the belly of the beast, we are encouraged to beware, to wrap ourselves in homeland security and superficial patriotism, and to see the world as us vs. them, civilization vs. barbarians, good vs. evil.

"I battle," wrote Fanon, "for the creation of a human world— that is a world of reciprocal recognition." This is precisely the common vision glimpsed by this yeasty ferment of political narrators— to value every human life equally. They reject the notion that Iraqi lives are not as sacred as American, that the massacre of 7,000 Muslim boys and men taken out, hands bound with wire behind their backs and executed at Srebrenica on a single day in July 1995 can pass unnoticed. Did we know? Did we respond? Are not their lives equally worthy to those precious lives lost in the World Trade Center on 9/11?

They are storing memories in their hard drives, these young

activists, naming the savage, "shock and awe" bombing and razing of the ancient civilian town of Fallujah as a war crime akin in its barbarity to the leveling of Guernica, the caging of two million people—largely African-American and Latino—in prisons in the U.S. in the name of public safety as racism, the appropriation of women's sexuality and reproductive health care as the province of the state as blatant violations of human rights. These voices sing the truth they see, they rap their words into arrows carrying secret messages, they seize their burden as intellectuals and stuff it into their wandering backpacks, they practice and they yearn (as we all do) for reciprocal recognition.

Dr. King, at his most radical, the year before he was assassinated, said: "The greatest purveyor of violence on this earth is my own country." That was four decades ago, yet it is perhaps more true today. The greatest purveyor of violence on this earth is my own country. For those of us who have the unique responsibility of living in the U.S., whether we call ourselves Americans or reject the narrow association, whether citizen or exile, anarchist, Marxist, artist, environmentalist, queer, feminist, or Buddhist, our tasks include building independent opposition and alternatives to the endless war on terrorism and the centralized and secret federal, militarized state, that must, of necessity, accompany empire both at home and abroad.

This resistance can take the form of humor, art, militancy, or door-to-door organizing but the stance is what Edward Said called "a spirit in opposition, rather than in accommodation." It is a choice to be vibrant dissenters, to question, to engage in what Foucault calls "a relentless erudition," to remain insurgent, independent of the powerful to try to "speak truth to power." It is the dead opposite of silences and aversions, of expediency, of orthodoxy and slogans, of mandatory patriotic nationalism.

HISTORY AND MEMORY

These young oppositionists ask embarrassing questions. They expose the pieties and dogmas of the powerful, stand on the side of the marginalized, silenced, and powerless. "To act is to be committed, and to be committed is to be in danger," wrote James Baldwin in *The Fire Next Time*. Today's young activists are awake and alert to the death and destruction done in our name, but they agree with Baldwin that "it is not permissible that the authors of devastation should also be innocent. It is the innocence which constitutes the crime."

Rejecting innocence, they come up against the need to understand history and to document their own memories.

As digital children at the end of the Cold War, coming of age as witnesses to at least three open wars and multiple additional U.S. invasions (Bosnia/Kosovo, Somalia, Haiti), teen observers during the collapse of expectations for a world of peace, awash in the gilded '90s extravagant consumerism of video games and shopping malls, they joined and helped to cohere the global justice movement exposing the WTO in Seattle in 1999, partying into the millennium, maturing as political activists at the moment of 9/11—these authors command our attention. They chronicle their own time, now the time for all of us.

It is fitting that the authors of *Letters* assume what the Nobel laureate Wole Soyinka of Nigeria calls "the near intolerable burden of memory." Memory and documentation require imagination; they reject amnesia.

How do today's young organizers deal with their own near intolerable burden of memory? Especially in the U.S., which has been called the United States of Amnesia? We don't know *who* we are or *where* we are. We talk of "minorities" but today's "minorities" are the majority in the world, on this continent and soon within the United States. We are in the midst of gender role transformations eroding the binary edges of female/male, urging us to rethink stereotypes and pieties. Can we find Afghanistan on a map? Name the six countries that border Iraq? We are urged to pay attention. Remembering and forgetting are both political acts.

Letters is an unreconciled book, filled with contradictions and uncertainties, unfinished, in motion, still becoming. It involves choices, blind spots, and problematic absences. It is not complete, nor regimented, but can be tasted as fragments, revelations, a view of the landscapes and habits of some young activists.

This book teems with history and memory, etched by the young. It bothers, agitates, and alarms. "Art hurts," wrote the great poet laureate of Illinois, Gwendolyn Brooks. "Art urges voyages." These activists' tales are being told, their global fabric woven. They write to their parents, each other, to the sixties, to the Movement, and to their future selves. As with any edited volume, voices are missing. But the invitation is open for dialogue. And the hunger for discussion, for community, for public space is explosive.

NO NOSTALGIA FOR THE "SIXTIES"

Amid the dichotomy of new and old, we are the parents (yes, literally), aunts, godmothers, and conjurers of these young activists. They, miraculously and perhaps foolishly, are not dismissive. As a cacophony of voices, these young militants are sharply intense, embarrassingly earnest, skeptical, fiercely independent, and contrary, beyond oppositional. They want, perhaps, more than we can give. They seem to be willing to let us join in.

A few ruminations from an aging "sixties" Midwest gal to young activists.

I reject feeling nostalgic for the bittersweet struggles of the past.

It is clear that the sixties, which was never really The Sixties, is being wielded as a bludgeon against you, a barrier, a legendary era that can never be equaled today. In fact, the sixties was annually declared "dead" by the pundits of *Time* magazine and *Newsweek* beginning in 1963 and throughout the mid-seventies. During the subsequent three and a half decades, there has been a relentless campaign to promote four myths about those radical social upheavals. These legends about the so-called Sixties must be on the table to be scrutinized by today's young activists. The generation of *Letters* needs us to be real with them, to let go of disabling illusions.

First, the sixties is enshrined as a heroic time of huge demonstrations, militancy, and organizing. It was never all that.

Sixties activism was almost always small, isolated, surrounded by hostile, angry crowds. The groundbreaking actions of the students who joined the Student Non-Violent Coordinating Committee (SNCC), the women who stood for an end to patriarchy, and the veterans, draft resisters, and deserters who defied the military machine, are legendary now because they were right about history and morality. Overwhelmingly, their courage was the quiet kind, the inventive sort, often unrecognized, not showy. Millions took a step away from the path well traveled, left the career track, lived on subsistence pay, learned to talk to strangers about politics, went to the point of production, invented communes, built schools, dug into communities, revived midwifery, seized and exposed the universities, were arrested, broke with family expectations and tradition. Black Panthers, GI organizers, environmentalists, Young Lords, gays and lesbians—the anarchy, the imagination, the gravity, the invisibility to the media, especially the failures, are familiar to today's young activists. So is the sense of isolation, the inadequacy to the task, the frustration with not being heard, the drowning in the American la la machine. The inability to stop the relentless escalation of war and occupation each and every day for a decade. The enormity of the hold of white supremacy on American life, North and South, inside and out. Divisions among ourselves, worst of all.

At the height of 1968's upheaval, activists at Michigan State felt dismayed that they were not strong and powerful, like those in Ann

Arbor. Militants in Ann Arbor measured themselves unfavorably against the struggle at Columbia in New York. And at Columbia or Cornell or Berkeley, organizers were unhappy that they were not meeting the high bar set by the May Day events in France, where workers and students brought the government to the brink. The challenge now, as then, is living as a radical organizer in your own time, your own place. The difficulty then and now is working away during what the great educator and founder of Hylander, Myles Horton called "Valley Times" while longing for "Mountain Times." It involves simultaneously acting and doubting.

Today's episodic massive organizing achievements can similarly be followed by eerie calm, business-as-usual, invisibility, the sense of never having been. Global solidarity and inventive militancy among AIDS activists, followed by . . . labor rights and global justice shutting down the World Trade Organization in Seattle, but . . . brilliant unity and tactical zaniness at the '04 Republican National Convention building toward . . . the devastating deflation of electoral defeats and setbacks to independent organizing . . . GLBTQ direct action and exuberant breakthroughs followed by counterreaction and withdrawals, momentarily washed up on the shore. . . . This was true also for all but a few seconds of the roughly fifteen years that constitute the sixties. The consciousness of today is both ahead of and behind the peaks of the past. That was prelude. Now is where we stand.

Second, and paradoxically in counterpoint to the above romanticization, there has been a relentless thirty year campaign to demonize and criminalize the sixties. Militant resistance is portrayed as criminal, mass rebellion transformed into mob action, courageous choices derided as self-serving, moderately outrageous comments in the heat of the moment seized upon and repeated *ad nauseam* as if they were the whole story or true. Fine leaders are degraded and their contributions dismissed due to personal limitations and all-too-real flaws. This is the organized, contemporary, and legal companion to the illegal, secret Counterintelligence Program (COINTELPRO) of the FBI which used disinformation, harassment, and "dirty tricks" against the predominately white Movement while using assassination, infiltration, and imprisonment against people of color. This demonization of activists was the pretext for physical assassination and character assassination. It finds us still with scores of political prisoners unjustly incarcerated from that time. The sixties was, in short, neither that good nor that bad.

Third, the struggle has been commodified, sold back to us as clothing, music, drugs, and film. It is trivialized, sucked of content, leaving only the husks of oldies, tattoos, and faded murals. What remains invisible is surviving for decades on twenty dollars a week, living communally, doing what had to be done without funding from foundations or the approval of program grants, stepping off the career track, risking exile or courts-martial, turning Left off the interstate. These were and still are choices made by the privileged as well as the modest, first-generation college, working class youth and immigrants who comprised the Movement.

Fourth is the lethal, deceptive telling of sixties' history as if it were predictable and known, smoothing out the turmoil, the turbulence, the anarchy, and the ethical choices. The pat illusions that: We all opposed the Vietnam War, or We all were relieved that civil rights were granted to African Americans, or The media helped end the Vietnam War.

But history is seized, not given, change wrenched as a result of struggles from below. The women who challenged the mangling of our bodies—the sisters did not know how it was going to turn out. The youth on the freedom rides, the lunch counters, the voter registration drives, urban insurrections, demonstrations against police brutality, struggles for Puerto Rican independence, Chicano liberation, Native American land, resources and dignity—no one knew how it would turn out. The young men who resisted the draft, who deserted the military, who fought in Vietnam and returned to join the antiwar movement and threw their medals back at the White House, the veterans who today warn and educate about the dread of real war—they did not know how it would turn out. Dr. King himself was an angry, developing radical—a constant work in progress, not an airbrushed saint.

When we think about historical moments, of course, we each read ourselves into it in heroic ways. It's so obvious now. We all imagine that if we had lived during slavery, we would have been a catalyst for emancipation, we know what we would risk. Similarly, in our hearts we believe that had we been alive in Europe at the time of Nazi Germany, we would have been part of the Resistance, we would have hidden refugees, we would surely have stepped up to the historic challenge.

What are today's crises of human rights and how will we be remembered? For what we did and for what we failed to do? How do we narrate and act in this historical moment? The young authors of *Letters* are living in their time, challenging the renewed U.S. project of empire. If we are lucky, we will be with them, riding the next waves.

IMAGINATION AND HOPE

Being a revolutionary, a radical, an anarchist, a rebel requires imagination, now more than ever.

Today, the United States constitutes 4.8 percent of the world's people, yet controls 60 percent of the world's wealth. And 1 percent of world's richest receive as much income as 57 percent of the world's poorest. As Venezuelan President Hugo Chávez likes to note, if the rest of the world consumed oil at the current rate of the U.S., all the oil (and & reserves) would be depleted in some nineteen days—an ongoing ecological disaster that cannot last.

This inequitable and unjust situation can only be sustained by naked force, domination of resources, media, finance, culture, and, critically, the sense that there is no other way—that global U.S. dominated neoliberal capitalism is *inevitable and unending*.

The savage U.S. war and occupation of Iraq, and of Afghanistan, the permanent war against "terrorism," the militarization of the economy, culture, and institutions, and the consequent erosion of democracy, transparency, and liberty at home are normalized, presented as a given, a natural phenomenon. The very notion that we will go along, collude, itself requires us to respond with urgency. Five years ago, the U.S. spent as much on its military as the next fifteen countries combined. Today, the U.S. spends as much as *all* other countries combined.

To stand against this plunder in the face the drumbeat of such overwhelming certainty that What You Do Won't Make a Difference requires a radical leap of audacity, of imagination. It is essential to the project of empire that people cannot imagine another way, that the inevitability of peoples' powerlessness is overwhelming.

This idea, then, is the ultimate subversion, this imaginative notion of popular efficacy. To act in defense of humanity requires us to think, as the World Social Forum claims, that Another World is Possible. Indeed, Another World is Necessary. Of course, no one can deny the military, economic, and cultural power of empire. But what seems invincible can be riddled with crises. South African apartheid is overturned. Franco's Spain becomes a beacon of transformation. Venezuela charts a new peaceful, democratic, Bolivarian revolution, altering relationships throughout the continent. We need not be excessively romantic to insist upon trying to act with awareness and unity with the people—the marginalized, excluded, and impoverished—who are rescuing themselves, and who agree with these young activists that the humanist solutions go beyond the borders of any single country. New thinking is required: revolutionary democracy, reinvented socialism, transformed relationships and economic structures.

With its powerful young Arab-American voices, *Letters* rejects the new racist categories, the "othering" of Arabs, Muslims, and immigrants, shreds the good vs. evil perspective of the Bush/Cheney/Rumsfeld administrations; the book dismisses the "lesser of two evils" rationale for U.S. torture, detention without trial, the horrors of Guantánamo and Abu Ghraib. It gives face to Arab Americans, struggles openly with the Israel-Palestinian claims to the same land, and humanizes. It is bound together by the notion of radical change and the hope that activism and imagination can, as Susan Sontag wrote, "train, and exercise, our ability to weep for those who are not us or ours."

Letters uses hip-hop and cultural transformation to break down walls. It includes Xicana and Third Wave voices, lesbian labor organizers, and the anguish of wrestling with Jewish and Israeli identity. It has letters to unknown parents killed by U.S. wars, to imprisoned parents, to both oblivious and adoring parents. *Letters* narrates being a teacher, a Muslim, punk rocker, working in Honduras, growing up in Texas, rejecting integration, becoming an organizer, an agitator, a mobilizer, an imaginator.

These *Letters* share what the late, luminous poet June Jordan wrote of as "a reverence for human life, an intellectual trust in sensuality as a means of knowledge and of unity . . . aspiration to a believable, collective voice."

These young narrators offer here their history, their memories, imagination, and hope. "I have hopes for myself," wrote Gwendolyn Brooks at the age of fifty as she encountered the young Black Freedom and Black Consciousness movement. Because I have hopes for these young militants in *Letters*, because I, too, have hopes for my sons and granddaughter, because I have hopes for comrades young and old, for people throughout the world, and for you. I have, also, hopes for myself.

INTRODUCTION

Dear Reader,

The future is now. We are the ones inheriting it, writing the history, fighting the battles, learning the lessons and planning for the struggles ahead. You'd better listen up. And quick. Previous generations of radical movements set out to change the world, and our activism takes shape on the backs of what those before us did. We learn from their successes as well as their failures. We are a new generation of rebels.

Watching the $40 million coronation of Bush's second term, one might be lulled into thinking that our generation is apathetic, narcoleptic, peripatetic, lethargic, sophomoric, and generally soporific. The fact is that our generation is energetic, frenetic, epic, apoplectic, enthusiastic, and more precisely eolic. The winds are blowing, and the weathervane points in our direction. This is your personal invitation to get up close and personal with twenty-first-century social movements and the people making it all happen.

The possibilities for activism in support of progressive social change are expanding and infinite. Today's social movements are so broad based and diverse that no one voice could possibly do them justice. Mainstream discourse tends to isolate today's young activists in the all-too-neat dichotomy of black-clad-crazy-White-anarchists vs. naïve-liberal-White-do-gooders. Even the Left bestows young activists with its own ultimatums, often telling us, for example, that Labor is the only voice of and for the Movement. And yet the reality is infinitely more complex. Today's social movements are on the frontlines of working for racial, economic, gender, environmental, and global justice. Some of us work in unions, but the U.S. labor movement does not define our generation's struggles. *Letters from Young Activists* brings together dozens of visionaries from across the country as they dialogue with the past, engage with present realities, and imagine a righteous future.

The writers included in *Letters From Young Activists* are people ten to thirty-one years old, whose activism emerges from our poor, working-class, and middle-class backgrounds. We are everywhere, but are concentrated on the coasts. Some of us were born into politically conscious households but most of us found politics at a young age through friends or music scenes; our negative experiences with police, parents, or teachers; or because we couldn't stand by and watch the injustices that surround us. We are Black, Puerto Rican, Chicana/o, Salvadoran, Palestinian, White, Haitian, Chinese, Indian, Tamil, and Native American—and we are all, in some sense, responsible for the future of the United States. We are atheist, Christian, Jewish, spiritual, pagan, Muslim, practitioners of Santeria and Ifa—and yet we have a common faith. We proudly declare that we are transgender, lesbian, queer, gay, bisexual, heterosexual, and hetero-flexible—are you sure you aren't one of us? We are preppy campus organizers, dumpster-diving punks, immigrants, former prisoners, the children of prisoners, Rhodes scholars, Iraqi war veterans, labor organizers, hip-hop heads, vogueing ball queens, and club kids—and these letters open our doors to you. Our movements—from women's rights to antiwar, from overhauling the criminal justice system to practicing international solidarity—directly impact and implicate you. Won't you come in and join us?

In the summer of 2003, the three of us had never met but were faced with the common challenges of living in the heart of an aggressive empire on the attack at home and abroad. We were all engaged in our local communities in a range of organizing activities, but looking for a way to do more. We were tired of the frightfully arrogant and completely off base ways in which mainstream discourse defined the issues young activists are thinking about, questioning, and struggling with. We were looking for new ways to connect our local organizing to a broader national and international Movement. Simply put, our generation of activists needed a platform to define ourselves.

The three of us have diverse political perspectives and personal backgrounds. Still, as three men, one Black and two White, we could not possibly purport to represent the broad movements we are a part of. Given our desire to include as wide a range of perspectives from the Movement as possible, we enlisted the help of some elders to constitute an all woman-of-color advisory board. Kai Lumumba Barrow, Yuri Kochiyama, Elizabeth "Betita" Martinez, and Gwendolyn Zoharah Simmons generously gave their time, support, and resources to this project. These dynamic sisters have long histories of work within radical social movements, as well as support for the work of young people. Their lives and work are the true example of the art of mentoring, helping give young people, so often marginalized, a voice. They so clearly understand the meaning of dialogue, of helping teach without standing in the way, of recognizing that movements can and should be respectfully intergenerational. Thank you mothers, thank you sisters, thank you.

Just as the most successful protests and organizing rely on not one voice, but many, so too does this book. We chose to solicit letters because the format creates a level playing field for potential contributing writers. While activists associated with the academy have played a vital role in social movements, many books by and about activists often drown out the grassroots. By doing a book of letters, we hope to create spaces for all activists, especially those not traditionally looked to for social or intellectual commentary. The following letters have a range of approaches and voices, but the format itself introduces the possibility for dialogue to take place. Letter writing is one of the oldest traditions of story telling; blending the personal and the political, they offer the greatest potential to speak to the widest range of people.

As individuals, each of the three editors has a sustained history of organizing and activism in a range of political movements on our campuses, in our communities, and in our country. Dan has worked as an antiracism and prison activist in Florida and Pennsylvania and spent several years as the editor for *Onward*, an internationally distributed anarchist newspaper that emerged out of the global justice movement. A graduate student in Philadelphia and a member of the anti-imperialist affinity group Resistance in Brooklyn, Dan continues to write and organize in support of political prisoners and against racism and patriarchy. Chesa is an antiwar and criminal justice activist and has used campus organizing, writing, public speaking, and travel abroad to organize his global communities. Chesa is currently working in support of the Venezuelan democratic revolution and living in Caracas. Kenyon has worked with FIERCE!—an LGBT youth of color community organizing project devoted to stopping police harassment and gender profiling of queer youth—and served as the Southern regional coordinator for Critical Resistance, the national prison industrial complex abolition organization. Kenyon now works as the communications and public education coordinator for New York State Black Gay Network. We all draw on extensive networks of activist contacts, from South Chicago to the Deep South, from university students to political prisoners, from movements based on rural development to those rooted in urban gender identity.

Our recruitment process for securing the letters was divided into three broad phases. First, we each invited individual activists whom we knew would make valuable contributions to particular sections of this project. Next, we sent out an open solicitation across e-mail listservs and Web sites to invite contributions from a still wider range of activists. Finally, with the help of our advisory board, we recruited writers to fill any remaining gaps in content and diversity of voices. Inevitably, there are holes in content and gaps in the diversity of backgrounds and perspectives represented in this collection. Such errors represent the limitations of this kind of project and our own mistakes and shortcomings, rather than those of the Movement itself. In order to give voice to more writers than we could possibly fit in one book, we built a Web site—www.lettersfrom youngactivists.org—where you can find a range of letters we wanted to make public.

We hope that the collaborative nature of this book will make the sum greater than its parts. Like any successful protest, the group is more powerful, inclusive, and complex when organized and brought together as one. This, then, was one of our primary tasks as editors—to organize dozens of letters and different authors to make common cause, to draw on and celebrate the diversity of the contributors and at the same time unify their words and struggles.

Young people have historically played a major role in progressive social change, and our experiences in a variety of social movements are vital to understanding what the world has in store for it. From ending sexual assault to stopping war and building counterinstitutions that mirror our political beliefs, young activists are involved in a wide range of thinking, writing, discussing, marching, building, protesting, critiquing, going to jail for, and organizing around issues that are critical the world over.

In *Letters from Young Activists*, the Movement is broadly conceived of as those forces united around opposition to imperial war and oppression, and through our support for participatory democracy and freedom from exploitation and violence. This Movement is not yet as cohesive or powerful as it will need to be to bring about necessary change—but the journey has begun. Our generation is capable of putting forward a diverse yet coherent political platform, one that is antiracist, pro-feminist, queer-positive, democratic, and that challenges the forces of militarism, authoritarianism, and rapacious capital. Under this broad political umbrella, we can break the isolation new activists often feel while supporting existing organizing.

Despite this broad political unity, the Movement is far from monolithic. Indeed, we must take on the Movement even as we focus on challenging oppressive U.S. political-economic institutions and cultural imperialism. Young people across the country create the space to be (self) critical of the Movement, to present cogent arguments on its strengths and weaknesses, and to suggest new directions for activism. We challenge reductionist one-dimensional images of what an activist is, does, or looks like. Above all, social justice movements today explore the issues and debates facing the world. In articulating the frameworks through which young people approach the issues of today, we draw on our experiences and backgrounds, discussing the issues on our terms, as organizers at the forefront of social justice struggles.

A diversity of voices, perspectives, and motivations is strength for our Movement. Incorporating such a collection of voices is something inherent to all of our political goals: to create an open, democratic, and diverse society where human potential is allowed to flourish. As we push forward with our vision of democracy based on a fundamental restructuring of the political, economic, and social order, we face many obstacles. We on the Left will need the power of unity if we are to survive the current onslaught of neoconservative attacks. And make no mistake: we are under attack. The hundreds of millions who are marginalized, exploited, and excluded the world over, along with those working to support them, currently face aggression that is unprecedented in our short lifetimes. The Bush administration combines three political trends: religious fundamentalism driving our country toward theocracy, the regressive transfer of wealth to benefit a narrow elite within the global elite, and the reformalization of an imperialist police state occupying not only foreign countries, but also our communities here in the homeland. This assault on the poor, on people of color, and on the Left drove the three of us and millions more to redouble our efforts as part of a global resistance. The neoconservative imperial project presents itself as the only possible way forward, inevitable, taken for granted—but our generation of young activists has a vision for another world, another world that is possible.

Our vision and hope, our work and struggle, are the future. From globalization to the war on terrorism and beyond, our generation of activists is compelled to action in the midst of a rapidly changing and unique political moment. Mass mobilizations like the battle of Seattle, the Republican National Convention protest, and the World Social Forum gatherings bring trade unionists, environmentalists, community organizers, health care workers, teachers, peace forces, human rights lawyers, HIV/AIDS activists, native leaders, students, artists, musicians, Indymedia journalists, hipsters, and hippies together. And yet these flashy protests are just one small part of our political work. All of the organizing-agitating-planning-strategizing that takes place in between these explosive events receives considerably less attention but has a profound impact on all our daily lives and on mainstream discourse. For example, while the media have paid little attention to the massive prison organizing of the last decade around draconian drug laws and mandatory minimum sentencing, many states have begun decarcerating their prison populations using the rhetoric of these grassroots movements. Although young people play leading roles in these movements, they are fundamentally multigenerational—as is the Movement itself.

Of course, someday soon we will no longer be young—since we

began this project, Kenyon turned thirty, Dan began a PhD program, and Chesa left school to enter the workforce. Some of us may ourselves become a defining part of the mainstream. But as we age we will continue to look for new and engaging ways to model our political principles in daily life. If we can shape a future world that is more consistent with our values, we will redefine the mainstream to reflect our perspectives. In so doing, we challenge the "natural" political trajectory: young, dumb, and full of revolutionary aplomb; old, wise, and—what else?—conservative. We are carving out a different future, for ourselves and for our world. Today we draw on lessons from previous generations in order to respond to the present reality, even as we hurl toward antiquity. Effective activism is rooted in an understanding of the events of the past, strategies for the present, and a vision for the future. As we young activists dedicate our lives to building a better future, we also find ourselves steadily becoming part of the past. Activists and movements come and go, yet activism and the Movement are continuous; that is, they have a past, present, and future.

Just as we build from the past, our actions determine our personal and public future. This continuum exists both within our lives as individuals and over time between generations. The organization of the following letters attempts to map this dialectical relationship between generations. The book begins with an intimate, deeply personal chapter engaging our parents about our political work, moves on to a series of chapters that dialogue with the present, then, bringing the narrative full circle, the final chapter provides the space for us to rhetorically engage our future selves. As we move forward in life we all make difficult decisions and compromises. Our challenge, and yours, is to live our lives in a way that does not make a mockery of our values. There is no time like the present to act.

With hope and determination,

Dan Berger   Chesa Boudin   Kenyon Farrow

PAST:
LETTERS TO THE PREVIOUS GENERATIONS

In this section, young activists dialogue—personally and politically —with those who have often been the hardest to engage with: our elders, be they our parents, authority figures, or older activists in the Movement. Whether we come from families who support our activism or those that do not, the authors in chapter 1 convey to our parents the lessons we take with us from our families as we engage in political activism. A common theme in all the letters in this chapter is the value placed on family relationships, in passing on the struggle, in working against all hopes to be understood by those who raised us. Whether our parents are working class or middle class, activists or apolitical, U.S.-born or immigrants, they have helped shape our lives and have given us tools we use daily in our organizing. In chapter 2, young activists take aim at the authorities in our lives. From letters addressed to the first Black woman secretary of state to the patronizing adults who disregard the rights of young children to the elites attacking educational institutions, the authors in this chapter challenge notions of power throughout society: who has it, who should have it, and why. Inevitably some authorities our generation of activists is struggling to dialogue with—from the police to prison wardens, from university presidents to agribusiness executives—are not included, but this chapter begins a process of engagement. The last chapter of this section addresses the multi-generational aspects of the Movement. Authors here give thanks to those activists that have come before, even as they critically examine how veteran activists do (and should) relate to our generation. Our legacy from the social movements of our parents' generation, those of the 1960s and 1970s, features particularly prominent in this chapter. The letters here serve as constant reminders of the prospects and challenges of building intergenerational Movements.

1

LETTERS TO OUR PARENTS

David Gilbert 83A6158
Clinton Correctional Facility
Box 2001
Dannemora, NY 12929

October 2004

Dear Dad,

Happy birthday. Though Clinton Max is one of the last places I would like you to celebrate turning 60, I take solace in the fact that your circumstances are largely a product of your own commitment to progressive political change and to the inherent value and equality of all human life. I deeply respect your commitment to your principles, your willingness to sacrifice yourself in the hopes of creating a better world for future generations of children, including me, your only son, even while staring a life sentence in the face. I'm proud of you for standing up for your anti-imperialist and anti-racist politics.

However, your decisions had real human costs including the murders of three fathers and husbands, and the traumatic disruption of untold children's lives, my own among them. When you and Kathy were arrested for the 1981 Brinks robbery, I was just fourteen months old. I know that politics motivated your participation, but the action was nothing to be proud of. I was too young to fully understand what it meant when you were sentenced to seventy-five years to life and my mom to twenty years to life, but we were already on a journey together. I, too, would become an activist.

Twenty-two hard years later in September 2003, I was in your prison on a visit when we celebrated the news that Kathy Boudin was released under parole supervision. We were both jubilant. For you, I know, it was a moment of pure, unadulterated ecstasy. For me, the knowledge that you will not be eligible for parole until you are 112 years old made the joy bittersweet, made the shadow of the armed guards on the walls surrounding us that much darker.

Neither of you were armed; neither of you directly hurt anyone; neither of you played a role in planning the robbery; and neither one of you intended for any of those three men to be killed. Yet, I had to turn my back on you and listen to the steel gate slam shut behind me, even as Kathy was enjoying her first minutes in freedom. Starting with her plea, she has consistently, publicly expressed her remorse. Why has it always been easier for you, from the time I was three or four years old and continuing up through our most recent visits, to express your remorse to me personally and privately than it is do so publicly?

Maybe if I had been old enough to talk, I could have convinced both of you not to go. Maybe if I had understood what was going on at the time of your trial, I could have convinced you to let a lawyer defend you, despite your political objections to participating in the trial. Maybe, just maybe, once those three families know how sorry you are for their losses and the role you played in them, they will be able to forgive.

Of course, I don't really remember those early years, a time that irrevocably changed all of our lives. I don't remember becoming part of a new family. I don't remember when I realized my good fortune at having fallen, a bit messily at first, into the home of Bill Ayers and

Bernardine Dohrn with the support of their two sons, my big brothers. The fact that all four of my parents—and all of you really are my parents—shared a long political history going back to your organizing against the war in Vietnam with Students for a Democratic Society and the Weather Underground, made it much easier to build a relationship with you and my mom in prison.

On the other hand, the difficulties of growing up in such a logistically complicated, politically controversial, and spatially far-flung family are also a part of my inheritance from you. Rather than focusing on this negative legacy—the tragedy, the failures, the mistakes, my childhood problems, or the ongoing burden of maintaining a relationship with you from the distance incarceration creates—I choose to focus on the positive side of what my parents' sacrifices, mistakes, and political activism have engendered. This legacy includes a wide range of principled life choices, a profound commitment to humanity and equality, and an emphasis on reflection and self-criticism. It includes as well the ability to laugh and love, to enjoy life's pleasures while fighting society's injustices. Perhaps most of all, it includes optimistic, open-minded engagement in local, national, and global politics. It is this legacy that has done the most to place me in a position to continue your struggle for a better world while avoiding the kinds of mistakes that led to the murder of those three men and to your life behind bars.

Growing up, my family's dinner table conversations about a recent suspension of a classmate at school, urban renewal projects in our neighborhood on the south side of Chicago, or the role of the U.S. military in Central America made local and global politics intimate family affairs. Learning to view the world through a political lens was much broader than simple participation in electoral politics. I didn't have to study civics to learn that there are responsibilities that come with political freedoms, that living in the heart of empire imposes particular obligations, that members of civil society have a duty to participate in inclusive, public debates as part of the fertile and dynamic democratic process.

Political participation and engagement are the lifeblood of any democratic society. Over our country's history, the right to vote has been expanded dramatically from a narrow elite class of land-owning white men to include most citizens—with prisoners being an obvious exception. Ironically, increasing access to the vote has been mirrored by decreasing participation in elections and civil society in general. In the high stakes 2004 presidential election, for example, just 60 percent of those eligible actually voted, making it the highest turnout since 1968, the last presidential election that you would have participated in before going underground. The widespread concentration of global corporate power is eroding political freedoms. This erosion leads many individuals, families, and cultures to withdraw from actively participating in civil society or teaching their children to think critically, undermining the health of our political system. I was lucky to grow up in a family where politics matter.

Of course, as I write this, I can hear you telling me that it is not just about apathy, but also about repression, about the systematic elimination of alternatives and progressive leaders. I read Walter Rodney's *How Europe Underdeveloped Africa*, Eduardo Galeano's *Open Veins of Latin America*, George Jackson's *Soledad Brother*, Ward Churchill's *Agents of Repression*, William Blum's *Killing Hope*, and how many other books you suggested? I know that living through the Chicago police and the FBI murder of twenty-one-year-old Fred Hampton, the rising star of the Chicago Black Panther Party, in his sleep, and the U.S. military napalming of entire villages in Vietnam drove you down a long, long road from pacifism, where you spent the first seven years of your career as an activist, to revolutionary armed struggle in support of third world liberation movements.

Though I know them only as photos, I will never be able to get the images out of my mind of you in the days after your arrest, black-and-blue all over from the beatings the police administered. I will never forget that once you were in police custody and no one was watching they shoved a shotgun in your throat and did much worse to the members of the Black Liberation Army who were arrested with you. So believe me, I know that fighting oppression involves a lot more than just raising awareness and getting people engaged. But the version of revolutionary violence to which you let yourself be driven in 1981 is surely far off the mark. Neither of us are cynics; we both believe in humanity, in the potential for positive change, in every person's capacity to do "good." I also believe in peaceful, democratic revolutions, although I know even these must be willing and able to defend themselves by any means necessary. I have seen one in action here in South America.

During the past few months, as I traveled over land from Santiago, Chile, to Caracas, Venezuela, you and your political legacy were with me. If I had grown up with different parents, that journey might have been nothing more than an adventure vacation. Instead, I was constantly looking to understand the challenges of local circumstances and the beauty and resilience of the cultures that developed in response. You helped teach me the value of an open heart and mind. In a sense, you enabled me to learn from that bus driver in Antofogasta, Chile; the single mother in Manaus, Brazil; and the youth activists in Caracas, who reminded me that Venezuela's democratic revolution is peaceful, but *not* disarmed.

Having you with me on life's journeys not only encourages me to appreciate the luxury of my freedoms, but also to learn from the world around me and to actively search for ways to play a positive role in it. You and your experience helped me realize that staying put was never an option, not after all we have seen and lived. Because of you, I can see myself, with one foot in Yale or in Oxford and the other in Latin America, as a possible conduit for resources to flow against the current, back to the poor countries and communities I have known. Your legacy encouraged me to stay here in Venezuela and dedicate whatever skills I may have to supporting the Bolivarian revolution in the face of ongoing U.S. intervention. Once I spent a bit of time on the streets of Caracas, it became abundantly clear that the majority of the people, especially the poor people, support President Chávez—that he has a democratic mandate to lead this country, as his victories in two presidential elections and a recall referendum should have already proved to the world. Moreover, I had a chance to see his progressive social programs in education and health care, his endogenous economic development, and his staunchly independent foreign policy in action. I know of no other government in the world today as progressive and as brave in the face of an empire on the attack. There is no place I would rather be. Is that my legacy from you?

Che Guevara would have described your revolutionary spirit as guided by love. My ability to carry your spirit with me wherever I go, a skill necessarily learned from too early an age, means you are and will always be with me. Your presence, your spirit, and your example give me solace as I prepare to face the temptations, the tough decisions, the struggles, the losses, and the joys in the years to come. From Amsterdam Avenue to Auburn, from Hyde Park to Attica, from great ivory towers to Great Meadows, and from the revolutionary streets of Caracas to the snow-covered razor wire at Clinton Max, I am sending you much love.

your son,
chesa

St. Paul
January 2005

> *He who lies here, it said, marched*
> *Not to conquer a foreign land, but*
> *His own.*
> —Bertolt Brecht, "The Tombstone of the Unknown Soldier of
> the Revolution"

Dear Mamma and Babba,

I am writing to you with radios silenced and TVs turned off. It is winter already here in the Midwest—that salt-stained season of ice and wind, of short days and long nights. And tonight, I am at a loss for words. My apartment—only two blocks from school, redbrick, half-furnished and half moved into—seems foreign to me. I'm constantly on the move these days, silent and sad, both moved and paralyzed by these pictures in my head, the ones that can't seem to get past my tongue. I'm dazed tonight, and images of Fallujah's skeleton haunt me. Gaza's misery follows me from room to room, telling me to write it all down. Even the words "election" and "democracy" make my stomach turn. I am at a loss for words and so I write to you in the hope that my silence does not deafen me nor define me, but strengthens me instead. It is at times like these that I turn off the news and I try to become my own medium. I pick up a pen, a book, or a phone and I listen before I talk; listen to the words, the paper, or the voice on the other end of the line. Because when the lies and the injustice have me pinned to the salty concrete, cracked and at a loss for words, I listen and then I speak.

All I can say is that I miss you and my sisters, and I think of you all endlessly. I am trying to study hard but find myself struggling to study at all, so I study struggle instead. And it does not escape me that I am fortunate enough to study it while others live it; so I breathe it, dream it, talk it, write it, love it, spread it, and sip it. But still I cannot honestly say that I live it, at least not the way you and Babba did in Beirut. I do not struggle to stay alive and I do not live the struggle the way those cats you guys have known over the years did; the ones who lived for it and died for it. Fallen brothers and sisters assassinated, incarcerated, and exiled.

And in Palestine today it's the same ol' shit: Resistance exterminated. Trees as old as the U.S. Constitution uprooted swiftly to the din of U.S.-supplied machines of war and destruction. Dirty ethnic demolition funded by my tax dollars and linguistically cleansed before it can be reported. It is a system subsidized by complacency and complicity. You raised me through it all, protected me with books and laughter, protest and outspokenness but it is still difficult to live with it day in and day out because it is everywhere in America. And because I still sleep most nights—most of us do—even as Palestine's topography is remade in the image of demagogues and war criminals. How can we bear to sleep?

There are no tanks at my door and no police at my throat, only TVs and radios telling me that Palestinians are terrorists—that we do not really exist, that we don't get it (be it democracy, peace, history, facts, life, grief, or whatever) and don't deserve it either. Telling us to stop asking questions. No, the army of occupation I deal with on the daily is the kind that infiltrates every house, wins hearts and minds, slips in and out unnoticed through satellite dishes and cable lines. It tries to strangle me all the time but I resist. It leaves me gasping for air—with the realization that this occupation army is not of this world, as it does not yet react to stones or demos, or bullets, just cash and I ain't got it. In fact I ain't got much to throw at 'em except some words. I even got a slingshot, too, but words, once slung, just bounce back, deflected into thin air. I have written to the generals, soldiers, and spies of this army but to no avail—they edit me out. They edit too many of us out. At best we are exiled to the twelfth paragraph of the fourth story on page twenty-three, or banished to the streaming headlines on the bottom of the screen. So we've demonstrated, snot-nosed, frostbitten in the winter, sweat-soaked in summer protests, and yes! I've voted, hated, loved and yet . . . the occupation continues worldwide.

I do not live the struggle, I just live with it, and often I regret not being in Palestine, on the ground. Then I ask why I am not even on the streets of Minneapolis? Why am I not out there every day with banners, setting roadblocks with tires aflame, handing out pamphlets, building alliances, winning friends? There isn't one answer: When the time is ripe. Pick your battles. The best offense is defense. Know thy enemy.

And so on and so on. So I realize there isn't really any one way to fight this army 'cause it has never been fought before, at least not in its current mass-produced, high-speed, online, live-feed, electronic, and digitalized manifestation. So we must give them a taste of their own medicine; share stories, resources, and lessons from Chiapas to Ramallah to Quebec; from Caracas, Kinshasa, Soweto to Tibet; Alabama, Rio, Baghdad, and Chile. The list goes on, never stops, and it ain't easy! No one said it was easy! As my man James Baldwin reminded us: "to act is to be committed and to be committed is to be in danger."

Even as I write to you there is a fire brewing underground. You know it is there, you have seen it. It is a movement full of beats, full of photos, music, poets, vets, and rookies in the struggle, full of hope and hard work. Yet this fire ebbs and flows under the constant hail of misinformation that is dropped from blaring TV screens that buzz and spin overhead; spit out by the Pentagon and White House spokespeople whose second nature, it seems, is that age-old trade: warmongering. All of us in this movement (these movements), we fish for truth, knowing it by sight and smell and sound, but never seem to catch it in time for prime time. It wriggles away, and today, I feel as if this country, my home, is wriggling away, too, into the hands of this dastardly army.

I know I am never doing enough and that I have much to learn, but I know that I am still learning, and that with your help I will find my own way to fight. I know you understand that, and that is what pushes me onward when the windchill plummets and when lies pass for truth. When body counts chill but never make the news; names that never make the story. It is cold in America.

My warmth is what I learned from you guys and from Bill and Bernardine, from Brecht and Baldwin, Malcolm, Edward and Eqbal; from the baseball field and from my ancestors, too; so I try to remind myself that nothing comes easy and it has been this cold and bleak before. You brought us here over twenty years ago, running from Sharon and civil war in Beirut, through checkpoints, airports, and scarcely furnished apartments. We moved west via D.C., NYC, and then Chicago, and the

Chi became home but now I question if it is not indeed my time to run again. And yet, I know that the battle is inside me, and that, above all, it needs to be fought right here in America; it needs to be fought slowly and wisely, in, out, above, below, and around the system. I know it is not just about Palestine. Rather, Palestine is about everything; it is about so much more than Arabs and Jews, and until we can make this an international struggle about human rights, human dignity, and freedom from racism and foreign military rule, then we are not doing enough. We cannot do it alone. Palestine is about everything.

You always taught me to fight against injustice, question it and work to defeat it. But you never stopped reminding us all of the importance of knowing what we want in addition to what we want to get rid of. All I know is that this war must end. The occupation (of Iraq, Palestine, the poor, and our airwaves) must end! We must oppose the U.S. Empire and the robust, corrupt, complex, and yet diabolically simple prison system it has put in place. We must turn this system on its head, here at home.

In truth, I know that you know all this already. I know you have heard it (and tried it) before but as I said, I am still learning, so bear with me as I try to put it all together, stumbling and tripping along the way. The glue I use is because of you, and it carries voices and stories, names and faces. It tells me: "This is your home my friend, do not be driven from it." So I will not be driven from my home, not here, not in Palestine, nor anywhere else. And if my meandering letter is any indication, I expect to stay moving in the coming years—escaping history and causing trouble. I love you and miss you.

In love and struggle,
Your son,
Ismail

Querida Mami y Querido Papi,

Now that you two have been separated for more than ten years—you, Papi, living back in El Salvador, and you, Mami, still living in the United States—I wanted to express my appreciation for the support you gave us, for bringing us up the best you could. And I just want you to know how much I love you and that I do not hold any anger for any mistakes you ever made with us.

My first memory of you, Papi, is hitting Mami and giving her a bloody nose. I also remember the last time I saw you abusing her, when she made you look at us (my two sisters and I) crying, and she asked you if this was the kind of life you wanted us to grow up in. I couldn't even talk yet, but I understood how powerful it was that Mami used words to make you think, to make you actually stop and look at us. That day I learned the power in standing up for yourself.

There are many things that were hard for me to forgive you for, Papi, but I understand the pressures you were under—you in your late twenties and Mami in her early twenties—as poor immigrant parents trying to survive in the United Snakes of America. But I do remember how much you helped with household chores, the cooking and cleaning.

I want to thank you for all the stories you shared with us as kids. As a little girl I could only imagine your experiences of walking to school on a dirt road with no shoes, of building toys from any scrap objects you could find—because no one could afford to buy toys. And I am so thankful that you took us to El Salvador in 1992, right after the so-called peace accords were signed after a twelve year civil war. We lived there for almost a year and, being twelve years old, I absorbed so much of that experience: The soldiers I saw on the street with guns, the openness and friendliness between neighbors, the delicious foods, and I will never forget how sad I felt seeing so many kids my age or younger selling stuff on the streets or just plain begging for food or money.

There is one bus ride in San Miguel, El Salvador, that remains tattooed in my memory. A little boy, no more than ten years old, got on the bus, stood at the front and center of the bus, pulled out an instrument, and began playing and singing. My reaction, as a twelve-year-old not having seen anything like this before, was to want to laugh. Nobody else was so I held it in. I asked you, Mami, why he was singing, and you told me it was to make money. It was like someone knocked the wind out of me. I wanted to cry, because I felt so sad, so ashamed that I had wanted to laugh, and so angry that everyone was so desensitized that all they could do was look out the window trying to ignore the boy. As I think about those people now, I realize that maybe they just did not want to make eye contact with him because it would remind them of everything else that was so unjust in the world. . . .

Looking back on that trip, I realize that just how growing up in El Salvador affected you, in a powerful way, my being born and raised in the Mission District of San Francisco, California, to immigrant parents has affected me in a powerful way. I remember growing up and wanting blonde hair and green eyes because that was the image of beauty I saw reflected through Barbie dolls, in magazines, and on TV. But thankfully, I grew up in a multicultural region like the Bay Area and the culture of resistance here taught me to love myself, to fight the seeds of self-hatred and apathy that are planted in youth.

But whether you grow up in San Miguel or San Francisco, people everywhere just want a way to meet their basic needs: health care, food, a decent wage to survive on. I see you, Mami and Papi, how broke you are, after all these years of hard work, how much you sacrificed yourselves. I guess sometimes that's why I feel guilty, like I should just find a job that makes good money so I could take care of you two like you deserve to be taken care of. But no matter how broke I get, I still can't see myself working somewhere that is not in some way contributing to making this world a healthier place for children to grow up in. The way in which our taxes are used to pay for wars makes me frustrated enough. The least I can do is try my best to buy from fair trade stores and family owned businesses instead of corporate-owned chain stores. The least I can do is work at a place that is about social change.

The realization that not everyone has this privilege to choose what type of job they want makes me feel even more obligated, while I am young and have no kids, to use my time and money in ways that support positive change in the world.

But I am determined to be financially stable while doing something I love (and help you and my sisters of course, just as we have been helping each other even though we're all broke). And everything I love to do revolves around contributing to make this world a healthier place to live in, where people would have free health care, healthy options for food, get paid a fair wage for their work, and where everyone would live in a way that respects Mother Earth. Since high school, I have been involved in community organizing and/or advocacy on various issues: increasing ethnic studies, interactive curriculum and funding in education, advocating against gentrification in our neighborhoods and the criminalization of youth, the right for gay people to marry.

One of the main reasons why I have become more and more dedicated to fighting injustice is because I see how scattered our families are and I know our family would not be so scattered and struggling if it weren't for all the wars, unjust economic policies, and pollution they grew up under and in which we continue to live in today. All this experience reinforces for me the interdependency between local and global communities, which is why I am currently working against corporate globalization and all the free trade agreements and privatization policies that they are trying to establish. Corporations basically want more freedom to pollute the land, water, and air and pay workers as little as they wish, among other things. I am not being unrealistic; I understand that countries need to trade in order to get their needs met, but there is no reason why trade needs to happen at such an unfair level! Families are torn apart because people are forced to immigrate, children starve because their family business cannot compete with a corporate monopoly.

I take the time to write this letter because these are things I want you to understand about me before any of us pass on, because the way war and pollution are increasing in our world so much more now than ever before, our lives can be lost at any instant. But I also want you to understand the beautiful, powerful movement for justice that is on the rise all over the world. Although we continue to live in a chaotic world, we also continue to fight for our rights! And that is what I want you to understand about me. I am happy: All the friends I have made and the experiences I have had to travel, have shown me that there are *definitely* more people wanting justice than wanting to destroy it. Whenever I get depressed, I find inspiration in the many diverse communities I feel a connection with: community organizers and activists, poets, teachers, elders, and youth. To stay energized, I attend theater and independent film shows in addition to some of the mainstream movies, I dance to hip-hop, rock, cumbia, and reggae, and sometimes it's good to just kick back and have some drinks.

There is one last thing I would want you to understand about me. And there is no easy transition into the topic. I just hope that by the time you have read this much into the letter, you will understand why it has been so hard for me to tell you this: I like women the same way I like men. I don't like labels, but for lack of a better word, I identify most with being bisexual. Growing up I remember how the words *maricon* and *marimacha* were used, and it wasn't a good thing. I remember the lesbian couple that used to live downstairs from us when we lived near Geneva Avenue. It was something that was joked about, and being no more than nine or ten years old, I understood that two women being together made people feel uncomfortable, which told me I should never publicly acknowledge the feelings I had. Just as I had crushes on boys and famous actors, I had crushes on girls and famous actresses. It's something I clearly remember but because of the queerphobia I was growing up in, I remember having to justify to myself why I was so interested in some girl. Thanks to rebel ancestors, like Cherríe Moraga and Harvey Milk, who fought and died fighting for gay, lesbian, bisexual, transgender, and other human rights—there were resources available for me in high school where I could explore these feelings. I first accepted this aspect of myself when I was in high school, but it has taken me until now to feel strong enough in who I am to finally be able to tell you, Mami and Papi, that I am a woman who likes women in addition to men. So now, if you have any questions about it, please ask me.

I don't know what else to say (or write); I just want you to feel proud of what my sisters and I have become. We are survivors like you are survivors. My two beautiful, intelligent, compassionate sisters have now become mothers, making you grandparents. Maybe my being bisexual is one of the reasons why I have not yet become a mother. Relationships get complicated when you are a woman like me. Just like Latina women experienced racism in the mainstream women's liberation movement, how they experienced sexism in the Xicano/a movement, I have experienced homophobia in addition to racism, sexism, and classism. But as I struggle through my journey, I give thanks for the many blessings I have, one of which is having parents like you. You have shown me that even though we grow up with obstacles in our way, we also grow up with privileges (as you reminded me anytime I didn't finish my food, *"Sabes cuantos niños y niñas se estan muriendo de hambre ahorita?* Do you know how many children are starving right now?"). And you taught me how we should use our privileges for good, to help ourselves and our communities. I always remember how Papi would hire day laborers anytime we had to move to a different apartment. So thank you, Mami and Papi, for planting in us the seeds that have given us strength to branch out into the sky.

We all continue on our journeys . . .

All my relations,
Kaira

28 November 2004

Dear Mom,

This is the kind of weather you'd like. The sky is dotted with patchy storm clouds, and the cold air snaps in my lungs as I walk down these tree-lined streets. Fall sun spills across the neighborhood, and the cracked, uneven sidewalks near my apartment are blanketed in the bright yellow, orange, and red of fallen leaves. When the rain picks up, the leaves and their colors get smeared all over the streets, cars, and stoops of this squat Brooklyn neighborhood. Right before dusk is my favorite time of day, because the sun is low on the horizon and the sunlight is diffused, the red-red bricks of the buildings stand out in brilliant contrast to the gray storm clouds. Winter is lurking just beyond these moody fall days, and I'm quickly preparing myself for the shocking cold and raging blizzards yet to come.

I think of you on days like this, when the weather and the colors of the world are so striking, because I know you'd appreciate it all as much as I do. You're the one who first taught me to be aware of the details, to pay attention to the simple things that are fundamental to a good life, like fresh bread and clean air, running out in a thunder storm, breathing in the pungent smell of fresh cut grass, lying quietly on one's back and watching the stars turn about and fall. It was you who taught me how to dance and listen for the songs of crickets and frogs on a summer night and bake cookies and put on mascara without making a mess of my face. You taught me to appreciate the world by courting the wonder of it.

And so this past weekend, as I walked down the street in the drizzling rain, high on coffee and solitude, I began to fret about how little you now know about my life. I'm here in the concrete world of New York City, while you are 3,000 miles away, cradled in the high mountain desert valleys of the Sierras. We are separated by geography and time and by the deep ache of a rocky history that is neither eased by distance nor assuaged by expired calendars. And yet we are bound, inextricably, through memory and blood and love, and through a beautiful but painfully strained friendship.

I want you to know what animates and motivates me, because I think it's the most honest, genuine way to share myself with you. You already know a bit about *what* I do—that my paid job is fighting to abolish prisons and the war on drugs, that I attend meetings, organize protests, coordinate fundraisers, harass policy makers and write and rant and stir up trouble. And you jokingly tell me that when you see footage of a protest on television news—even if it's in the middle of Kansas—you look for me in the crowd, like some activist version of "Where's Waldo?" (If only I could be everywhere at once!) But I get the sense that you imagine me as just being opposed to things popular in the United States, like McDonald's or prisons or Christmas. I'm seen as the contrarian kid in the family—the one with a contrary gender, a contrary sexuality, a contrary worldview that is just plain oppositional to everything "American." At the same time, I'm also "understood" in our family as the kid with a pronounced inclination toward "civic duty" or "volunteering;" I'm the one who is constantly "fighting injustice," as though I have some sense of it that the rest of our family lacks.

The irony is that I see myself as precisely opposite. I define my life by what I am *for*, not what I'm *opposed to*. And I'm prepared to fight for what I believe in—life, love, freedom, justice—*for everybody*. It just so happens that the political and economic system under which we now live is antithetical to the things I hold most dear, so I've sought out people who are just as willing to fight for freedom and justice as I am. That's how I found the Movement, how I came to learn that there are tens of thousands of people in this country—and millions around the world—who are fighting tooth and nail, heart and soul, to build the world we believe in. The Movement is a kind of bridge between where we are now and where we want to be. It's the vehicle to take us there.

I came to understand that I am *for* things through two core lessons that I learned from you. The first is that the setup we live under now is *wrong*. Some people have a full, sickeningly overflowing table while the rest of us are left to fight each other over the remaining crumbs. And what's more, the vast majority of us—the non-ruling people of this world—are left to fight each other *because* a gluttonous few have claimed the whole table and even the crumbs as their own. I came to this realization early in life, both because children are quick to identify blatant injustice and because our family so often had to fight for what little crumbs we could get. The second lesson, which took me a long while to grab hold of, is this: people designed things this way so *people can undo it, change it, transform it*. But it's like one of those big summer barbeques we used to have—it doesn't work unless everybody brings a little something to contribute and takes on a task so all the food gets made.

In those rolling hills and rural farmland towns of California's Central Valley, my life was dramatically shaped by school kids laughing at me because I wore clothes from the free box at the Baptist Church; hearing social workers make snide remarks to you; cops harassing us all the time, often storming into our house; friends and family getting hauled off to jail or prison as a regular part of life; the courts treating you like a pariah because you didn't have money; and by the daily stress caused by surviving but inches away from utter disaster. These experiences sparked within me an immutable fury about the hardships we faced, which I came to understand as the injustice of poverty in a class-based society. From day one, you taught me that respect and compassion should be accorded to everybody—especially to those people who didn't normally get much of either. So I could not accept, as a child (or now as an adult), that anybody needed to have money or status in order to be treated like human beings. And yet at every turn, our humanity—and that of those in our community—was challenged as though it lacked merit, like we needed to *prove* our worth.

You don't need me to tell you that poor people are treated by the government and society at large as expendable. Nor do you need me to tell you that poor people—most often poor people of color—are scape-goated for problems caused by the concentration of wealth and power in so few hands. We're kicked off welfare or sent to decrepit schools or have to suffer through pneumonia without any visit to the hospital, and why? We live in the richest country in the history of the universe! And yet tens of millions of people in this country don't have enough to eat, are without health care, cannot afford a college education. We are drowning because the cost of living continues to rise and our thin pocketbooks can't keep us afloat. And all the while, the most attractive job options for the people in little towns like yours are to guard other poor folks in prison or become military fodder. There are billion-aires who have more money than whole countries, and more than half the world's people live on less than $2.10 *a day*! It does not take a child's innocent and honest sense of justice to know that this situation is utterly foul, but it takes a level of denial only an adult can muster to pretend like this is how things *should* be.

We are told time and time again that if you work hard enough, you can "make it." The implication is that if you're poor, you're a lazy schmuck who clearly hasn't worked hard enough to pull your shit together. But I watched you bust your ass to make a dollar, and few people I know worked harder than you. And I grew up around some of the most beautiful people in the world—people who built houses or whole neighborhoods, served coffee for nickels and cleaned the toilets of rich people and fixed cars and kept vegetable gardens in their back-yard so there'd be food in the summer. We lived with people who worked and worked and still, even then, gathered cans to recycle so we could buy an ice cream sandwich and rent a video on a lazy Sunday afternoon. If this farce about "pulling ourselves up" were true, then with all the work you've done you'd surely be able to reach the moon.

We can keep telling ourselves that it's not our fault, but the incred-ible hatred for poor people in this country, the exalting of the rich, the utterly wretched paternalism of charity—it all starts to exact its toll, seeping into us like some virus. And it becomes difficult to not imagine ourselves as being responsible for not "making it" in this, an economy designed to ensure that so many people never "make it." It's designed so that millions are, instead, chained to destitution and despair. In this context, charity is a sham because it means that the rich and well-off can make themselves feel better about the fact that the very setup that affords them their wealth also impoverishes millions of people in this country and billions of people around the world. Charity is like placing a Band-Aid on an amputated leg and hoping it heals.

We didn't take much charity—we took care of each other. And you were the organizing force behind that network of women and men who worked together to survive and live. I saw you organize multifamily outings on shoestring or nonexistent budgets and coordinate child-care and ridesharing so folks could get to the store, welfare office, and the DMV all in one day and without having to drag their kids along. I paid very close attention to the ways you so carefully listened to people, and I started to ask myself why we were the ones going to jail, passing on college because it was/is too expensive, going without health care, suffering through a welfare system that is designed to strip away one's dignity, all the while explaining ourselves to the cops and courts. Why must poor people "prove" our humanity just to get a few food stamps from the very system that keeps us hungry in the first place?

I know you carry guilt and shame because you were not able to pro-vide us with the lives you wanted to provide for your kids. I wish I could strip this guilt and shame from you. I would cast it into the sea and watch it sink and disappear into the seaweed, because you have already given me the world. The conflict and distance between you and I is real and painful, but it is not born of poverty and struggle. Poverty certainly exacerbates some problems, but we have survived and thrived, and I refuse to settle for anything less than living fully. This is part of the legacy you gave me to carry. You taught me how to fashion joy out of thin air, how to laugh and cry and work and love. And in the face of a world that is often so horrific and unfair and corrupt, aren't joy and love and the ability to laugh in the midst of utter catastrophe weapons for us to wield?

We can change this wretched situation; we can utterly and completely transform it. We can reclaim control over our lives and communities and destinies. I think the biggest step, for people like us, is to believe not only that we *can* take control of our own lives, but that we have a *duty* to do so, and we already have much of what we need to make it a reality. Everyday I wake with a stronger feeling that this world is turned on its head, and we need to work together to make it right. The world we want is not out of our reach. I know you understand this feeling. When I showed you the videos of the global justice protests against the World Trade Organization in Seattle in 1999, you said it reminded you of a distinct feeling you had in San Francisco in 1970—that the tipping point for real transformation was close enough for you to taste. I continue to make my home in the Movement because I am hungry, and that taste is heavy on my tongue.

You taught me to look at the simple details of the world to understand the complex ones; you showed me how to distill the bulky mess of living into chunks that I could hold in my hand, feel the weight and shape of, and understand with my gut and heart instead of just my head. And I suppose this is why, in the course of our estrangement, I have been so reserved in sharing with you the details of my own life—my friends, my day-to-day fears and hopes, my latest questions and feelings about gender, who I fall in love with, the tidal shifts in my dreams and goals. I keep from you the simplest of details about my world, just as you keep yours from me, and so we've become intimate strangers. But I assure you that despite our estrangement, I am still your child, and I am trying to do right by the love you have given to me. And I am trying, with all my heart, to alter this upside down world, Mother, not because I am opposed to everything, but because I can appreciate the fierceness of a thunderstorm, take in the vibrant colors of fall, smell the saltwater on the wind, and be wild and reckless with my laughter.

I promise you this, Mom—I am wielding these weapons you gave me, and every day I am learning to use them with greater precision. I plan to be thoroughly spent by the time I die, because I want nothing less than the world in our hearts to be born, and if I can contribute to that birth I will be fulfilled. Sometime, you and I will get to the dirt and clear it up. For now, I just wish you could see this storm rolling in over the horizon, and hear the thunderclap above these bony Brooklyn rooftops. If you were here right now, you'd ask me if I want to go walking in the storm, and I'd tell you yes.

Love, always love,
your kid,
gabriel olga

Dear Mummy—

It's late. I know you're waiting up for me as I attend yet another activist meeting. Tonight it's the Blackout Arts Collective. We are planning our national Lyrics on Lockdown Tour, combating issues surrounding the prison industrial complex. The meetings are more frequent and urgent. I come home hoping for the opening—the spark in your eye that matches mine when I mention what I was out doing. It rarely comes but I still hope you will say, "I am so happy you are doing this."

Instead, you ask, "Why do you have to do this? Is it paying?" You ask why I'm out so late. Did anyone accompany me home? A swirl of questions—some I've answered a million times, some that have no answer, some that need no answer. I can never quite articulate to your satisfaction why I need to be involved in these activities. So I will try to explain it to you the best way I know how.

All my life, you have taught me to work hard and aim for the top. Be the best, be fair, and don't let people treat you badly. I watched as you, a foreigner in this country who arrived in the early 1970s from Haiti, struggled to make sure no one took advantage of you. You would aggressively remind people that just because you had an accent, it didn't mean you were stupid. You commanded the respect you deserved just like anyone else.

The reason I do this work is because there are so many people like you who face the same challenges you have faced and who have no voice. I don't need to be their voice—they have their own. But sometimes we need people to help us find that voice. That's what I do. I help people build their voice so they too can make sure no one takes advantage of them. You taught me to be proud of my Haitian heritage, even though many in America and other parts of the world look down on us. The truth is, many of our people are marginalized in the United States and at home. In Haiti, we are plagued by politicians who claim they want to help the country progress, but behind closed doors, they are corrupt. They sap the country of precious resources to satisfy their greed. In the United States, we have had to fight (and are still fighting) for equal rights and opportunities. Remember in the 1980s, we fought for the right to donate blood? Imagine that. Because the government felt we were a "high-risk" AIDS population, we were banned from donating blood. The activists of those days won that battle, but there are others still raging on. Our brothers and sisters struggle to gain political asylum are turned away, but refugees from all countries, Haiti and elsewhere, should all have an equal right to asylum. Some have been detained at Guantánamo Bay and some even die in other detention centers. Our brother Rev. Joseph Dantica is one who recently suffered this fate—a fate that could have been avoided had he been treated justly. In Miami, upon arrival as a refugee, the eighty-one-year-old's medications were taken away, even after his condition visibly deteriorated, causing his death. Young and old are subjected to this kind of inhumane treatment. Right around the corner from us in a Queens Village public school, an assistant principle, after breaking up a fight where a fourth grade Haitian student from a bilingual class was involved, made all of that student's classmates sit on the floor in the cafeteria to eat their food, sans utensils. When they began to cry in protest, she snapped back that they acted like animals in their country—and she would treat them the same way.

You see, Mummy, there is so much work to do to uplift our people. I must fight everyday. It's a job that calls me to fight 24/7. I fight for Haiti and with Haiti by writing to expose the truth about how our people are mistreated. I fight with organizations like the Movement of Independent Haitians for National Reconstruction by creating programs that will help our people progress in this country and at home—whether that be through education, social services, or cultural activities. As an artist, our struggle and our history is the subject of my work. When I go around lecturing, my job is to dispel the myths people have about us. I fight to make sure that people understand that there is more to Haitians than AIDS and poverty. I fight so that people can see that besides our accents, our music, and our language, we are not so different. I fight so that the world can understand that we were the first Black nation to gain freedom from the bondages of slavery. I fight because in 1804, slaves who had been stolen from all over the continent of Africa fought so that I could be sitting here with the ability to read and to write you this letter. Those newly free Haitians would have wanted you to understand how important it is to continue this kind of struggle. Our forefathers/mothers—Jean Jacques Dessalines, Toussaint L'ouverture, Henri Christophe, Defilée la Folle, Catherine Flon—they knew that as long as there were people who had power over us, we would continue to be disenfranchised. They sacrificed everything to turn the odds to our favor and win. More than two hundred years later, we still pay for our audacity. We still pay for rebelling and conquering the colonizer. We pay in blood and in spirit, generation after generation. The monetary debt we paid to France to secure our freedom proved that. The U.S. occupation from 1915–1934 proved that. The economic embargo the United States placed on Haiti proved that. And most recently, the hand the United States played in ousting our democratically elected president (whatever feelings we may have about him) proved that. We've never been given a break, but we've never asked for one. We never shied away from working hard for freedom and peace. So, I believe we deserve better, just like you've always taught me.

Mummy, this is not easy work. There is a great deal of danger. Especially after 9/11, everyone's actions are monitored. The government is now allowed to scrutinize any organization for what is considered "terrorist" activity. These days, going against the grain can land you in jail quickly, even when you are exercising your constitutional rights. We are all taught that freedom is for everyone, but is it? The United States claims this and sends our young brothers and sisters out to liberate other countries in the name of freedom: the same brothers and sisters whose ancestors were denied freedom for over four hundred years in this very country. At the same time, countries like Haiti have remained in need of support for decades. Many other countries have just turned a blind eye. Since we're not a hot commodity or a valuable enough resource, not many are willing to help.

The most influential powers are interested in two things: Money and power. Behind the money and power are cowards who could care less about whether or not there are people in Haiti who can't store food longer than a day because there is no electricity. They are not concerned that in the United States, Black women are the fastest rising population in the prison industrial complex. Other young activists and I target the government for the role they are playing in the underdevelopment of Haiti with letter campaigns and by supporting the work of organizations like the National Coalition for Haitian Rights, which battles daily to create change. We educate people about what's going on in the community because we believe that when people have knowledge, it's one step closer to change. We target the government for turning a blind eye to human rights violations by protesting and calling up government officials, demanding change. We target the police for locking up our brothers and sisters unjustly. We target big business for building more prisons and fewer schools by exposing them and getting people to boycott their products. Since we choose to target these constituencies, since we choose to demand that they change, we will always be targets ourselves, and we will always be in danger.

Even within our communities we face adversity. As a woman, you gave up so much of yourself and your dreams for your children and your husband. I watched as you played your part as a dutiful wife and mother for over thirty years. I watched your contemporaries experience sexism and racism on a daily basis. Living in America, the first couple of things that anyone sees about you and me is that we are women, and we are Black. I'm on a mission to make sure women can enjoy the same rights and privileges as men. I'm on a mission to make sure my children (if I ever have any) don't have to be called or even thought of as niggers and bitches or be victims of a system that is set up to lock them up instead of educate them. I want them to be proud of who they are without that being considered a dangerous thing. I don't know if all this will ever happen in my lifetime. If I don't try to change it, it will always remain the same.

I want you to know that the values and morals you've instilled in me are reflected in my actions, in everything I do. The lessons you taught me, all the wisdom you gave, all the anecdotes illustrating right and wrong serve as strong influences. At the end of the day, we activists just want the world to be right for everyone. When the world is right, we all can live a better life. I know that's what you want for me. A better life than you had. You may think this "better life" is easily obtained because you struggled, but it's not. The struggles have changed. We're not on the cotton fields, we're in the prisons. We're not getting lynched, we're being electrocuted. We're not being sold, we're being bought by corporate America. We're being hired, but not promoted. If we remain complacent about all these things, we'll never have a better life.

A better life, to me, doesn't mean more money. The question you constantly ask me is, "How is this all bringing you more money?" I always respond that it's not always about the money. Sometimes it's simply about the work that has to be done. If we all sit back, enjoying the fruits of the Civil Rights Movement and the Black Power movement, no one will be addressing the issues that still plague us. Equal opportunities within the education system. A truly transparent and just judicial system. The elimination of racial profiling. These are only some of the things that prevent us from living that better life.

Mummy, I want to tell you not to worry, but I know you won't stop. If I had kids, I would worry too, especially knowing what I know. But, if you feel uneasy about what I do, I just ask that you understand and support this work. As you worked hard so that I could have that better life, I feel like I must work hard so that the next generation doesn't have to deal with some of these challenges we still face. I know when the time comes, they will have their own issues and I will be there to support them. And I ask the same of you.

Kenbe/Love,
Ella

2

LETTERS TO AUTHORITIES

Dear Secretary of State Condoleezza Rice,

When I first decided to write you, I was ready to go for the jugular. I wanted to let you know, in no uncertain terms, just how much I disagreed with your political positions, abhorred your relationship with the Bush clan, and anything else I could think of. I decided I was going to look through every nook and cranny, leave no stone unturned in search of what would be some faulty move, a misspoken word, or some sort of flaw that I would use to turn you out on paper. I downloaded whatever I could find on you: commencement addresses, interviews, speeches, and your famous remarks to the 9/11 Commission. I even went to the bookstore, and purchased some Right-wing puff piece posing as a biography. Just as I was preparing to write, you were nearing the end of your tenure as National Security Advisor, and nearing your Senate confirmation as the new Secretary of State. And I was poised to give you what the Black gay children call a "read."

But then a strange turn of events occurred that profoundly changed my intent for writing this letter. Oddly enough, I was reading your biography on the flight to your second hometown, Denver, Colorado, where I was giving two public talks: "Same-Sex Marriage and Race Politics," and "Gentrification, Prisons, and Anti-Black Racism." My talks were attended by members of Denver's Left—from liberal Democrats to punk-anarchist radicals. And here I was, Black revolutionary that I am, giving talks to almost exclusively white audiences. Your name came up both times, and I didn't come anywhere near mentioning you in my talks. Two different white people asked me the same identical question: "What do you think about Condoleezza Rice?"

Why did they care what I thought about you? Then it hit me like a ton of bricks. These white people wanted me to do what I was planning to do with this letter: Finger-point, neck-bob, and hand-wave. Call you a traitor or worse, a "Tom." Dog your personal appearance. And in doing so, I would be met with thunderous applause. On both the Right and the Left, Black people publicly scolding other Black people for being cultur-ally or politically backward is what's hot! On the Right, Ward Connelly's crusade to end affirmative action in higher education in California, and the success of writer John McWhorter's disturbing Right-wing books that label virtually anything that Black people do as pathological. In mainstream pop culture, it's J. L. King's sensational and tabloid-ish runaway best seller On the Down Low to Bill Cosby's public rants about poor Black people. Even the Left has not been immune from this trend. Lately, many very prominent Black Left intellectuals have publicly scolded the Black community for not being more involved in post-9/11 immigrant detention and antiwar organizing, as if policing and impris-onment, poverty, and HIV/AIDS as issues have significantly decreased or become insignificant for Black people in America since Sept 12, 2001. Whether Right or Left, the message is, if you're Black and have some-thing shitty to say about somebody else Black, you're likely to find an appreciative (and mostly non-Black) audience.

So, why are American politics (on the Left and Right) at a place where white people can use Black people to justify their own racist hatred of Black people? And is it even possible as Black people to articulate critiques of other Black folks, in ways that won't be manip-ulated by mass media on the Left and on the Right, to the ultimate detriment of us all? Are the media and the white American public really interested in preventing HIV infections among Black women and challenging homophobia? Or are they interested in salacious tales of Black sexual pathology? Is the white Left really interested in my analysis of your political legacy? Or are they interested witnessing a Black man publicly denigrate a Black woman?

And now that I understood that this was the game I was supposed to play, I could not bring myself to do it. Not in Denver, and not in this letter. I didn't give them what they wanted. As they paused, eagerly anticipating if I would take the bait, I calmly stated, "While I disagree with most of her choices politically and personally, I also understand that America offers Black people very few options, and she has chosen one of the few options we have to ensure her personal survival. What other options has America offered a genius Black girl born in 1950s Birmingham, Alabama?"

And it is this question that brought to bear the reality of my own life, my own situation, and how strangely similar it is to yours. Among other similarities, we were both "smart Black kids."

Now, there are many smart Black kids in and out of American public schools. But you get designated "a smart Black kid" not only because you show some signs of above-average intelligence (which U.S. public education defines as the ability to take standardized tests, memorize by rote, and regurgitate "facts" as fed to you), but what's equally important to gaining the title of "smart Black kid" is that you must also know how to obey. You know as well as I do that there are many Black children who are highly intelligent, but don't play the game well or at all. The prisons and the grave are full of smart Black people who either didn't know how or flat out refused to "behave" in a system that is designed to physically or symbolically isolate the smartest and most well-behaved (through public school "tracking" or providing "opportunities" to attend private school) and to let the rest sink or swim as they may. If you are termed the "smart Black kid" doors open for you, teachers and principles and guidance counselors work (or do what they are supposed to for all their students) to see that you have every opportunity to succeed. I was tracked into the honors program, and then encouraged to attend private school through the A Better Chance program and my own mother's tenacity and ingenuity. You must have skipped several grades to graduate from high school at age sixteen. And I know from reading your biography, that you also were very "obedient" and had the support of nearly all the teachers you came across, both in Birmingham and later in Denver, where your family moved when you were thirteen.

We also know something about living under the threat of violence. Your circumstances were somewhat different, though, knowing you were ten when your childhood friend Denise McNair and three others were murdered by some white racist who planted a bomb at Birmingham's 16th Street Baptist Church. You described living in Birmingham as living under terrorism, as bombs were exploding in Black neighborhoods all over the city for years. Growing up in Cleveland in the 1980s, I did not fear white mob violence (unless I crossed the train tracks from my housing project into Slavic Village), but I remember being ten years old, like you, and having police helicopters shine lights from high above on my frail brown body, their bullets shoot into the night, wondering which one of my friends or neighbors those bullets would strike. It is an experience I, and many poor Black people, liken to terrorism as well.

Our families did what they could to get us, you and me, out of our respective predicaments in order to save our lives. You, in Birmingham, in the 1960s. Me, in Cleveland, in the 1980s.

So, I think that we know something about each other. I think we know something about wanting better for your life than bullets and bombs. I think we know about being the "first Black" fill-in-the-blank. And we definitely both know about being the "only Black" fill-in-the-blank.

So here we stand, the Black Republican and the Black Revolutionary, poised against each other, facing off like some boxing match, knowing neither one of us much likes the sport, nor did we create it. But we know that the tickets are bought, and too high a price has been paid for the promoters to let us call it draw. But as we stare each other down, we recognize something familiar in the other's eyes. For we are two manifestations of what it means to be Black, to have to grapple with your existence in America and make choices based on what you know are really fucked up options. We have both spent a lifetime proving we are smart enough, competent enough, good enough, but we still have no means of self-actualization that is not mitigated by white-dominated institutions that we must negotiate with in order to do what it is we feel passionate about. All Black people in the United States make choices and make more concessions, for we know that the battle for self-realization is never fully on our terms.

But inevitably, I will again, be distracted from my task by someone asking me, "What do you think about Condoleezza Rice?"

And what I think about you and your chosen occupation is precisely this: Your ascendance to the role of secretary of state, for me, simply is what it is—a reflection of a racist society that isolates brilliant Black people from themselves and forces them to serve America's imperial interests. What happens next is that the Left or the Right, depending on which trajectory the Black person has chosen, will use that person as an example of how politically or culturally misguided Black people are. In my fight to rebel against that fate, I find that I, too, am trapped by the options I have to do what I am also good at—which is to work to ensure that no other Black children, traumatized by bullets and bombs, feel they have to abandon everything they know and love, and attack another Black person's limited options in order to save themselves.

May you truly know peace,
Kenyon Farrow

Dear Ex-President George H. W. Bush,

I don't remember the mortars, the bombs, the bodies riddled with bullets. I don't remember the babies crying, even though I was one of them. I was born out of a war that might not have been were it nor for your support back when you were running the CIA and then as vice president. Unlike the countless other babies whose cries joined mine back then, who are statistics of collateral damage, I have been blessed with the advantages of a U.S. citizenship, a loving family, and access to the best schools. Ironically, through your support for the illegal, brutal U.S.-Contra war against my native Nicaragua, you gave me access to these privileges. Your war landed me with parents unlike any others, even as it killed my biological parents.

Between 1980 and 1990 a civil war between the Sandinistas and the Contras tore Nicaragua apart. The United States took part in the war, aiding the Contras with planes, weapons, and other military equipment, and by mining Nicaragua's harbors and undermining its economy. As a Sandinista, I do have a particularly biased opinion of the war and of your support for it, but by any objective standard, and according to numerous international bodies and courts, the U.S. participation in that war was illegal. During ten years of war, thousands of men, women, and children were killed, both Contras and Sandinistas. Your support encouraged the Contras to callously take thousands of lives, my biological parents among them. When parents are killed, babies are left orphaned. Amid the chaos of war, babies were left to fend for themselves, some hospitalized, some abandoned in their homes or in the streets. What twist of fate let me escape the violence while so many could not? When my parents chose to adopt, they knew they wanted a baby girl who had no siblings and whose parents were not alive. I fit the criteria and I was there practically waiting for them. Coming together and joining lives didn't prove to be as easy as finding one another. I had been waiting for them with a friend of theirs for three months; finally they came to Nicaragua and on November 8,

1985, we met and became a family. I was granted an exit visa by the Nicaraguan government, but since you were waging war against the Sandinistas, your government did not give me an entrance visa into my new home, the United States. But we managed, and my parents walked right through customs without saying word. It wasn't until five years later that I actually became a U.S. citizen and began to live my life in the United States legally. Each day I am thankful for my blessings, and each day I think of all those who do not have blessings to be thankful for. How can I come to terms with the fact that I benefited from the violence and inhumanity that I so abhor?

The war in Nicaragua may just be a footnote in the history of U.S. imperialism, but it drastically altered the course of my life and millions more in Nicaragua. War inevitably leaves countless innocents maimed for life, or dead. Few people whose lives are touched by war are as fortunate as I was. When I acknowledge this simple fact, I simultaneously accept the responsibility that comes with my privilege. I have a responsibility to take a stand against senseless killing, war, and the death penalty. The knowledge that most orphans will not be as lucky as I was calls me to action. I was able to harvest privilege out of the tragedy you sowed in Nicaragua. Every day I search for ways to stand up in solidarity with the oppressed. Though you would not have it this way, this is how I choose to live your legacy.

Sincerely,
Anna Kennedy

August 4, 2004

Dear Staff, Teachers, and Administrators,

Welcome back to a brand new school year. For some it may be a new beginning with new students; for others, it may mean familiar faces and back to old ways. This year when you introduce yourself to your students, patrol the halls making sure everyone is safe, or have a friendly conversation with a student I hope you try one new thing.

I am entering my sophomore year in high school. That's over a decade of attending Berkley schools. I've had many amazing teachers who have encouraged me to enjoy learning. It is obvious that they love their work. However, there are times when teachers have neglected to teach about becoming a considerate citizen. Sometimes I have had to be the teacher and teach my peers (and adults) about respect and tolerance.

Every day when I get up to go to school, I get a little scared. I am not afraid of the teachers or of any particular students. But there is one thing that happens every day that disturbs me and makes me want to shout out. When I walk out of a classroom and step out of doorway I cross my fingers hoping I won't hear a student call someone a "retard." Because every time I do, a sharp pain goes through my chest. When a student chooses to call someone a "retard" they do so knowing that the word has a negative connotation and refers to a group of people that are less respected in the school. It is a put-down to all people with disabilities. People believe that having a disability and being in special education is one of the worst things that could ever happen to anyone. My twenty-year-old brother Micah has a cognitive impairment. Every time I hear the "r"-word I get the chills and become upset. It's not because I think that the student using the "r"—word is referring to my brother, but because they've learned that it is acceptable to use that word. The problem is that it is NOT okay to call someone a retard.

Since the Civil Rights Movement and the end of Jim Crow, white people have learned that it is unacceptable to refer to an African

American using the word "nigger." It took a great social movement to brake down barriers for African Americans. Some things have changed. Now in school we read books like Richard Wright's *Black Boy* and learn that differences are not deficiencies and discrimination against anyone eventually hurts everyone. The same must happen for people with disabilities in the workplace, in the neighborhoods, and at school. Because when we live, work, and learn with people with disabilities, then we begin to learn their struggles and stories. It will also take a movement for people to respect, appreciate, and realize that people with disabilities are a part of human diversity.

Only since 1975 has the public school system been required to educate students with disabilities. We still have a long way to go. Schools still make up excuses to not allow a person in a wheelchair to go on a class field trip, because it is "too much work" to make the appropriate accommodations. There are often no signers or brailed programs at assemblies. For people like my brother who can't read, schools have yet to spend the money and properly use adaptive technology. Disability history is not taught in our schools. Few people know Justin Dart, the father of the ADA (Americans with Disabilities Act) or Ed Roberts, the father of the Independent Living Movement. Yes, there have been advances. At Berkley, I have had speakers with disabilities come and speak about their lives including Sarah Triano, who organized the first disability pride parade in Chicago in 2004, and Norman Kunc, who speaks about inclusive education. Right now my brother is one of the first students with a developmental disability to have a post-secondary high school experience at a university. But there is still a long way to go. It will take the complete ending of segregation of people with disabilities. When people with disabilities are fully included in all classrooms and actively participate in all school events, only then will students learn the person behind the label. As one of my brother's friends said, "I never knew people with disabilities had similar interests as me," until he started hanging out with my brother.

Every time I hear someone use the"r"-word I have to make a decision: Do I walk up to the student and say, "It's unacceptable to use *that word*." The person usually stands there trying to recall their words. I stand there wondering why I have to be the one telling them this. Then I continue. "I hope you stop using the 'r'-word because—just like you would probably never call someone the 'n'-word—you shouldn't call someone a retard. It is unacceptable."

By not saying something to students who use the word, you, the staff, make the "r"-word acceptable to use. It also makes me wonder what they think of the students in special education. You are implying that people with disabilities should not receive respect. When a teacher does, however, choose to criticize a student on using the "r"-word, they are showing that every person is worthy of dignity.

At a camp I attended this summer, one camper constantly used the "r"-word. Not able to stand it any longer, I finally asked him to stop. His response was so powerful that it forced me to write this letter to you. He said, "Retard is the only word I can get away with at my school." I was shocked and appalled. But I had no reason to be. In my ten years at Berkley—I've only known ONE teacher who has ever said anything to a student, in front of me at least, when the "r"-word was used. Granted there are probably teachers who may have heard a student using the "r"-word and pulled them aside and told them to stop. I commend all of you who have done that. Unfortunately there haven't been enough teachers and staff doing it, especially in front of the classroom, the hallways, or during conversations. Once again, it is not only choosing to stop students from using the "r"-word in the classroom, but questioning the values that lead you to choose words to be more or less harmful. A child shouldn't know they can get away with using any derogatory word in their school.

I hope I won't have to be afraid to walk down the halls of Berkley this year. I hope there will be another option when I hear the "r"-word. Maybe this year there will be another group of people—the staff, the teachers, and the administrators—behind me. Maybe they will be there when I can't or don't say anything to the student using the "r"-word. Maybe they will be the ones standing up to the student telling him or her it is unacceptable to use that word. I shouldn't have to be afraid to walk down my own school hallways because I might hear words that should not be tolerated in our building. School is a crucial place where students learn not only academics, but also social values.

Changing the culture of any high school to promote values of respect and responsibility does not happen over night. It happens little by little. Students will bring what the teachers, staff, and administrators teach them into the larger world. Especially, students will learn not to use the "r"-word, when they meet and begin to know someone with a disability. When students with disabilities are integrated and included in the classroom, with the proper supports and parental involvement, the classroom becomes a more caring, thoughtful, and respectful place of learning. As the disability movement says, "A community that excludes even one of its members is no community at all."

Maybe there will be a day when I'll walk down the hallways of Berkley High School and I won't be scared because I'll know that there's a group of people, not only teachers, but also my fellow classmates, who have learned to accept each other's differences and use respectful language. Maybe then there will be no sharp pains through my heart, only a satisfied smile.

Sincerely,
Emma Fialka-Feldman

February 9, 2005

To Governor Arnold Schwarzenegger:

Wake up! The United States educational system is in an enormous crisis as your government continues to make educational budget cuts. The United States has money for war and prisons but not for our schools—it is not providing all students with a quality education. California, one of the world's largest economies, is now rated as forty-eighth of the fifty states in the amount spent per pupil on education.

I believe it is the fault of the United States educational system that my mother has been on the streets since she was thirteen years old; that my parents and many other parents divorce; that I, and many other children, have been sexually molested; that incest continues to occur; that my mother, like many others, abandoned my siblings and me; that my mother, father, other parents, and youth have been in and out of prison; that my sisters and brothers work at fast food restaurants; that my sisters get pregnant at a young age; that my cousins and friends are dying because of gangs; and that the cycle of violence continues.

The time has come when parents, teachers, students, and community organizers/activists, regardless of race, class, gender, and sexuality, are demanding that our children's education become a priority nationally, statewide, and locally. I know this unity is possible, for I witnessed and participated in the Fast4Education, which began in the Bay Area, California, in 2004.

The Fast4Education is a grassroots civil and human rights movement committed to ending inequity in public school funding. The Fast4Education believes that every child has the right to an education. It will use any peaceful means necessary to make equitable education a reality.

It was with a commitment to these values that parents, students, and teachers organized the seventy-mile march from Richmond to

Sacramento on April 9–16, 2004, demanding a meeting with you. We could not face our schools without the libraries, counselors, and music and sports programs that the school district wanted to cut. But you ignored us. So nine of us decided to engage in a Fast4Education from May 10, 2004, to June 4, 2004, on the front steps of the capital in Sacramento. Our three demands to the state of California were that:

(1) California provides equity in education funding. The formula for funding schools must account for the socioeconomic levels of the students.
(2) California restores the $2 billion dollars under the 1988 voter-approved Proposition 98 to properly fund public education and give our children what the constitution requires for their education.
(3) The West Contra Costa Unified School District debt is eliminated.

Do you think that these demands are unfair? Some people thought these demands were unrealistic but others knew that what we were demanding was really only crumbs in this nation of plenty. People who agreed with these goals helped to make the Fast4Education a success. Those who believed in Fast4Education included K–12 grade students, undergraduate and graduate students, professors, parents, teachers, community organizers/activists such as Dolores Huerta, Catholic priests, American Indian Movement members, politicians, doctors, and hundreds of others. They helped in various roles, such as meeting with the state superintendent, negotiating with the legislature, contacting the media, taking care of the fasters, documenting paperwork, phone banking, and many other tasks.

As a community we agree to do our part to make the educational movement a success. As our governor, you should be as concerned as we are about education, but instead you make promises to our children and then continue with budget cuts that will only cause harm to kids.

After twenty-six days of fasting, the Fast4Education achieved major state legislation supporting our demands. A bill seeking to ensure equity among all California public schools passed overwhelmingly, and you signed it. This bill also reduced the interest rate paid by the West Contra Costa Unified School District on state bailout loans from 6 percent to 1.6 percent. You also agreed to visit schools in the Richmond area and to meet with the fasters.

However, the success of the fast comes with a bittersweet taste. You are not following through with your word. As our governor it is your responsibility to assure that the meager amount of funds that the state budget allocated as a result of the Fast4Education be used for the appropriate improvements needed at our schools. This has not taken place. Our schools have yet to see improvements, even after the legislation passed. You never came to visit the schools and apologize to the children that you ignored after they marched for eight days during spring break. You have joined the established history of presidents, the CIA, the FBI, and all others tied with the government in a tradition of false promises and lies.

As a twenty-year-old, third-year undergraduate student, I fasted for twenty-six days in a pacifist protest for positive changes in the educational system, letting the state know the serious consequences of its economic cuts that will keep schools still separate and still unequal. Many motivations led me to fast, but overall I did it because I care about the education our children are being deprived of, and because I want to improve that which they are receiving. Nine of us put our bodies on the line for the lives of all of our children.

Participating in a water-only fast for more than a few days endangers one's health and life, for it can lead to stomach damage, organ failure, blindness, and possibly death. But I took that chance for our children. Fasting is a serious stance to take in response to the serious problem in this state's value system. I did this action believing in the power of a fast, the support of the community, and the lives of our children.

Stop hiding behind your fancy desk and listen to us. Listen to us, because we live in a very violent, capitalistic, patriarchal, heterosexist, white supremacist country in which innocent lives are exterminated every second. I truly believe that in order to lessen the cycle of violence the movement needs to make education our number one priority.

The educational system is in need of a transformation. For example, ethnic studies, as opposed to white history, could help lessen the cycle of violence that the system perpetuates as part of the colonial/imperialist project. If money were given to schools to incorporate ethnic studies in the K–12 curriculum, rather than military recruitment, students would be taught about community roots, self-determination, and issues that are real to their lives. If today's education system was revolutionized, there would be more leaders like Dolores Huerta, Lolita Lebrón, Pam Africa, and others. The reason you and other people in power in this country do not want us to learn about people who look like us and who have made a difference is because that would inspire millions of non-whites to follow in those footsteps.

I agree with Tupac Amaru Shakur, as quoted in Michael Eric Dyson's *Holler If You Hear Me*, that "There should be a class on drugs. There should be a class on sex education, a real sex education class, not just pictures and diagrams and illogical terms. There should be a class on religious cults. There should be a class on police brutality. There should be a class on apartheid. There should be a class on racism. There should be a class on why people are hungry." If these topics were covered in schools, there would be people organizing around these issues instead of perpetuating them. As governor of California you should be very concerned and supportive of our public education. You have the opportunity to fix the funding for public schools—do it.

Furthermore, education needs to be given more attention because the school system is sexist, racist, heterosexist, poverty-stricken, drug and gang infested, abusive, and violent. There exists low-quality education, lack of concerned counselors and teachers (both teachers of color along with uncaring, racist teachers), crowded classrooms, racial fights, and low expectations for non-whites. Schools look like prisons, water fountains do not work, and bathrooms are unsanitary. The impact that these school conditions have on our students is permanent. Students feel like they do not fit in, uncomfortable/scared/fearful, bad about themselves and their culture, pain, anger, trapped, frustrated, unsafe, no love, defensive, depressed, stressed, and full of hatred toward school.

We need to be there for future generations because the way they deal with these conditions is by isolating themselves, smoking, drinking, committing suicide, losing weight, gaining weight, becoming aggressive, internalizing oppression such as sexism, fighting, passing down the negativity, selling drugs, creating negative relationships with their parents, failing in class, not attending regularly, or expressing outright frustration with school. Students should be getting help, but instead they face bad jobs and living conditions, having to deal with stereotypes, suspension from school or expulsion, making their parents suffer, jail time, probation, and police brutality.

It is tragic that you, like most policy makers in California, seem content that our students are not succeeding and make their situations worse by passing laws that have reduced urban tax bases, denied "illegal aliens" access to health care and education, ended affirmative action in the public arena, eliminated bilingual education, and criminalized youth as adults. To this list could be added the national No Child Left Behind Law and the Patriot Act. As a student, future teacher, and one of those who fasted for education, I am concerned with all these issues that are affecting the ability of our children to learn; thus, I believe that the educational movement can no longer be still. It is called a movement for a reason.

I urge you, and will do so again and again, to please wake up, because the truth is that the educational system in this country is in need of help and the public education in California is in crisis. May 17, 2004, was the fiftieth anniversary of the *Brown v. Board of Education* decision in which the Supreme Court declared that segregated schools were inherently unequal and therefore unconstitutional. Yet the reality is that many of our schools are still separate and still unequal. This is not justice!

The time of a Civil and Human Rights Movement for Education is here. We need to demand an increase in school spending. For the future of our children, our state, and our nation, public education must be supported.

Truthfully,

Jessica Vasquez

Hey kids,

Some grown-ups just don't get it. They act like we're still babies when we're seven or something. They like to touch us too much and pinch our cheeks or pat our heads, and they act like we don't know anything. I'm a big kid who knows stuff, and I want to be treated like a person, not a baby.

I think grown-ups should listen to me. I'm smart. I know a lot. I will not tolerate being treated like a baby!

I spent my whole life hanging around my mom and her friends. I've been on marches—always had my own sign, too. I've been to the Southern Girls' Convention. I worked to make my school recognize Women's History Month when they were going to ignore it. I know how unions work, and I think kids need one!

First, I think all kids should read *Click, Clack, Moo: Cows That Type* by Doreen Cronin and Betsy Lewin. This book tells all about union organizing. A bunch of cows get together and use an old typewriter to demand electric blankets. Duck is the neutral party. He takes the letters back and forth between the farmer and the animals. The cows get tired of letters, and they go on strike. The chickens strike, too, and the animals win. When animals stick together, they get what they want! So I think kids should get together and try to get what we want.

Here are some good demands:

1. Stop treating us kids like babies. This should stop at four years old, or maybe it should never happen!
2. Spend more time with us. You're always too busy. Try harder to take a little time off for us.
3. We should have a say in things our family does.

Sorry, I can't think of any more. But that's a good start.

Kids unite!
Chloe

Chloe Cook Joy

3

LETTERS TO OLDER ACTIVISTS

Dear older activists,

I hope this finds you well. I'm writing this letter, first and foremost, because I want to offer a long overdue thanks to those of you who have mentored not only me but so many of my comrades over the years. I wouldn't be the person I am today without your support, your critical nudging, your passion, and, maybe most of all, your personal examples as people who have grown older without giving up your radical political commitments. You have played crucial, if often uncelebrated, roles in our lives and in expanding the possibilities for building broad-based transformative social movements. You don't get thanked or acknowledged enough for this work.

Mentorship isn't something that is talked about much in many of the radical circles that I inhabit. Maybe that has something to do with the fact that I come out of a largely white and middle-class anarchist scene, rooted in the punk rock subculture. With many good reasons, this scene tends to be very suspicious of authority and expertise, and it really values self-reliance. For many of us in this scene, especially men, our first lessons about power were based on our battles with some of the most immediate sources of authority in our lives: our parents and teachers, both of whom offered little in the way of exciting and empowering models of cross-generational learning. I have no doubt that this goes a long way in framing how we think about learning from and with older people.

But mentorship is increasingly on my mind. Partly this is because I'm getting older myself, and I'm starting to wonder how I can nurture and support younger activists. There is a whole cohort of radicals like me, moving into our later twenties and early thirties, who are grappling with these and other related issues. I increasingly find myself in conversations about sustainable long-term movement-building as many of us look to history and think toward the future, imagining lifetimes of struggle. In these terms, mentorship seems vital. Undoubtedly, another part is that I've been able to learn and work with people, including some of you, rooted in other social locations and political traditions that are more richly multigenerational. Experiences like those make me realize that many of the political spaces I call home suffer from a lack of cross-generational dialogue and learning.

Pointing to this lack is of course much easier than proposing alternatives. Identifying and enacting radical models of mentorship is tremendously difficult work. Am I wrong to think that you, too, struggle to find and build these sorts of models? Do you, too, get lost or confused sometimes when you try to put them into practice? I suspect that, even for those of you who have successfully developed strong mentoring relationships with us younger activists, there are lots of ongoing unanswered questions.

This brings me to my second reason for writing this letter. In the spirit of egalitarian exchange, I want to offer you some of my own gentle critical nudging. That is, I don't just want to thank you. I also want to make some requests of you, to challenge you to think more seriously about yourselves as mentors.

I especially want to encourage you to be more open about your uncertainties, your mistakes, and your struggles. They might seem inconsequential or quietly regrettable to you, but they have much to offer us. The Left in this country, at least in my experience, suffers from much mutual and bitter recriminations, self-righteousness, and posturing. There aren't too many visible models of folks who are courageously and compassionately self-critical. But we can learn so much from those who are willing to talk honestly, humbly, and directly about their mistakes and sources of confusion. I know I've learned some of my most memorable and challenging lessons from some of you who haven't been afraid to acknowledge ways that you've messed up, miscalculated, or misunderstood. I think many of us could use this kind of fearless openness, particularly from those of you who, like me, are relatively privileged. I'm talking about the courage to be self-critical, vulnerable, and willing to admit mistakes, all in the process of taking risks. This is something I'm trying to learn how to do better too.

I also want to emphasize something that is easily overlooked: we have a lot to learn from you, but there is also much you can learn from us. Perhaps one reason that some of us are suspicious of mentoring relationships is that we aren't satisfied with the prevailing models of apprenticeship that we experience at school, at work, and elsewhere in our lives. I think there are times and places for apprenticeship, especially when it comes to learning specific skills from people who are more experienced. Yet I definitely empathize with other young activists who worry, along these lines, that mentorship simply means you tell us all of the answers and we receive them. This is what radical educator Paulo Freire called the "banking concept of education": a fundamentally flawed view that those who know deposit knowledge in those who don't. Of course you have so much to share. I respect that. But your generous sharing has to be rooted in a context where we listen to each other, where we collaboratively grapple with questions, where we learn together. The radical mentors who have most impacted me are those among you who, in this way, genuinely see cross-generational learning as mutually enriching.

There is just one last request I feel I have to make. Here, I can't be so gentle in my nudging. I've noticed that some of you struggle more with mentoring than others. I see this, negatively, when you sometimes give "advice" to us younger activists that sounds more like condescending lecturing than sincere sharing. Those of you who do this are often socially positioned in ways that lead you to feel deeply entitled to your expertise. And when you wield your age, experience, and achievements with self-righteous certainty, I find it hard to trust you. I'm thinking, for example, of some of you who are veterans of the often-mythologized "sixties." There is certainly much we can all learn from the 1960s, as well as from many other historical moments. But the danger lies in romanticizing or demonizing the past, turning it into something that wholly trumps our new and creative ideas in changing circumstances. Young activists don't need your status plays or your simplistic impositions of your past onto the present. Rather, we need you to recognize self-consciously how your past forms you, how it shapes your experience and understanding of the present in both limiting and illuminating ways. Please share that with us.

I hope for this letter to be a beginning, an opening. I spend a lot of time studying histories of U.S. social movements, and I recognize from this that cross-generational relations among activists are frequently fraught. Yet I also see that, in general, younger radicals lose out when they don't have access to the lives and experiences of older radicals, and, in turn, older radicals lose out when they don't have access to the imagination and energy of younger radicals. In fact, I would go so far as to say that sustained radical movements are necessarily multigenerational; they need storytelling, coalition-building, skill-sharing, collaborative reflecting, and all of the other things that mentoring relationships can foster. So, more than anything, I encourage you to reach out and share yourselves and your lives. Start thinking about how you can mentor younger activists. I'm sure you'll find people willing to listen. And for those of you who already are, thanks again. Consider how you can deepen and extend your work. In either case, remember the importance of openness, dialogue, and mutual respect.

I believe that's the soil where rich cross-generational learning can grow. Let's meet there.

In solidarity,

Chris Orr

Dear Daddy,

I overheard you yesterday on the phone in our living room. And you said something that made me stop short on the stairs. You said that if someone had told you that black people would be in this situation ten years ago, you wouldn't have believed them. You wouldn't have believed that our communities would still be without adequate institutions. That young people would still be struggling to receive a quality education in public school systems. That even though violence was at an all-time low, the arrest rate for young black men was still high.

When I heard that, I sat down on our living room steps. I had been coming to ask you a question, perhaps about the election, maybe about dinner, but after that I couldn't remember. I was stunned. Ten seconds turned into ten minutes, and I simply sat there thinking about your life and by extension, my own. You left, and I went upstairs to begin writing this letter. I didn't understand how my father, who has touched so many lives, could be so discouraged about our situation. Haven't we come a long way? There are things to be happy about, particularly the young people whose lives you've touched, and there are a lot of us.

I remember the nights we spent at the Denise McNair Community Center in Cleveland, waiting for you to come back from the drug patrols in King Kennedy. My three sisters and I would try to wait up for you, but eventually we would fall asleep wrapped in blankets while listening for you to come back. I don't think that we realized how dangerous those drug patrols were; to us, it was just what you and the brothers did almost every night. King Kennedy was the most notorious housing project in Cleveland, but you couldn't have explained that to me at the time. The downtown neighborhood was known for drugs and violence. The apartments were dilapidated but the neighborhood was still alive. Children still waited for the bus in the morning and came home in the afternoon. There were still corner grocery stores and take-out restaurants. People were surviving in spite of the violence.

On the nights that you patrolled King Kennedy, the Denise McNair Center was our hangout. We would play games on the floor and roll around in the desk chairs. We would mess with the walkie-talkies and the bull horns from the anti-gang violence rallies. The Center was an unassuming storefront on Woodland Avenue. It didn't tell the story of the movement inside. The sign didn't illustrate the strategy sessions about how to get drugs out of the neighborhood or the community members that came daily to report their problems. The storefront was the starting point for anti-violence marches; the meeting place for former gang members and a place the elderly could feel safe. Only the name, Denise McNair, in homage to one of the victims of the Birmingham Church bombing, gave voice to the activities within the Center.

My sisters and I were still young, so we didn't realize the enormity of what was happening around us. Over beef rib dinners from the mosque and candy, we would gossip about our day and eventually doze off to the sounds of the two-way radio. Pretending to be on the other side of these conversations was one of our games. We would laugh, not realizing the true meaning of what was happening in our city.

It finally became real when I turned sixteen and realized that the shootings, the killings, and the funerals had become part of our daily lives. One after another you would go, making a pilgrimage to gravesite after gravesite, mourning the loss of yet another young life. We would stand in the cold, in the neighborhoods shielding our candles from the wind in vigil after vigil. You vowed to have a candlelight vigil for every young person killed as a result of violence, and for the last ten years, you've kept your promise. I would read the obituaries that you left in your kufis on top of the TV stand. They were young high school students who wanted to be musicians. They were middle school students, simply caught in the crossfire. They were sons and daughters who happened to wear the wrong color into the wrong neighborhood. There was Paul Wallace, who was stabbed getting off the school bus, and Abdul-Hakim Chui, who was murdered for his coat. Then there was my cousin Darryl. It wasn't until after his death that I began to understand why this movement was an obsession for you. Why you would wake in the morning and ask me at the kitchen table, "Did you hear about the stabbing at John F. Kennedy High School?" or leave in the middle of the night mentioning only that there was shooting in Garden Valley apartment complex even right in our neighborhood of Mt. Pleasant. And I wonder how you will ever let this movement go. When will you trust us enough to take over the mantle? Maybe the better question is, when will we trust ourselves?

Despite what people may say, we are the present and the future of activism in this country. The culture of bling-bling, the 22-inch spinnas, and the Crunk Juice haven't blinded us to the fact that our communities are hurting. They haven't softened the blows of 9/11 and the resulting pre-emptive strikes on Iraq. Those events reminded us that death would continue to be a constant in our lives. Even though some of us have escaped the violence in our neighborhoods, many would be sacrificed to the war on terrorism. In 2003 the streets were filled with thousands of young people protesting the march toward the war in Iraq. Oftentimes, those efforts were even led by students devoted to saving the lives of young people like themselves. It was through these actions that we began to question the wisdom of our leaders and their willingness to send young, poor people of color to fight in a war against other young, poor people of color. It is a similar struggle to the one that your generation faced in Vietnam. History has described that war as a galvanizing moment, a time when the people were able to change the government, although it took time. For our generation, the war has meant division. Our country has been split down the middle by the War on Terrorism and the subsequent reelection of George W. Bush. I look to the legacy of commitment to change that you have left us for strength, but I can't help but be discouraged. Is this how you and your generation felt at the beginning of the war in Vietnam? Or when Malcolm X was assassinated? Or when Emmitt Till was lynched?

Every day I ask myself what there is to be optimistic about, and my first thought is always hip-hop. It has become a way for young black men and women to find unity and to learn through our culture. Some of our family members have moved out of the hood and some have stayed there. I lived between the city and suburbs. As I grew older, I spent my weekends split between enrichment programs and rites of passage at the neighborhood community center. I never truly left the neighborhood behind, because I was a daughter of the legacy that you left me, and I always had those voices in hip-hop to remind me of my community and my responsibility.

We are the first generation of black young people to struggle with the different life possibilities due to the large-scale integration of higher education. According to the *Journal of Blacks in Higher Education* the racial gap between black students and white students pursuing higher education is decreasing. In 2001, 54 percent of black high school graduates enrolled in college within 1 year, compared with 64 percent of white students. In 2003 58.3 percent of black high school graduates enrolled in college within the year, compared with 66 percent of white students. Even this small rise in college participation rates is being threatened by President Bush's threats to cut funding to the Pell Grant and other funding opportunities for students who need it the most. These assaults on youth have made our work as young activists more urgent.

The question for our generation remains, how do we uphold the legacy of our fathers yet speak with our own voice? How do we stay true to our values of working for social justice and still prosper? And that is why I'm writing this letter to you. We need your wisdom, but not just your wisdom, the wisdom of all of the elders. I know that we're in danger of becoming too focused on what we have, forgetting about the gain for all of our people. Even elders have tried to convince us that we've reached a pinnacle of success because we have a number of CEOs of color or because we have people of color in the government. But what do those positions mean if we don't have real change in our communities?

We also need understanding. We are a different generation, and hip-hop is our culture. You may not understand the music, but we need you to appreciate the value in our collective voice. There are those artists like Mos Def, the Roots, and others who have taught us the power of youth voices and the strengths of the hip-hop community through their music. But it's important for you and others in the black community to understand that even those artists who seem to fall into the stereotypes reveal the complexity of our world. P. Diddy's "Vote or Die" campaign galvanized millions in the 2004 election, because it used hip-hop, which has become the global language of our generation. Although some have questioned his motives and his values, his method of using hip-hop as a political tool is one that all of us should be able to support. Acceptance that this is the voice of our generation is the first step in the conversation. As long as you deny this, we will continue to speak different languages. And the lack of a common language has meant that some of us feel disconnected from you and the struggles that have brought us to this point.

I rode past King Kennedy the last time I was in Cleveland, and I didn't even recognize it. The torn-down buildings that used to house drug salesmen and gangsters have been replaced with town homes. And the street names have changed to commemorate the work that you and the brothers did there. I saw new street names commemorating Omar Ali Bey and other brothers who spent their lives working for our future and remembered the sacrifice. The housing authority seemed to have given up until you and the brothers began your drug patrols. But I think that your effort showed that the struggle to unify our communities left us broken, but not dead. Maybe that's why you're discouraged, because it seems like we've come so far, and seem to be turning away from the progress we made. I want to tell you that we will not give up on the struggle. We need your faith in us as well. Without your faith that we can succeed in making this world a better place for our children we will not have the vision of our elders and the blessing of our ancestors. I don't want you to lose hope in the next generation.

Love,

Najah A. Farley

Dear elder activist,

Ironically, I did not have any life goals until I ended up in jail. I had survival goals—street "respect" and a basic level of survival (read: materialism). I truly felt my options were limited, so I chose to sell crack on the streets of New York. Like all life choices there were consequences to choosing to be involved in street life. One of the consequences of choosing street life is jail, which is dehumanizing. In jail you are a commodity with a number—my number was 441-93-00647—not a person with desires, needs, potential, and talents yet to be realized. Another reality of being incarcerated is being away from my family and loved ones. Especially when there are times of need or family crisis. Weeks into my jail bid at Rikers Island, my aunt and cousin passed away a month apart from each other. I could do nothing to help my family through our loss—no hugging, crying, grieving with my family in our times of need. Finally, within the last five years both my brother and best friend were shot and killed on the streets, and my closest friend is in jail in South Carolina serving life. In this letter I want to try to make a connection to some of the failings of activists of the past and the "rites of passage" of street culture that so many youth of color go through every day.

I learned how to survive oppression with employment, education, and life skills support from a youth program based out of New York called Friends of Island Academy. With this support I realized that I could be whatever I wanted. I could rise above the "glass ceiling" of the street economy. It was this consciousness and support that has helped me to find direction. My life goals are to teach and inspire other youth of color to find their own path, instead of having to "walk the plank" of this world's warped perception of us.

I became an activist because oppression influenced the way I perceived my options and self-esteem from an early stage in life. For me, as an African American man, there is no way around the issue of slavery. One can start with a contemporary perspective on the impact of oppression. Currently there are a range of ways in which oppression impacts people of color, from a lack of economic opportunity, to intentional miseducation of our youth (necessary to hide the sins of yesterday), to political disenfranchisement, to the prison industrial complex, to the intentional facilitation of the distribution of drugs into our communities. Conversely, one could look at the past to see the impact of oppression. It matters to me that our people were forced to work for four hundred years for free and we have yet to be compensated for our contributions to the American society and economy. It matters to me that an estimated fifty million Africans died coming to America across the Middle Passage from Africa. It matters to me that our people began to organize to give voice and offer solutions to our issues, here and all over the world, and that our leaders were assassinated, to neutralize our strides.

Today we see the impact of not having voices like Malcolm or Martin to speak to our issues. Since our two most prominent leaders were killed, African Americans have not had leaders who speak for or represent the collective good of the African American people. For example, presently in America we are experiencing an education, employment, affordable housing, health care, civil rights, and human rights crisis. We clearly do not have leaders to speak on behalf of the people. An example of this is a provision in the Voting Rights Act of 1965, which says that African Americans' right to vote has to be renewed every twenty-five years and is up for renewal in 2008. There is no one to call to task the government and other social forces who oppose the needs and priorities of the working class and communities of color. It matters to me that our children can never be taught our true history by a government-sanctioned curriculum because it would undermine a founding pillar of American history and society—slavery and oppression. It matters to me that the lynching of African Americans was this nation's second national pastime. It matters that I know my family's surname is not Washington.

I am active in this struggle because I have to be. When I was on the streets I thought life was all about me trying to fit in and being "down," but later realized I lacked an understanding of the plight of my people and of the nature of the prison industrial complex. Now I believe the plan of the rich corporate elite is to control the agenda, resources, and direction of the United States and the world at the expense of the dreams and hopes of the masses. I will not be a passive participant in allowing oppressive situations to exist locally within the United States and throughout the world. I will not condone the invasion of Iraq. And I am active in the struggle because the generations before me resisted oppression—whether we are talking about more recognized resistant movements like the "civil" rights struggle of the 1950s and 1960s, the Pan-African movement of the 1900s led by Marcus Garvey, or the numerous undocumented slave rebellions and uprisings. (Don't believe the hype! We always fought back!) The legacy of activism is filled with successes and failures that we have inherited from those who were active before us.

You can find good or bad, success or failure, in almost every situation in life. I am in no way, shape, or form attacking the past or the efforts that were made to achieve the legacies that we have inherited from elder activists. I am simply basing my perspective on some of the legacy that we have inherited from those who came before us. It is my contention that integration hurt the African American community. Instead of us insulating and reinvesting our dollars within our community and then building our political base around our economic base, we fought for integration, which ultimately became a great hole in the pockets of our communities. I choose to see this shortcoming as a beautiful lesson we must learn from, in order to make progress for future generations. Ultimately, elder activists were unable to create and control institutions that would have given young people like myself opportunities for work and become acquainted with our African culture. We are in need of institutions that will provide for our intellectual, psychological, and economic needs. Since we live in a time where Africans in America do not have institutions and systems to counteract the continued (although altered) system of oppression against our community, our people will continue to fall victim to the present day "slavery system." I believe that the present day prison industrial complex is that very beast.

The insulation of our economic base could have yielded results that would have been beneficial and necessary to our communities. A self-contained economy could have created jobs such as counseling companies designed to help our youth work through their specific and general issues that have risen up as a result of legacy of slavery. If our community had founded a national bank, we could have financed everything from home ownership to business venture capital. Lastly, we could have created a not-for-profit "watch dog" whose purpose would be to look out for our collective best interests by informing us of upcoming political developments and working with us to influence the debates in the spiritually dead and morally corrupt Washington, D.C. All of these examples I have given would have created jobs and stimulated the economies of our communities. If we would have implemented any of these ideas we would be better off than we are today. I am not being naïve in thinking that the system would not have devised plans to neutralize our strides. We know they have and will always continue to do so as long as they have an economic interest at stake.

I do not think that activists from the past could foresee these circumstances playing out the way they did. But, all things being equal, integration was not good for the African American community. To counter these institutions we are preparing youth of color to see themselves in healthy ways. We are also better preparing our youth to understand the prison industrial complex and equipping all our youth with the tools to lead productive lives.

Nonetheless, elder activists in the struggle have accomplished tremendous strides. Three areas in which I believe elder activists were successful were cultural consciousness, resistance in the legal arena, and survival. First, the Black is Beautiful era facilitated a connection to our African heritage, a healthier view of self (as a people), and music that reflected us culturally and politically. Second, the human rights activists of the 1960s were exceptional at providing organized resistance in the legal arena, endowing us with a rich history of legal victories like *Brown v. Board* that we used to help ourselves. Institutions like the NAACP were vital in gaining many of the freedoms that we take for granted today. Finally, activists from the past were successful at surviving as a people. I feel I inherited the spirit of activism. I know its spirit is alive and well because it is both part of my consciousness and the consciousness of others. Activism is alive and well within many of us! Ultimately, the activists of the past were successful because we are still remembering them and talking about the lessons we learned from them.

In peace and struggle,
Marc Washington

Marc Washington

PRESENT:
LETTERS TO THE MOVEMENTS

Today's Movement is complex and diverse; young activists work in a variety of movements, each with their own particular strategies and tactics. And yet, we are all part of one Movement. Authors in chapter 4 explore culture and the Movement; of particular concern here is the relationship of youth culture, both hip-hop and punk, as crucial reference points for many young activists today. In working to build a broader, more cohesive Movement, letters in this chapter also reflect on the role of art and spirituality in social change efforts today. Following a similar thread, authors in chapter 5 examine the role racial, gender, sexual, and religious identities play in propelling us into activism—even if such struggles lead to conflict within the Left or within our communities. Yet, as the letters here remind us, issues of identity are often at the root of our social justice work. Reflecting on the Movement means challenging it; even as we work to build a new world, our movements are limited by the world we inhabit. In chapter 6, authors confront the serious epidemic of sexual assault and domestic violence, prevalent even within the Movement, while trying to find alternatives to relying on the oppressive criminal justice system. Letters here also call the Movement to task for neglecting its responsibility to be self-critical, or for elevating workshops above actual political work. At its best, self-reflection improves our ability to effectively change our world, and so in chapter 7 we turn to the War on Terrorism. Here, veterans of the war and of the Movement passionately challenge U.S. imperialism, from military occupation to the abuse and rapes at Abu Ghraib to an increasingly repressive home front. While opposition to the War on Terrorism provides the most striking example of the international quality of the Movement, it is far from the only instance of it. Indeed, today's movements are as global as the global capitalism we oppose. In chapter 8, authors highlight the leading role played by people and movements outside of the West, whether it is the Bolivarian revolution in Venezuela, opposition to the Israeli occupation, or the HIV/AIDS prevention work throughout Latin America and the Caribbean. Letters in this chapter are especially concerned with pushing the United States to play a positive role in the international arena. Given the enormity of our goals, the Movement will need to be firmly grounded in a vision of a new society using practical strategies for getting us there, and with new forms of egalitarian leadership—from youth, from women, from poor people, and from people of color. Authors in chapter 9 grapple with the tough questions of leadership, cautioning against postmodernism and liberalism in favor of a Movement that commits itself to winning new ground. The intra-Movement dialogue and debate of this entire section is a reminder that progressive change is on the horizon.

4

LETTERS ON CULTURE

Dearest Hip Hop,

What's up? It's been a minute since we had a sit down together. I mean, I still see you at shows, we give each other a pound, and sometimes we even kick it at my spot and listen to records. But it ain't like it used to be. You've changed, and I didn't want to admit it. I been thinking about it a lot lately. I see you everywhere I go, and you all up in folks' mouths that don't have no right to call you by your true name, 'cause they don't know even half the game. Sometimes it feels like you forget where you came from, or someone's trying real hard to make you forget who you were, and that you coulda been more than a contenda, back in the day.

Oftentimes, I wonder if you even remember the times when we would hang out at the cement city schoolyards in the south, South Bronx, plug into a lamppost, scratch scavenged sides simmering with stolen sounds and spit street science and inner-shitty subversion all night, and say "fuck you" to the popo as they rolled by, afraid to disturb our anti-govern-mental groove, un-regimented rhymes, and anti-authoritarian azz shaking.

You were born a bad azz bastard b-boy/girl, a historical hybrid full of as many countercultural contradictions as the project physicians that brought you into creation, built from bad breaks and basuras, cross colors and krylon. You were salvaged from garbage cans and demolition dumps, boosted in bulky parkas, and borrowed from our mom's 45 collection, scrawled on the stank subway 6 train, and plastered on piss-filled platforms and sacred playgrounds.

You were our ten-point program, our list of demands, a declaration of existence, our statement of resistance, a shout (out) from those whose tongues had been previously tied by the shitstem, a voice for those who were not supposed to be seen or heard. Because you existed, we persisted. And you were as rebellious as a riot, as insubordinate as us, a borrowed black-brown-boricua bible tribal tone poem pieced together from the samo shit talk and sabotage spanglish, a ghetto griots god-guided tour of every gutter and all-borough bombing. You were just as hard as Harlem, as bad as the Boogie Down and Brooknam, and as stunning as Strong Island, St. Albans, and Shaolin,

You were the terrible twin of punk, Afrika Bambatta in a "Never Mind the Bullocks" T-shirt and afro-hawk, Ramalzee and Lee and the urge to get free, Dondi as a spray can splash Gandhi, Grand Master Flash and The Clash, both poles of Basquiat, painting primal anti-products on barrio billboards, ex-vandals drawing skelly courts on stolen streets.

You, the eternal outlaw, couldn't/wouldn't be placed in a box, and illegalist artists never got paid, but still they played and sprayed on reclaimed walls and project halls liberated in the name of nobody but ourselves. We boldly emblazoned our names and claims to fame in forty-foot-high letters on private and city property. Back then, no one would give us a permission wall or permission to be (who needs their permission to be free?) so we just took it. We stole that space just like our labor, our blood, our babies, our culture had been stolen from us since foreva and eva, amen.

We couldn't afford (to pay for) instruments or attention, so we scratched on vinyl; we had no canvases, so we painted on overpasses;

we had no ballet classes on these crazy calles, so we made do with our own bold (b-boy) bodies and cardboard boxes. We stole back space and sound as reparations for the countless creations crafted by people of color then co-opted and commandeered by culture vultures with calculators, and the DJs and MCs of the APOCalypse didn't give a damn if their utterances got any farther than that little slum schoolyard where they first plugged in their two turntables and a microphone, powered by our war-words and spit. In our cheap converses, appropriated adidas, low-budget levis, and cool co-op kangols, we created a counter culture that you couldn't get over the counter. And back then no one wanted you over the counter anywayz, not Virgin or the Tower (of Babel). Not Sony or MCA or Atlantic, BMG either. Not white (washed) boys in segregated suburbs straining to grasp slum syllables while stretching our sold salvation army skins to fit their permanent privilege. Not music moguls and mass-media mobsters who buy our muse for their amusement and market our azzes for mass consumption to the highest (and lowest) bidder.

Back then bling wasn't the thing, and the only platinum was a Piñero poem about a black woman with a blonde wig on, and there was no half-nekked salt-shakin' sistas on MTV (or BET and VH1), and fuck Bentleys, you couldn't even catch a cab on 125th street and Malcolm X Boulevard. There was no corporate conglomerate to vomit back (and forth) our surreality, and no preacher-pimp publishing company would touch you with a ten-foot billboard.

But nowadays, I see you on every (clear) channel of the tell-lie-vision, on (and off) every stage, hear you laughing (and crying) on the radio, watch you acting (and re-acting) in movies, hawking your "hip hop" franchise fashions like French fries, your basketball shoes like rhythm without the blues, soda pop and pimp juice, and a million other mega-million-dollar marketing schemes you're tied into and tied up in, and I am faced with a painful question: You started out rebelling against the system, pounding on the doors of perception, but was that only 'cause you couldn't find the key to open the door? And now that you smacked the doorman and snatched the key, art turned alchemy, it's solid platinum, hanging from your neck like a slave chain. Sure, sometimes I think I see the old you peeking out shyly from underneath your worn kangol, a glimmer of a vision in your eye, now obscured by the "bling" and all them other material things. And I swear I can still hear you spittin' sweet sedition way left of the de-funkt dial on my battered boom box, but just when you about to bring the noise, it's inevitably drowned out in a bottle of counterfeit Courvesoir and a cup of (jim) crow. Tired of living the amerikan nightmare, you wanted the amerikan dream, so a microphone became just another way out the hood, like a basketball or a kilo or a fast car. In the end, you weren't tryna bust out of the shitstem, only bust the door down to get in.

Yeah, you coulda been a leader for a people who will lead themselves, a real synonym for black power, the anti-nigga machine, the Moses for the massive, the true king (and better) of New York. Man, you was beautiful, full of innovation and inspiration, rebellion and redemption, energy and possibility, but never beyond belief. Because you were something to believe in, in a world with nothing left to believe in.

We made ragtime and blues, jazz, be-bop, and rock-and-roll and soul and funk and ska and reggae and salsa and more, music designed to blow minds, while the Man built factories to manufacture our minds. But music does not belong to man, man belongs to music, and we thought hip hop was different anyway, because it resisted and existed outside of the maquiladora and the machine that our papis and mamis slaved in. Hip hop said fuck your factories, and FBI files too, and your idols and idea of fun. Yeah, hip hop, like Malcolm you were our shining black hope for forging our own damn future. Remember, long before the motor boats on the French Riviera, and the champagne on Thursdays, and the "cribs" designed by Trump and the R&B hook some random chump crafted, before you was rich and famous, when a nickel bag cost a dime, you was just a semija dropped in some abandoned lot that no one ever thought would take root. But Tupac was right, roses do grow from concrete, and that rose in Spanish Harlem song wasn't as corny as we thought. You flourished, feeding off the ghetto garbage, dumpster diving and stealing from supermarkets, a rebel without a pause, and we hoped that would be enough. And for a New York minute, it was. For a minute.

I hope you don't get it twisted, cuz I still got mad love for you. How could I not? We been to the mountaintop and the project rooftop together, we rode and wrote on the subways and highways before we went our separate ways. We saw a promised land of free meals, free lands, free minds, free hands, and back then we really gave a damn. I still remember how we held our boom boxes and ghetto blasters high as our head and wherever the beat fell was our traveling autonomous zone. And we did it all on our own. Now that was fame. Remember?

Peace,

Dear Punk Rock Activism,

We go back a long time. I don't exactly remember when we met. Maybe it was when a local band handed out animal rights fliers between songs at one of my first shows. Or maybe it was the day I opened a box of mail-ordered records, put one on, and a woman screamed out a question at me with more passion and hurt than I had never known. "Do you know what it's like to walk down the street at night? Do you know what it's like to feel the threat?" (Spitboy). No, I guess I don't.

I learned a lot from you. It was from poorly copied feminist fanzines, snatches of lyric sheets, and limited edition record sleeves that I received my politics. True, my parents' progressivism, their stories of '60s glory, played their part, but it was you who gave me a politics of my own. You threw it all at me at once. "The flag is soaked in bullshit and lies, and the decrement of a million dead [Struggle]. When the system starts to crack, we've got to be ready to give it all back [Chumbawamba]. Somewhere along this line we were stripped of identity, creativity . . . trapped in the 9 to 5 . . . We're all in prison in these free countries of ours [Chokehold]." You taught me that it was all connected years before any college professor mentioned the words "interlocking systems of oppression." You were there, Punk Rock Activism, when my Bad Religion T-shirt got me kicked out of high school, and I sued. You were there when I snipped a picture of two boys kissing—probably the first I'd ever seen—from a queercore zine, and pasted it into the school newspaper next to an article I'd written denouncing homophobia at school. And I thank you for that.

But you put some confused notions in my head, too. Do you remember when I was eighteen, living in my first punk house, and that older kid from out-of-town changed my life through late-night political talks and the books and bands he introduced me to? "Where do you get all this stuff?" I asked him, while plying through his books about Kropotkin and newspapers explaining how to scam free food and bus tickets. "Oh, you know, from infoshops, or just people in the anarchist scene," he answered, disinterestedly. I must have seemed big-eyed and naïve when I asked him what these "scenes" were like. "It's a lot like the punk, actually," he told me. "People usually live in collective houses or squats. And they do events, but instead of putting on shows for bands, they have speakers or show movies and have discussions. Or they write zines, but they're about politics instead of music." I was totally fascinated and wanted to be part of what he was talking about. Thinking back now, I realize how this moment cemented a simple, problematic equation in my head: Punk=Anarchism=Activism.

That same year, in that same filthy, freezing house, I started my first activist organization. Big surprise: it was a Food Not Bombs chapter. We were earnest, but the group quickly shriveled and sedimented, like the vegan slop we never got around to cleaning out of the pots after the "sharings." Our numbers shrunk because folks could quickly see it wasn't serving a purpose. We had launched the group because we sensed that it was what our kind of activists were supposed to do, rather than to meet local needs or challenge specific conditions.

After the Seattle WTO protests, it was amazing how much you seemed to change, Punk Rock Activism. Suddenly there was a flurry of mass mobilizations, black blocs were everywhere, and people were actually noticing. For about a year, it seemed like we were part of a new mass movement, not just an activist scene. But then the routine started to set back in, and we began discarding the tentative alliances with the unions, NGOs, and poor people's community groups. It was disheartening when summit mobilizations began to feel like simply one more modular, prefabricated activist effort, undertaken with little local connection or critical self-reflection, like so many chapters of Food Not Bombs, Anti-Racist Action, Critical Mass, and other punk "franchise activism" projects did throughout the '90s.

As much as I want to convey appreciation for how far you brought me, I can't help but express some disappointment, too. It's not just my own, but that of a lot of my friends as well. The problem, Punk Rock Activism, is that you're just not that effective at making lasting structural changes. No doubt, you've done a lot for us personally—given us a community, assured us we're not crazy for feeling out of place in our home towns. But some terrifying shit is going down these days and you can be—you *need* to be—more effective.

Recently I was reading an amazing book called *A Promise and a Way of Life: White Antiracist Activism*, in which an older generation prison activist named Bonnie Kerness asks the author, "Have you seen white kids running about with punk hairdos and green hair and rings in their nose? I have had an opportunity to work with some of them, and they are not serious. Not in the least." Punk Rock Activism, she's talking about you! And she's talking about me—at least me at one point in my life. At first I was hurt and angered by her comments, and I reacted defensively. But at the same time, I knew she was at least partially right. Kerness goes on to ask us some questions directly: "What is your goal? What is your strategy? Who are you changing?" She says, "They think that organizing is throwing an event, and it is not. Not even close. Running around and yelling 'smash the state' is not necessarily productive in terms of organizing a mass movement."

These are serious questions, and Bonnie Kerness is hardly the only one asking them. For the last five years, after every single summit or meeting we crash, other radicals have presented the same constructive criticism: direct action activists need to be organizing locally, working with communities most severely and directly affected by globalization, and connecting local issues to global ones. Otherwise, they argue, we won't be able to build the kind of mass movement required to win real changes, and the priorities and needs of the most oppressed won't be central to the struggle. If the movement isn't about self-empowerment and changing conditions of oppressed people, it's not radical, no matter how bold the slogans on the T-shirts or how daring the direct actions.

I get the sense that you don't understand or agree with these criticisms, so you dismiss them. I can hear you saying, "What do you mean, we don't organize locally? In between summits, we hold benefit shows, plant community gardens, create infoshops, screen political videos, hold anti-sexism discussion groups, and lots more. Anyone is welcome. Plus, many of us squat instead of paying rent, we're vegan, we don't drive cars—we connect everything we do in our daily lives to our politics."

This is where the conversation usually breaks down. The problem is, you and your critics are using a lot of the same words, but you mean different things by them. In my experience, there's a tendency for kids who get politically active through punk to conflate the concepts of "activism" and "organizing." But there's a distinction between the two. Basically, *activists* are individuals who dedicate their time and energy to various efforts they hope will contribute to social, political, or economic change. *Organizers* are activists who, in addition to their own participation, work to move *other* people to take action and help them develop skills, political analysis, and confidence within the context of organizations. Organizing is a process—creating long-term campaigns that mobilize a certain constituency to press for specific demands from a particular target, using a defined strategy and escalating tactics.

Organizing people is different than organizing (coordinating) projects and events. It's not that these efforts lack merit, but rising out of our youth culture scenes, as they typically do, they are often invisible, off-putting, or irrelevant to other constituencies. We've been satisfied talking to ourselves, not organizing anyone, and not building bridges to other groups and organizations for far too long. Why are we seemingly unable to do these things? The reasons are complicated and multiple, but I want to propose one to you right now, Punk Rock Activism.

You've blurred the line for us between oppression and exploitation on the one hand, and alienation on the other. We both know that in the United States, punk is overwhelmingly a white and middle-class subculture. You channel and encourage the rage, anger, and disillusionment of largely privileged youth—and you are right to do so. But along the way, the racist police brutality, the poverty of minimum wage, the violence of rape and war that others feel becomes almost one and the same with the emptiness of consumer-culture, the stultifying pressure of middle-class expectations, and the boredom of cul-de-sac suburbia that we, much more immediately, feel in our lives. Oppression and alienation are connected, of course, but they certainly aren't interchangeable.

We equate our activism first of all with rejecting white middle-class culture and try to withdraw our participation from it. We work to solidify an identity in opposition to the mainstream, and have that identity validated by a like-minded community, hoping others will follow the cue. Our thrift store fashion, contempt for manners and hygiene norms, and our dumpster-diving, nomadic lives make sense in this context—they're efforts at creating a "culture of resistance." The problem is that the Punk=Anarchism=Activism equation taught me and others that our personal choices constituted good activism, and that the world of social justice work—at least the worthwhile kind—was circumscribed by the scene.

But is being a radical about creating an alternate identity or is it about organizing masses of people? Is activism for you or for those most affected by systems of oppression? The easy answer to these questions, which you've provided us with, is "Both." The problem is that, in practice, these two directions often contradict one another. Effective organizing requires being rooted in a defined community, and (at least initially) minimizing differences between oneself and those one is trying to move to action.

While community might be the most natural of concepts for some folks, it's entirely troubling for us punks. What kind of communities do unions and other groups usually see as natural constituencies to organize? Workplaces, religious congregations, schools, neighborhoods, and ethnic or immigrant groups top the list. But punks, in serving their first goal of rejecting "the good life" on offer and expressing their contempt for mainstream values, work as little as possible and change jobs frequently, hate and mock religion, endlessly drop in and out of other people's communities, and are predominantly white and U.S.-born. As for organizing the white middle- or solidly working-class communities punks usually come from, we rarely live there or identify with them once we can get away. Our instinct is that those communities are the problem, not part of the solution.

Without doubt, seasoned radicals can't expect young folks to know how to organize instinctively. Developing winning strategies and negotiating class, race, and other divisions is incredibly difficult, and needs to be taught. The problem, it seems, is that for all you're worth, Punk Rock Activism, you don't know how to teach these skills, and we often don't know where else to look for them. So, while many organizers from other backgrounds and traditions have stepped up to the challenge, our assumptions have, in large part, kept us disconnected and sometimes created obstacles for the broader movement.

I know this is a lot to throw at you. I hope you can recognize that this criticism comes from a place of love. I also hope you'll realize that it's not an either/or I'm calling for—but rather an acknowledgment that activism and organizing, that overcoming alienation and fighting oppression, are always in tension, and that we need to be conscious of that tension when we engage in our work. You still have the power to politicize young people as you did for me and hundreds of others I know. You have the potential to *help* develop us—not just into activists, but also into organizers, changing rather than abandoning the places and people we come from, working in solidarity with people that are struggling daily to force the boot off their own necks, working for collective liberation.

Punk Rock Activism, you remember this one, right? "Boy/Girl Revolutionaries, that's what you told me. So show me!" (Huggy Bear).

So show me.

Towards victory,
Andy Cornell

Andrew Cornell

My dear sistas, brothas n sista-brothas, my dear comrades and allies, my dear lovers n friends in the Movement,

I am young. I am passionate. I have energy. I am full of fury and rage. And I want to put my heart in this Movement but sometimes I feel like there is no room for it. I fight for freedom 'cause I got this feeling in my gut. Because when I close my eyes and sing "Freedom!" I can see a light.

Because I believe there is more than the history written by the literate powerful. I believe that my ancestors' histories of resistance are written into skin, blood, bone, and muscle. And that these histories will survive, even as libraries are burned and indigenous tongues are lost to (neo)colonization. I believe there is something beyond our tangible bodies. Something that capitalism fails to explain. I feel that something.

There must be room for more than analysis and critique in this Movement. Room for more than shouting at—and tearing down—power. And this Movement's vision, like love, must be infinite and far-reaching. Our analysis and struggle cannot narrow and splinter. We can no longer afford to allow the Right-wing to connect the dots for us.

While I resist and battle transphobia, homophobia, and misogyny, I shudder at the gay marriage and pro-choice movements. Somewhere in the gay marriage debate love and spirituality have been lost among legality, money, and assimilation. I am angry at the gay marriage movement's failure to interrogate the history and present of an institution that sanctions rape and deems a dutiful wife her husband's laborer. I am angry at the pro-choice movement's failure to interrogate the history (and present reality) of "scientific" experimentation on women of color and poor women's bodies. I am angry at both movements for framing queer, trans, and women's liberation as the rights to become more successful capitalists. We cannot afford to continue participating in superficial dialogues concerning trans, women, and queer rights that are irrelevant to third world people and people of color, including those who are queer and trans, in the United States. Our issues cannot be limited to abortion and gay marriage. We must fight for our rights and all peoples' rights to love, live, and desire.

But love cannot thrive in the presence of war. My fight for liberation means that I must also fight for the right to simply exist. Therefore, I must battle the U.S. war machine, and it's so-called "War on Terror." But, the war on terrorism does not begin or end with this war against Iraq. It accelerates a Christian Right Nationalist agenda that includes destruction and control of the earth, human bodies, and consciousness. It seeks to control people physically, economically, and spiritually. As domestic violence and gay-bashing heightens in a culture of fear and violence; as our access to health care becomes even more limited; as women's rights fade; as people of color communities become even more susceptible to police brutality, racial profiling, detention/imprisonment, registration, and surveillance—those who were most vulnerable inside and outside of the United States before are even more vulnerable now.

We need to confront religious fundamentalism and the bigotry it espouses. We can no longer allow religious institutions to manipulate peoples' prayers to build nations, wage wars, trap rebellions, and drown desires. However, battling religion does not mean our Movement should be devoid of spirituality. Churches, temples, and mosques have already stripped queer people of color of our rights to pray. We have been deemed scandalous and sinful. The transphobia, homophobia, and misogyny that got Bush elected is a spiritual assault. And while in response I plan on rallyin', writin', singin', marchin', learnin', and sharin', I also plan on engagin' in a spiritual dialogue. So I need to be part of a Movement that makes space for the spirit, rather than belittling it.

Too often our Movement only engages in intellectual critique, as if liberation is only for our minds and not for our hearts, souls, and bodies. When I find that sterile elitism spilling from my own mouth, when our Movement remains fragmented addressing the issues of a privileged few, I grow weary. But I still have faith. I have faith in a vision that is deep and expansive. I have faith in god, prayer, and magic. I believe in underground railroads and the many modes of resistance that power fails to recognize. I want to challenge myself to expand the sharp vision of critique that I use so often to tear apart powerful institutions and sometimes even myself. I want to use that vision to imagine and build other ways of being. I want to listen to my ancestors and dream of a better world for my descendants. And I want to pray—through dancin', rallyin', singin', chantin', marchin', fuckin', dreamin', feedin', ritualizin', love-makin', truth-speakin', movin' n bein.' I am writing this letter, because I have faith in us—in this Movement—and our ability to change and grow.

with much luv n respect,
xxxo,
marian yalini thambynayagam

Post-Apokalyptik

Spring 2005

Guwaadze` America,

I am striving to learn the art and science of asking better questions: of myself, of our people—and of you, America. This letter is in honor of that process. America, I have loved *you*—even as you were forsaking *me*. I have loved you, even as you were denying and/or justifying your trespasses against me.

Indians? I'll try to tell you about the living. American Indians are more politically dangerous than ever before. We have more money. We have more education. We know the political process better than our elders did at our age. And now, not only are we more cognizant of our political and social power—we are more capable of utilizing those media and technological resources available to us. My voice—informed by culture, struggle, and the history of that struggle—speaking to you is only one manifestation of a radical social movement whose seeds were planted long ago.

We are the children of the survivors. We are the children of the activists, artists, and literary figures of the American Indian Rights age.

You thought the movement was over? Nah. Just resting and gathering medicine. We remember the teachings of that era—the failures and the successes. We remember how it really went. Ours is a collective memory, and we remember all of it; only now, we are better prepared to utilize those teachings, and we are better positioned to implement our political power through art and the new media available to us.

Our developing cognizance of our political power means a stronger and more progressive future for young American Indians and human peoples all across this hemisphere and the next. With our active participation in the artistic and political communities of our cities, young people of all races and nationalities are able to see what can be done with a little involvement, a little organization, and a vested interest in protecting and developing our culture, community, and resources for future generations. Artistic and cultural endeavors taken on by the young activists/artists of today will determine and make way for a whole new culture of young people who are not only more aware of their own political and social role within American, and human, society—but who are ultimately more willing to utilize that role to effect recognizable, steady, and sweeping social change. Young American Indians in 2005 are dangerous because we can, and are prepared to, pick up where previous generations left off. We are the new warriors—of idea and of practice.

Our arsenal is made up of stories—stories of change the way our elders remember it, envisioned it and imagined it. And each story has its place. Movements, like stories, don't happen the way we plan them; they happen the way they happen. Most importantly we must see that there is no real division between now and then, between us and them. The American Indian Movement and the American Indian Rights Movement are still alive. They continue to live in the subtlest actions and words of the people—young and old. We still remember. And, utilizing newly acquired mediums, we are prepared to tell the story at all costs.

I was read to from a very early age. One of the first books I can remember being very aware of and involved in was *The People Shall Continue*—one of the only books written for children, primarily Indian children, outlining the story of Indian people and our history from creation through colonization into present day America. I didn't understand right away what the story was about, and much of the book needed a lot of explaining. But I knew that the story was *my* story, and if I worked to understand this "children's story," I would learn something about myself and my place in the world around me. The book was written by my father, professor and poet laureate Simon J. Ortiz. I didn't know my dad as I grew up, but I knew he had written this book and many more that have changed the way Americans and American Indians have perceived and regarded the Americas, themselves, and each other. I knew that even though he wasn't with me, he was working—living and dying—to tell the real story of our people, our struggle, and how we were surviving in spite of everything we'd endured at the hands of empire, and of the U.S. government. I now know that this is no simple task.

Once you recognize your responsibility to change the world for the people you come from—for the people who have given you every good, human thing about you—you don't question it. You just do it. Whether it be through media, art, or other communal modes. It is the responsibility of young Indian America to become well versed in, not just American history, not just American Indian history and policy, not just American Indian art history, not just our own individual histories. It is the responsibility of young Indian America to become well versed in what's happening in Indian policy and public policy and art policy *today*.

However, I often see young Indian people, and other young people of color, who don't realize what kind of political power they hold—in the artistic and cultural forms that they enjoy. They often neglect to see the music, the movies, and the art they are entertained by as the very tools that will change the things about their culture that they hate. I grew up in an urban neighborhood, a barrio, where most of the young people I grew up with didn't like the things that were happening in their neighborhood: the influx of drugs, gangs, violence, and all the things plaguing urban communities.

Now, my contemporaries and I are at a precipice. We make up a culture of mixed-heritage, multilingual young people who recognize and
are cognizant of the very real issues of our communities. We make up a
culture of young people who are prepared to be the advocates for our
communities, utilizing the tools available to us and also instructing
those younger than us on how to better utilize those same tools and
the ones being developed even as we speak—to make things better for
our people.

Art is central to this process. To this young generation of Indian and
mixed-heritage artists, Indian art is not something to just view or purchase or be a spectator of. Indian art, and all art, is meant to be experienced and lived. Our art comes from the social, cultural, and political
struggle that we, and our ancestors, have endured to make a better
life for our people. We live the struggle, and our art is a depiction of
this struggle—for land, for freedom, for life. It has always been this
way, only now our art is also a vital depiction of the ultimate and
inevitable evolution of this struggle, and the evolution is showing us
that we have the power to determine our own histories and futures, to
change life ways, policy, and science and the way Indigenous societies
are perceived and interacted with throughout communities worldwide.

A huge and vital part of the strategic development and eventual
implementation of an activism curriculum within higher education,
especially American Indian higher education, is the teaching of the
development and histories of certain movements, their place within
society and the way we, as a society, have come to perceive "activism"
as it has changed and existed as a living entity in our communities.
This all begins with knowing the story. How far off is the *Institute of
American Indian Activism?* Not too far, if I have anything to do with it.

And yet, I've never called myself an activist or a "political Indian."
But I do not shy away from my role as storyteller and story-keeper. I
loved to be told stories when I was little, but I always preferred the
ones based in reality, or the ones that were made up around things
that had really happened to real people. And now I pay homage to that

with my life. Too many of our stories have been lost. When telling stories through film, theater, or poetry, I pay continual homage to the stories of our people that will never be told—those that have been lost to time.

I am not an activist, but I'll die artistically and politically active. Like so many before me, I am willing to speak up for those who have no voice, and if this makes you call me an activist that's okay too. I've never professed to be "revolutionary" nor *a revolutionary*—but I am prepared to fight for those stories that must be told for our way of life to continue. Our Indian life ways are built by and around our oral and written histories. We carry them with us so that we may go on.

Our story is our life. I protect stories. That's what I do. I am a storyteller. And in 2005, storytelling, like activism to a degree, is business. But far beyond the buying and selling of culture, even beyond the circumstance—intellectual, political, or otherwise—that brought *you* to *my* story of "Active Indianism," there remains the story of how we came to this world, how we fought, with our living, and dying, and speaking— to protect it. One has to be willing to fight and die to protect and tell *that* story as completely and accurately as possible. And I am.

I am an American Indian, but I am so much more than that. The worst thing you can do is underestimate the minority. Indians are not just Indians anymore. You can't *really* count us in this day and age. My enrollment number doesn't make me Indian. My family and my human history is what makes me Indian. A better name for us is the *Hanoh'*— The People. We are of mixed heritage and ancestry. Politically mixed. Mixed tax bracket. Mixed everything. We're everywhere, and we're more organized than ever.

George W. give you nightmares? The War on Terror got you down? Many things are frightening and unclear in this time of fear and murky political waters, but one thing is not: *you stand to gain with us on your side.* Policy and politics in the Americas have sought to eradicate us, and *we're not going anywhere.* Our survival is yours. Inform yourselves about what's happening, or not happening, in the Indigenous communities of this continent and everywhere. Our loss is yours. Our progress is yours. We won't underestimate our role in your societies. See that you don't neglect your role in ours.

And so, because I have learned your system and your doctrines well (perhaps a little too well) I have made a new religion. A religion of loving you with my truth, America. A religion of forgiving you for trying—and failing—to kill me, America. I *am* dying, but it's on my terms now. You are mine, America, like an abusive parent, or a tiny scratch on the roof of your mouth that you just can't seem to stop tonguing. We've been in this together for some time—and it's time to compare our notes, America.

Ha'ah, kaimah'tse, dza-dzenah wai ehmeh-nah eh-eh dzeh shruunu. Mahmeh, kuuyah kgu. Dahwaaheh`:

Yes, it's true, it is no longer today the same. Very much it has changed. It is good.

Dahwaaheh`,
Sara Marie Ortiz

5

LETTERS ON IDENTITY

la cultura contiene la semilla de resitencia que
crece en la flor de liberacion
*(culture contains the seed of resistance that grows
into the flower of liberation)*

Hey Samantha,

I know it's been a while, but I hope everything is going ok. Thank you for writing to me on my trip this summer; it was nice hearing about what was happening at home while I was away. I know it's hard to understand why I do the things I do, but coming from our background I have a greater understanding of how all these issues affect people. I want to do something to change it.

It's like when we were talking about our ancestors—they have taught us the Nahuatl concept of Tloke Nahuake ("together and united") and the Mayan concept of In Lak Esh, which means "you are my other me." These concepts say that we need to understand that we are all reflections of each other and that all our actions affect all those around us, our families, our communities, and our society. What we do and say holds far greater repercussions than what we're willing to accept, and so we have to do our best to be accountable and aware of how our actions affect others. If we fail to act, we fail to help others, and if we fail to help others we ultimately fail to help ourselves.

I think you're too young to remember, but Mom actually struggled a lot—both here and back in Mexico. She started working at the age of seven and then had to leave her home and come over here by the age of sixteen to work, as there was really nothing left in her pueblo. Here she worked in sweatshop after sweatshop, putting up with ten- to twelve-hour workdays, abuse from her employers, and INS raids to be able to survive and send money back home. And your dad, coming from Palestine, to a place unknown with no family or friends to rely on, struggled a lot to just make it here and then save the little he was able to, to send back to your grandparents. Many people and families have experienced this forced movement out of their homes and into unknown places that continue to be difficult.

Even after being pushed to leave our homelands, we face discrimination. One example of this is Proposition 200 in Arizona, which we are currently organizing against. If passed, this legislation would require all people in the state to present their birth certificate or passport to receive public services and to vote. I already told you about the people that die trying to pass the Arizona border because of the dire situations they face at home. And now this vague proposition, much like Proposition 187 in California, is trying to scapegoat our community by blaming the state's economic downfall on this migrating population. These immigrants contribute a vast amount to the economy, above and beyond what resources they are said to use. Same with our family; I know you don't remember mom ever being discriminated against, but remember how after September 11th happened, your teachers and other students were calling you all names, and some even still joke about it today, calling you a "terrorist?" This type of misunderstanding and misinformation about our communities has not only led others to act violently against our people but has also led policy

makers to implement laws that continue to scapegoat and disenfran-
chise many communities of color. It is these very policies that I am
currently working against because of the injustices forced on our
people. However, if I hadn't struggled through my own process of
reflection and growth in regards to my identity, I don't think I would
have learned so much about the world and why people all over the
globe are not only struggling against similar issues but creating
bridges between communities to overcome them.

Just as you are struggling with your identity, being in both
Raza/Catholic and Arab/Muslim cultures—where sometimes it feels as
if people try to force you to choose one—I too had to struggle with my
own identity. As I have both parents that come from Mexico, I know you
may think that it was easier for me to understand my identity, but it
wasn't. I remember getting into the punk scene in high school because
I was tired of everyone saying we should look or think a certain way, be
more involved in the church, or act more like young ladies. I didn't
seem to fit anywhere. Going to Mexico I was considered a *pocha* or *del
otro lado*, not "fully Mexican," yet here I was seen as "brown," as "Mexican," and not "fully American" either. It took me a while to actually
appreciate our Mexican culture, let alone understand the immense
history we're connected to through our ancestors and traditional ways
of spirituality and healing. As I learned about our ancestral past and
traditions, I felt I had found and gained a large part of myself that was
missing. I understood that labels imposed up on us—such as Hispanic,
Latino, or Latina—were not me and could never appropriately describe
who I was. Understanding the struggles that our ancestors, parents
and communities have been part of, such as forced dislocation, dis-
criminatory laws, and depreciation of our contributions as a people to
this nation, have motivated me to continue the struggle to pass on our
traditions and knowledge to ensure we have a voice and organize with
other communities against these issues.

You might remember our parents constantly telling me to focus on an
actual "career" and "realize" that life is hard so we need to concentrate

our energies on making as much money as possible and be stable. It was hard for Mom to understand why I was getting so involved with political actions and *indigenismo*, as this society had already shown to discriminate against our community and not allow for much socioeconomic advancement. But it has been this very understanding of my identity, culture, spirituality, and gender that has motivated me to struggle. Culture and identity allow not only for the development of a greater historical and, perhaps, international understanding of the world, but also how these distinctions and differences are valuable and can bring light to our similarities and connections. Our identities do not begin or end with us alone; they come from long historical struggles within the governments, societies, communities, and families they grew and evolved from.

For me, as a Xicana, the very concept of *Xicanismo*, or identifying as *Xicana* or *Xicano*, stems from a political identification with the '60s Chicano movement and the need to bring identity to the forefront of how a people have been treated, discriminated against, judged, and survived. This identity also speaks to the need of using this historical understanding to more critically analyze what is currently happening in our society and internationally, and to better implement interventions that will take into account people's voices, leadership, and means of healing to facilitate empowerment and self-determination.

When I join an organization, my *Xicananess*, my femaleness, my political awareness, and my international understanding of people's realities are what I bring to the group, to the analyses I provide, and to the activities I engage in and deem important. My own need to be aware of these factors provides an understanding that others, too, face these issues. Thus more collaboration between communities is needed to more adequately address discrimination and injustice. When I work with youth in my job as a social worker, I not only take into account their immediate needs, but how these needs are tied to the gender, culture, identity, familial and societal values, and other realities they are part of. This approach allows me to more effectively provide the resources they are in need of or don't have access to because of current societal conditions and policies.

Identity—be it your gender, ethnicity, sexuality, race, ability, nationality, spirituality or religion, or other facets of who someone is— is not predetermined by birth. It is nourished and shaped by our lived experiences in the families, communities and societies we are part of. Identity, as the Mayan concept In Lak Esh teaches, is not only an individual characteristic; it is manifested in our process of reflection and analysis, our practices and actions, and thus enacted as the assumptions, judgments, fears, limitations, or connections we place on others.

Our awareness of our community's historical struggles provides insight as to the strength we carry within ourselves and sheds light to the strengths other communities hold that we need to be aware of and advocate for to make well-informed decisions. Having dual or varied identities such as your own may be difficult at times, but it also represents a wealth of realities you are able to understand and experience and thus help others with. Always remember you come from a long line of strong people whose history, knowledge and work continue to contribute greatly to our society and to our development as people.

> *"If I stand tall it's only because I stand on the shoulders of those that came before me."*
>
> —unknown

In Tlaneztia In Tonatiuh,
(May Your Sun Shine Brightly) Guadalupe Patricia Xochihuiztli Salcedo

Sweetie,

Every morning, just as I am about to crawl out of your arms and our nakedness, I thank you. I thank you for creating a space where I can feel safe in my boxer briefs, white undershirts, baggy jeans, boots, and with my piercings and short shaggy hair hidden under baseball caps. It is hard to find places where I feel validated and confirmed in my gender identity and sexuality, especially when roughly twelve hours of the day are spent in a uniform that does not reflect who I am. So a vital part of me is left with you each day.

I wake up each morning to put on an outfit that is not truly me. I adhere to a dress code that has me wearing heels, silk bras, blouses, and form-fitting slacks. What does it mean to dress professionally? It translates into giving up my boyish self, the self I show when I'm with you. As I go through my closet brushing aside clothes that are comfortable on my body and you watch me dress, I wonder if you can still see me, the queer kid from NYC that you fell in love with. My concern is that this dress code forces part of my history and much of my identity into hiding. This seems contradictory because part of the struggle I am committed to is challenging and ultimately undoing the gender binary: a belief system that assumes there are only two genders. I believe, as someone once said to me, if there are six billion people in this world then there must be six billion genders. My gender is one of billions and can't be defined by a binary.

On my first day as a union organizer three years ago, long before I'd met you, I was directed by union leadership not to present myself in a manner that would make *me* an "issue." I was told that as a union organizer my role would be to help create a political space where workers can successfully organize their union, i.e., gain power in the workplace through collective action. So if my lifestyle would be the subject of controversy, it needed to be downplayed or camouflaged.

What part of my lifestyle might be considered "controversial"? Could it be the dyke club I went to last Saturday night where female strippers danced for the eyes of other women? Is it that I believe in anarchism? Or maybe it's the drag king performance I did for over one thousand people at the San Francisco Pride celebration, or the fact that I don't necessarily subscribe to one pronoun all the time. Or, perhaps it is as simple as you, the woman I am in love with. These are some of the things that my employer does not want me to bring to an organizing drive, in an attempt to protect the workers who are organizing their union. But this presumption not only undermines the workers' ability to judge for themselves, it assumes that there are no workers who can relate to me as I truly am.

Regardless of whether I reveal my full identity or not, discrimination exists in many different forms in workplaces, especially for those who cannot or choose not to disguise their identities. Throughout my experiences in organizing drives, it has become clear to me that, in addition to the boss's rules, the attitudes and behaviors of the employees themselves also affect the work environment. Bad working conditions are not only the result of material deprivation, but also, the emotional trauma of discrimination in the workplace. For example, the gay worker referred to as the "fag" nursing assistant from the west wing of the hospital suffers an unstable and oppressive work environment, in addition to the insecurities already resulting from a low wage and no health insurance. This is also true for Latina nursing home workers I know whose bosses have prohibited them from speaking Spanish inside the facility. At a nursing home in Sonora, California, the one African American nursing aide is commonly referred to as "the black guy." In the workplace, his entire identity is summed up by his race. And women commonly suffer gender discrimination—not only by their employers and coworkers, but also by their partners at home. So common is it for a husband to prohibit his wife from talking to an organizer about the union that union organizers across the country have dubbed this as the infamous "cock-block." In all of these cases, the workers are being stigmatized and oppressed because of their identity.

As you watched me dress this morning, watched me put away part of my identity, I thought of all the workers who get up every day and go to work in oppressive environments. The fact that I have to hide is emblematic of what the labor movement fails to address: the multidimensionality of all people, including the working people who are organizing the union. I am driven to activism because of who I am and the conditions imposed upon me and those around me, including conditions arising because of my queer identity in both my gender and sexuality. Other stigmatized individuals or groups in the workplace can be equally compelled to activism by their identity oppression.

Employers, mine included, believe "What is not seen is not a problem." This misguided assumption in the mainstream culture affects the way we think about ourselves and others in the labor movement. The disguise of my queer identity at work suggests that homophobia and genderphobia do not exist at the workplace, but this cover-up is the very intolerance it seeks to hide. In complying with the imposed dress code, I am denying aspects of my own identity: I am complicit in the discrimination that also victimizes me. Workers never get the chance to judge my identity for themselves because it has already been silenced before they encounter me. This homogenization of activists and organizers suggests that we are void of individual identities and experiences. This sterile depiction inherently limits the expression of employees with whom we organize. Sadly, the parochial focus of the union limits its ability to reach out and touch the lives of a full spectrum of people. And it limits my ability as an organizer to be fully available to some of the workers.

The marginalizing experiences of workers (and organizers alike) are neither acknowledged in the workplace nor by the union movement unless defensively vis-à-vis the boss. In my view, labor has to speak directly about the rights of queers, immigrants, people of color, women, and differently-abled people. These are the workers who are either part of our union or potential members. They are the hardest hit in terms of being the last hired, first fired, and most often excluded by labor unions historically. We need to take on discrimination in the workplace proactively—not just defensively and not just with the boss. How do we as a union (staff and members) support each others differences and struggles? The strength of our movement won't grow if we only talk about bread and butter issues, while ignoring issues of identity and power. The union can't function as a movement to build worker power if those in the labor movement are limited in how they can express themselves. Ironically, often economic power and stability are intrinsically linked to identity. We cannot begin to fight for the rights of those members who are discriminated against in the workplace because they are queer if we cannot even acknowledge there are union staff who are queer.

While I come home every night to share myself with you, every day at work I silence myself for "the sake of the movement." At work I miss out on the intimate conversations that are taking place during the day between union staff and workers. While my straight colleagues bond with workers over stories about their families, relationships, marriages, and children, I am silent with respect to my own life and our relationship. My guarded nature at work then impacts my ability to intimately connect with workers as the campaign develops. I am blamed for withholding. I wish I didn't have to be so guarded. I hate pretending with workers who I respect. It hurts not being able to talk about you. I love what we have, why shouldn't I share that? I'm angry because I'm not ashamed of us and I don't want to be forced back into a closet, especially a closet full of skirts and heels.

Yet I put on my "straight feminine" outfits every morning because I love being part of the labor movement, knowing of the ever-present potential it has to create powerful economic, social, and political change. When working-class people, who are marginalized in this country as it is, have moments of beating the boss, these victories prove to me that we can take on the battle to include all of our various identities in the movement. Often when workers begin to organize their union they fight because of their own self-interest, but as the battle progresses, workers unite and begin to fight for each other's struggles, connecting their neighbors' lives to their own. The strength of those who organize at the workplace demonstrates how the labor movement inspires people to come together even with their differences.

I am hopeful that we, those involved in the labor movement, will invest ourselves in the struggle to include our many identities. And, perhaps then parts of my identity would not have to be left with you every morning. I could go to work and talk about how happy I am to be in love with you. Sweetie, thank you for not losing sight of me as I transform my identity into that of a "straight" union organizer every morning. Into the night I lose myself in the comfort of your love, committed to begin my mornings in outfits more and more expressive of who I am. Who we are.

love you,
n

Nell H———y

Dear Progressives of My Generation,

I remember receiving an e-mail from a high school friend in late 1999 asking what I had been doing since we graduated.

"I am doing a doctorate in the sociology of religion, becoming more serious about being a Muslim and starting an interfaith organization," I wrote.

"Why all this religious stuff?" he replied. "What made you run off and join the flat earth society?"

When it comes to religion, such exchanges are all too typical. My generation of progressives has developed a rich discourse and a focused strategy around race, gender, class, ethnicity, and sexual identity. But we have barely begun the conversation on religious identity.

I remember many all-night discussions about identity issues when I was an undergraduate in the early 1990s. Yet, my friends and I rarely discussed religious identity—a shocking fact considering, during that same time, Bosnian Muslims were being massacred by Serbian Orthodox Christians in a murder-spree fueled largely by religious prejudice.

In a world dominated by conflict along the lines of identity, progressives need to develop models of multiculturalism that are respectful of the histories of particular communities while simultaneously promoting modes of interaction between groups that create justice for our contemporary, highly diverse, societies. The multicultural debate becomes self-absorbed and irrelevant when it is exclusively consumed by the question, Who am I? That question needs to be followed up with the questions: How do I (and my people) engage with you (and your people)? How does my history encourage me to contribute in unique and positive ways to all of humanity? Most importantly, how can I and my people join with you and your people to achieve a dream of collective social justice?

Answering that question will lead us to a better understanding of the role that religion plays in people's lives, informing the broader conversation progressives have on identity, diversity, and justice. Or else we write themselves out of the heart of the vast majority of humankind and render ourselves immaterial to both the bloody conflicts and the faith-based social change movements afoot in our world.

Conservatives have developed the most effective discourse on religious identity. Their faith-based organizing strategies played a major role in the elections of Ronald Reagan in the 1980s and Bush 2 in 2000 and 2004. Had progressives connected their justice agenda to religious values, following the example of Martin Luther King Jr. and more contemporary figures like Cornel West and Jim Wallis, those elections might have turned out differently.

I was raised in a devoted Muslim family. My heroes include a Hindu (Gandhi), a Catholic (Dorothy Day), a Jew (Abraham Joshua Heschel), a Baptist (King), and a Buddhist (Thich Nhat Hanh). Studying their lives has encouraged me to find the social justice resources in Islam. Conversations with my Jewish, Hindu, Christian, Mormon, and Bah'ai friends have helped me clarify my Muslim practice. I am convinced that, now more than ever, the possibility exists for people to be rooted in their religious tradition and in mutually enriching relationships with people from other traditions.

In 1998, I started an organization that would help young people achieve this ideal, the Interfaith Youth Core (www.ifyc.org). The purpose of the Interfaith Youth Core is to build a movement where young people from different religions can strengthen their own religious identities, build understanding across religious communities, and cooperate together to serve others. The IFYC is a Chicago-based nonprofit with national programs and an international vision. We want to put a big idea in the culture—if you are young and religious part of what you need to be about is coming together with people who are different from you to build understanding and cooperate to serve others. Like anything else, the organization started small, but our budget, staff, and scope have doubled in size each of the last three years.

When I started telling progressive communities about the Interfaith Youth Core, I was surprised at how dismissive they were about religious young people. It was as if they were saying, "Why don't you run programs for a population that matters?"

Unfortunately, religious extremists are well aware of how powerful programs for religious youth can be. Preachers in the bigotry-driven Christian Identity movement pay special attention to young people. So it should come as no surprise when we learn that twenty-one-year-old Benjamin Smith went on a shooting rampage that targeted Jews, Asians, and African-Americans on the north side of Chicago. The youth programs of those Christian Identity movement preachers are tearing apart the fabric of a diverse society.

Extremist Jews in the Middle East take pains to involve young people. So it should come as no surprise that the assassin of one of the great souls of the twentieth century, Yitzak Rabin, was a twenty-five-year-old Jew. The youth programs of those extremist Jews are destabilizing a peace process.

Muslim fundamentalists make explicit calls to young people, inviting them to study in their hate-filled schools and train in their jihadi death camps. So it should come as no surprise that most of the September 11 terrorists were in their twenties. The youth programs of those Muslim fundamentalists are creating a state of permanent war.

There is another, far more hopeful, storyline involving religious young people. I call it the faith hero storyline. It is astounding how young our faith heroes were when they began impacting the world. King was just twenty-six when he led the bus boycott in Montgomery. Gandhi only twenty-four when he led the movement against racist pass laws in South Africa. Jane Addams was twenty-nine when she started Hull House. All three were the products of progressive religious education, and in turn, founded their own progressive religious institutions and movements.

Young people of faith are going to impact the world. The only questions are, How and to what ends?

It reminds me of the truth in Gwendolyn Brooks's poem "Boy Breaking Glass," written from the perspective of a young person:

I will create
If not a note, a hole
If not an overture, a desecration

When we read about a twenty-two-year-old kid who fires a gun or detonates a bomb while whispering the name of God, we should take it personally. It didn't have to be like that. A progressive religious movement could have gotten to that kid before the extremists did. In every twenty-two-year-old religious terrorist, there lies a faith hero we failed to nurture.

I recently read an Indian journalist's account of the RSS, an extremist Hindu organization based in India. Fifty years ago, one of its young members murdered Gandhi, and more recently the RSS was involved in the killing of over one thousand Muslims in the state of Gujarat.

I was surprised at the intimacy of the article, and wondered how this person knew so much about the RSS. Toward the end, he confessed that he had been a member when he was a teenager during the 1940s. It was the twilight of the colonial era, this journalist wrote, and he wanted to be part of something larger than himself. He joined the RSS because it seemed like the only option for a teenager with a growing political consciousness living in an area where the more moderate Congress Party lacked an active youth wing.

If the interfaith youth movement achieves its ambition, that storyline will change. Young people all over the world will have access to programs that strengthen their own religious identities, build understanding between religious communities, and promote cooperation to serve the broader society. Religious congregations will use interfaith curriculum in their education programs. College campuses will start interfaith student councils. Boston, Bombay, Belfast, Baghdad, and places both beyond and in between, will have Days of Interfaith Youth Service.

Does it sound a bit too grand? The Christian Identity preachers, the extremist Jews, the Muslim fundamentalists, and the Hindu fascists do not play small. Why should we?

My own social justice work, as a teacher, an organizer, and a move-ment-builder, is based on the twin notions that God gave us both great gifts and great responsibility. I feel in my bones that this train called Earth is bound for glory. As one of the most important faith-based activists of the twentieth century, Martin Luther King Jr., often said, "The arc of the moral universe is long, but it bends towards justice."

Salaam,
Eboo

November 4, 2004

Hey Dan,

It was really nice talking with you last night. It seems like awhile since I've been able to have a genuinely good conversation with a friend. It helped me to talk with another American Jew about my experience in Israel. I have not been able to really process my experience there yet.

My trip to Israel was through Birthright, a program that brings Jews from all over the world to Israel for free to boost our relations with that country. Being a Jewish American visiting Israel, I couldn't help but think about what my relationship with Israel is and should be—of how Israel's policies relate to my identity as a Jew. As a politically conscious individual, I have been critical of Israel and have grown increasingly interested in the current situation since the second Intifada started in 2000. I went to Israel to explore how—or whether—I could identify with the country. Many Jews believe that preserving the state of Israel is essential to preserving the Jewish people, and thus they defend much if not all of what Israel does. Other Jews have no objection to a Jewish state but oppose Israel's policies, feeling that the country's actions have made us less safe. There are also those who do not feel a connection with Israel or feel that Israel has nothing to do with being Jewish. This spectrum includes both secular and religious Jews, Zionists and anti-Zionists. Given all the criticism that many Jews worldwide have of Israel, I wonder what sacrifices we have made in establishing a Jewish state. We have succeeded in preserving the Jewish people, but what part of the Jewish people? I ask this question without an answer. As Israel strengthens itself by building armies and occupying land, are we asking if something is being lost along the way? Further, what does it mean to be Jewish and critical of Israel?

While I stayed in Israel I roomed with an eighteen-year-old solider serving his last year in the military. He is one of the fighters in this war. He expressed his disagreement with his government; he hates the war and believes in peace—yet he said he would choose to fight in the army even if it were not mandatory (military duty is required in Israel for all eighteen-year-olds). When I asked why, he explained that his father had fought in the Independence War and the Yom Kippur War, and had served his country and his people. It was never a question for this young man whether to join the military. He saw the army as a way of serving his people more so than his government—a difference I understood, even if I did not agree with him. Like others I spoke with, the soldier also told me about how the violence in his society affected his life. He has buried friends and witnessed suicide bombs. As we walked through the streets of Tel Aviv, he pointed out sites where different bombs had gone off. He claimed he was so sick of shooting at people and watching people die on both sides. In mid-stride he turned to me and said, "Never ask a solider what he thinks of the conflict after he's lost a friend in a shooting or suicide bomb. Wait a few weeks and you'll get a much different answer."

The Jewish people historically represent a culture of modest resistance. Israel, meanwhile, represents a culture on the offensive: bulldozers destroy neighborhoods, airplanes shoot missiles into densely populated urban neighborhoods, and the government builds more walls, all obstacles from peace. The government is calling its latest "anti-terrorist" endeavor a wall, a security fence, or a trench, but it is a vast barricade and a symbol of domination. The Israeli military builds walls and enforces borders that extend beyond the Green Line—the cease-fire line established after the 1967 Arab-Israeli War—and cut deep into Palestinian lands. The wall has not put an end to violence or even put a dent in the terrorist factions that wish for the destruction of Israel; instead the wall feeds Palestinian (and world) outrage and anger toward Israelis. It is a blockade to solutions, a reality that inevitably postpones any efforts to foster peace.

I'm trying to get an understanding of how the situation got so bad and why it is still going on, with no end in sight. Israeli settlements continue to violate the Geneva Accords and countless other UN resolutions, while systematically depriving the Palestinian communities of basic resources. Palestinians continue to carry out homicide bombings targeting Israeli civilians. I do not believe that terrorism is a justifiable means toward statehood. I am appalled at the targeting of Israeli citizens as a means to an end; however, I cannot afford to turn my head from the terror and violence of the military occupation, which claims the lives of many Palestinian civilians. The Red Crescent Society reports 3,579 Palestinians killed since September 29, 2000, as compared to the Israeli Defense Forces figure of 1,042 Israelis killed in the same period.

Many peace initiatives have been proposed with various measures of success, yet violence from extremists has always overshadowed these attempts, whether it is Jewish extremist Baruch Goldstein gunning down 29 Muslims in 1994 or "The Passover Massacre," a suicide bomb that killed 28 people and injured 172 in 2002. Although, individual extremists play a large role in the violence, it is important to point out that the Palestinian terrorism continues to exist because Palestinians have no state, whereas most of the violence by Israel is by an established government that is not only recognized but also supported by influential governments. Both sides respond. Israel quickly responds with military action, such as Operation Defensive Shield (largest military operation in the West Bank since its occupation in 1967), resulting in an increasing number of attacks on Israeli citizens. This struggle is not only about water, land, religion, history, and politics. For many Israelis and Palestinians, the war seems to be about daily life in a military occupation, wondering if the bus in front of you has a bomb on it. It's about watching your friends and family die in Palestinian homicide bombs or Israeli military attacks.

The more I read, the more I learn about massacres and terrorism that both Jews and Arabs have committed. Arabs killed 10 percent of the Jewish population in Hebron in 1929. In that same time period, Jewish terrorist gangs began to evolve, such as the Irgun and the Stern Gang. From December 1947 to February 1948, Jewish terrorists mined passenger trains and tossed bombs at Arab civilians in cafés and markets, resulting in 138 deaths and hundreds more wounded. Many Jews called the Irgun freedom fighters, yet the Jewish Agency condemned the group for its terrorist tactics, such as bombings, assassinations, and other forms of terror against Arabs and British civilians and military. The Irgun fighters were later absorbed into the Israeli Defense Force. I find it incredibly ironic when looking at what levels of violence were justified in achieving a Jewish state and the violence we see today from the Palestinians, who view themselves as freedom fighters. David Ben-Gurion never moved against the Irgun and the Stern Gang until after Israel was established and secured, which is not what Israel is asking the Palestinian Authority to do. Essentially, the Israelis are asking the Palestinians to do something they themselves refused to do.

When the children of Palestine witness such brutality as what happened in Sabra and Shatila (2,500 people slaughtered by militias in 1982 under Ariel Sharon, defense minister at the time), they are being subjected to an atmosphere of violence and military presence. These children watch as their families are torn apart and their homes left in ruins. It is likely that they will grow to hate Israelis, and perhaps Jews, with vengeance, begging the question of whether Israel contributes to the creation of future warriors for jihad. The idea of violence fueling violence sounds so cliché, yet so apparent in what is going on in the Middle East. On my last day in Israel, we went to the Yad Vashem (the Holocaust Memorial Museum in Israel). Our tour guide said something that stuck with me; he said ten years from now, the world may say that what is happening in the Middle East now is a Holocaust of the Muslims. I thought that was a pretty profound statement, especially coming from a Jew that has focused so much on understanding anti-Semitic genocide.

In the end I find myself motivated and inspired to learn more about what it means to be Jewish. I guess this is the beginning: discussing it with friends, family, and elders. I'm currently studying Hebrew and planning a trip back to Israel to spend two months there, working and studying Hebrew. In today's world situation, Jews need to grapple with not just our identity, but also with actions of the state of Israel; Israel is part of a background that I am linked with. I am not personally opposed to a Jewish state, although I oppose many of Israel's policies. I feel the birth of Israel in Palestine set the stage for conflict and was more or less an occupation in itself, and yet I do not believe in the destruction of Israel. I believe Israelis and Palestinians can coexist in the same region, although it will take major political, economic, and cultural changes for that to happen. To eradicate Israel from the region will not bring anyone closer to peace. I support the efforts in creating a two-state solution. I cannot say exactly what those borders will look like, for it is up to those directly involved to establish such mutually acceptable borders, but I believe there must be a clear and coherent dialogue about current laws and structures that impede the self-determination of the Palestinians. No two-state proposal is sustainable without full Palestinian sovereignty. As a Jew I will continue to think critically, ask questions, and search for truth. It is my right as a human being to speak about my thoughts and experiences, and to engage in dialogue around issues such as these, for our own learning as well as our teaching. We either accept history as our future, or start changing our ways and making history a pivotal point to learn from mistakes made and create a more inclusive, conscious, and free world.

Dan, I was excited to hear that you had observed Yom Kippur. I did not, but if you were here I would have loved to have shared that with you. Recently I connected with the local Hillel after feeling unsupported and isolated in my community. I have enjoyed this, although the folks at Hillel differ greatly when it comes to discussing Israel. Well, my friend, I wish you a good day. Thank you for listening to my trail of thoughts. I would love to hear some of your ideas and responses.

Shalom,

Dear James Baldwin,

I sit here in the midst of planning and organizing. Events, meetings, fundraisers, and a scholarship are all being assembled to help us remember a dismembered young man. We don't know exactly what happened to him on the day he disappeared from his home. Nevertheless, we would soon learn that the many pieces of his body were being found scattered across Brooklyn. I was immediately disgusted at such a gruesome act. I was stopped by the realization that I met Rashawn Brazell at a neighborhood hangout—where Black Gay men gather—just two summers ago. I wrote about it on my blog, and others did, too. I began to see that it was through our online journals that word was getting out, and that if we wanted to do anything about this, we'd have to meet.

It was only a few weeks before all of us bloggers, activists, paid staff of community organizations, and shocked bystanders sat in a dimly lit restaurant; we were trying to figure out what happened to a nineteen-year-old that most of those assembled had never met before his death. We didn't know if he was "out" about his sexuality. I suspect the concept of being "out" never fit into Rashawn's worldview; excluding the actual act of loving other men, being "out" requires one to subscribe to a particular identity. James, in an interview you were asked if you were Gay. You replied by saying, "I love some men. I love some women. And some of them love me. I guess that's all you can really ask for." I would imagine Rashawn would say the same if asked. Anyway, we discussed what we could piece together from news stories: ". . . bits and pieces of nineteen-year-old Rashawn Brazell began popping up a couple weeks ago—first in a subway tunnel near Bed-Stuy, then later at a recycling plant in Greenpoint . . ." from *New York Press*. We berated some media for their careless coverage, like *Gothamist*, a NYC-based blog, which said that the murder ". . . leads us to wonder what other trash might be lurking down there." Being considered "other trash" is exactly what brought all of us together.

We were tired of being ignored in the mainstream media, and we could still refer back to another story that had just been run to compare how little Rashawn mattered in the eyes of the media. Only a few weeks before Rashawn's death, Nicole DuFresne was shot on the streets of New York's Lower East Side. She was a white woman from somewhere in the Midwest, and had come to New York to pursue an acting career. She became every broadcast media outlet's lead story, and a sound bite for every white politician. Her face was plastered on the front pages of all the newspapers in the city, until her alleged assailants confessed to the crime. It was the sort of media overkill that gives me a headache: "Wide-eyed white girl comes to New York to make it big and is shot down by a gang of 'ruthless' niggers with no morals."

Now, let's pair the coverage Nicole got with Rashawn's. The local gay newspaper wrote two pieces about him. All other stories were written in the context of subway crime; most didn't find the space to mention his name. I would never wish the coverage Nicole got on anyone; that's an overblown reality only fit for tabloid gossip. The point is that no life should be more important than the other. But when I phoned editors to get them to cover this story, or even simply take a look at the facts, I was faced with refusals. I was told their readership/viewership would simply not relate to Rashawn's story. One editor responded "call me when they find the head"—as Rashawn's head has not been found. Even as a media professional, I felt powerless, faced with the possibility that no one cared about this.

Eventually, once we held a vigil, a few mainstream outlets ran the story. Yet, I'm still bothered by the vast amount of resources it takes to run a story about a murdered Black man (Nicole DuFresne almost certainly did not employ a publicist), especially one whose sexual identity may not fit into a prescribed norm. What was most titillating for many outlets was that his killer might have been someone he met off of a chat line or Internet hookup site (that scenario has since been disproved). In other words, his death is not what matters. It is the idea that he may be participating in "degenerate" social activities, which then led to his death. As Black Gay men, our communities, networks, functions, sexual activities, kinks, and mannerisms are consistently pathologized by a system of imposed normalcy. Even in the midst of an extensive assimilation effort on behalf of the Gay mainstream (e.g., same-sex marriage), we are still outcasts. For editors, the story that would stick was not his life nor the respect it demands, but a consequence of his "social sin." Even now, I think of how his mother must have felt as she saw her son's memory tarnished. I don't know if his mother was aware that Rashawn loved men, or if he used chat lines, but her son's brutal death was being made his fault. That must cause her a pain I cannot know.

All my life, I've been faced with the alleged worthlessness of my own body. Most Black men can say the same, and we are constantly reminded of this farce through our nonexistence in the media landscape or through other disheartening situations. I grew up in England, surrounded by a white, conservative, and aristocratic family. I've had to fight hard to find my own worth. Half the battle is finding the worth of Black men as a group, a community, and acknowledging the strength and significance that we have to each other. But, I promise, not one of us who have gathered had to question Rashawn's worth. I have never seen so many people come together when one of us died, when it was still unclear *why* they died. Dear James, it didn't matter. We had come to affirm the life and existence of one of us, in spite of our conditioning that would have us ignore him.

James, I reckon that you might be here with us. That you might stand with us, meet with us, party with us as we attend to the subtlety of the situation before us. As we struggle to understand Rashawn's death, we strive to gain some greater understanding of ourselves, and our place in this world. We have all been forced to consider that when we die, we might be considered "trash" to be picked up with the rest of the garbage in subway tunnels. May it never happen again.

In prose,
Merv*

6

LETTERS ON OPPRESSION WITHIN THE MOVEMENT

Late November 2004

Dear Sue,

I know I didn't know you really well. We met at the arraignments in Columbus, Georgia, after the November 2003 School of the Americas Watch vigil. And then we talked on the phone a few times planning the Theater of the Oppressed workshop at the trials last January. I read your e-mails on the SOA Watch Anti-Oppression Working Group listserv and really appreciated what you offered. Your commitment to changing both U.S. foreign policy toward Latin America and institutionalized oppression within progressive organizations like SOA Watch motivates my own work on these issues.

I don't know what to say. I am still trying to process the news of your death—your apparent murder at the hands of another activist, someone I never met but was in my extended activist community. My grief mixes with anger, confusion, and conviction that we can no longer deny that domestic violence, sexual assault, and sexual harassment happen in our "progressive" communities.

I want to scream sometimes when people tell me that talking about sexual assault and domestic violence is a distraction from the issues and is divisive because they don't really happen here, and it is none of our business anyway. But in my polite middle class way, I speak softly and usually concede ground. I appreciate so much how direct you were and how you spoke your mind on issues of oppression. I hope in your memory I can speak more forcefully.

IT HAPPENS. As you said so powerfully in your e-mails, violence is ingrained in the structure of our society. Sexual assault and domestic violence happen in every community. And if we are going to stop them we have to be talking about them in every organization we belong to, every school, every neighborhood, and every church. We need to have community standards so people know what behavior is acceptable and that they will be held accountable by their peers. Those standards need to be included in every organizational newsletter and Web site, all church bulletins, nonviolence/action guidelines and school curricula. We have to shine a light through the shame that surrounds these subjects.

The words of your e-mails a month ago crying out for an end to male violence, for men in our communities to own and take responsibility for their violence, ring in my head. I feel guilty that I didn't write back and ask how you were doing. So often my life gets so cluttered with details and theoretical discussions I don't know what is happening in the lives of the people around me. I wonder how I can be part of any change in the world if I can't even help build communities where we both support each other and hold each other accountable. The culture of our society is against community responsibility and intervening in people's "personal lives." If we are going to decrease rape and domestic violence we are going to have to change this culture. We have to create a space where people can come forward knowing they will be supported. We have to take risks and tell people we know and love when their behavior is unacceptable. But I know you and your immediate community were doing this and had a plan to protect you. So I am facing the fact that I don't have the solution, only possible steps.

I read in the newspaper that you told a friend that you were working on getting a restraining order but that you didn't want him to go to jail. It is so hard to know what to do when we know how racist, classist, degrading, and unjust the so-called justice system in this country is. How can we turn anyone over to it? That is why I am working on the SOA Watch Sexual Offense Prevention and Response Team. You probably saw some of our e-mails about it over the listserv. We want to create a model for responding to violence (especially sexual) in our community that is an alternative to going to law enforcement. We are still figuring out what that alternative looks like. Ideally it will include a process for community mediation, the room for survivors to make demands of perpetrators and be supported by the community (including asking people to leave communities), and the space and acceptance for perpetrators to take responsibility for their actions and take steps to change. But this assumes voluntary participation by all sides, which is not often the case.

I am still trying to process how I feel about your attacker. I found myself asking, how could someone who worked to end injustice and violence commit such a horrible act? It forces me to acknowledge that we are all capable of violence and that my community is not special. We (progressives, activists) are not above anyone else and I can't think anymore that being an activist will protect me. It is a hard but necessary realization.

Part of me feels no sorrow at his suicide. But part of me wonders what in his life led to this act of desperation? What, if anything, could have we done as a community to intervene? In this "another world is possible" we talk about, how are we going to respond to perpetrators and to mental illness that leads to violence?

I don't want your death to be swept under the rug. I hate the uneasy silence that surrounds your name now. While I understand the fear of losing credibility by admitting that violence occurs in our "progressive" communities, if we refuse to talk about our violence—how can we expect to change the violence in the world around us? We have to air our dirty laundry if it is ever going to get clean.

Your death leaves me with more questions than answers, and your life inspires me to continue the struggle.

With love and respect,

Laurel

In memory of Sue Daniels

Dear Movement,

It's hard for me to write this. Hard to write of all the moments and to all the people I have known in the struggle, the Movement. It is difficult to sum up so many years and all my reasons for saying good-bye to you. Once you filled my lungs with air and hope and promises—not only resistance but also freedom—and I breathed for the first time with you. Truth is, I am unsafe here with you. "The work" has left me dry. My understanding and definitions have changed, and now I know that rallies and protests and boycotts and grants and programs and trainings and media packets and press conferences and campaigns can't win anything if we don't know how to talk to each other and how to trust each other. This is not the world I was told I could be free in. The world that touched me and held us all, back when I loved revolutions. I want you all to know that I loved the struggle, I loved the Movement, and what I thought we could be and could mean to each other. The thing is that the growing and learning and teaching and trust are real superficial here. Trust is an illusion here, and our work and our word become some commodity here, and the language of "empowerment" is twisted and thrown back at us like weapons to keep each other silent.

The problem I see is that we don't talk, never really did. They would be so easy to clean up if we just talked and let down our defenses. But not here, not where beefs last thirty years or more, sometimes over petty disagreements, jealousies, bad break-ups with former lovers, and other trivial nonsense. What's worse than having beef is that elders sometimes drag young people into the bullshit, and force them to take sides over shit that they are never told the truth about. When we treat each other with such contempt and suspicion, we do more damage to each other, to organizations, and to communities than the state ever could. To sum it up, we destroy the very thing we say we are trying to build. And we do it by not looking at, addressing, or acknowledging our internalized issues. What are we building? Where we going? Where are we safe now?

Here's my theory: As much as us activists and organizers like to think we are the people who are going to heal the world that is so damaged, it's not that simple. WE been fucked. We are like abused children that never learned to get outta that cycle. We were hit hard, no doubt, and in turn, we hit each other, our lovers, and our children. We have been torn, broken left bleeding, left out, shit on, spic'ed out, tortured, lied to, lied about, and iced. NO DOUBT. The trouble is we can't get over it. No amount of struggle and meetings and protests and trainings change that. Nor is any of it supposed to, DAMN IT! We hide in meetings and late nights, in flyers and newsletters and brand new DVD projects designed to let everyone know just how fucked we are?! None of it is designed to heal us. Nor is it designed to break our cycles of violence, silent or physical. We don't know how to deal with the nuances of our differences and the differences of our oppression. More importantly, we do not respect our differing perspectives on how we are affected by oppressions as womyn and men of color, as queer/trans folks, as resisters and survivors. But most importantly, we do not respect our different perspectives on how to change it. We don't respect the difference between the exploited and the super-exploited. People throw around the term "hierarchy of oppression" to silence people, to invalidate one's criticisms or disagreements, and it has turned too many resisters into nothing more than real good politicians.

There is a book called *The Toltec Book of Love*, and in it there is a chapter that describes us perfectly. It asks the reader to imagine a world where babies are born perfect, beautiful, and healthy, but the world is diseased. All the adults have sores that cover their entire bodies, making it very painful to touch and be touched. So from the beginning these babies are taught that to touch is painful. As they grow older they begin to develop sores of their own. It is normal to fear touching, and as they get older it is down right painful. We are all like that. We are damaged and hurting and to touch each other is painful.

We are a Movement trying to build a new society with new ways of seeing, relating to one another that are not hierarchical, oppressive, or dominating. But what we really are is a Movement built on defensiveness. When someone makes a mistake, hurts us, we automatically go on the defense, we make assumptions, and we attack. Why? We use our pasts, our oppressions, and our names to justify our aggression. After a while, all transgressions are defined as oppression, and it is all lumped together as something that must be purged from the movement cuz there is no room here for fuck ups. So the Sista that calls the cops cuz she is being beaten by her lover gets iced but NO ONE tried to help her or help her lover, who was hurting too. No one tried to stop it. One gets iced, the other gets ignored or excused, and the pain that put them there festers and grows, and finally there are more folks involved taking sides, making the whole thing worse. And there is more paralysis in the movement if the couple is of the same sex, or queer. We never deal with the abuse, nor is the abuser encouraged to deal with their own abused histories, which might actually prevent something. Way too often, we are not held accountable in a way that makes us deal with and understand how our oppressed histories manifest sometimes by making us abusers. But what we gotta remember is that this world is much like the world described in the *Toltec* book, our sores are our internalized shit, our defensiveness that does not distinguish between the state and allies.

I want us to address real issues—both our political visions and our personal realities—and see each other as part of the very real and important work we are supposed to be doing. I want us to put our insecurities, shortcomings, and shames on the table. I want us to transform them, to change them into lessons learned that don't have to be painful. I want to believe a man is a human being beyond his privilege, and his sexist thinking can be addressed, not at the expense of womyn. I want to believe a womyn's internalized sexism can be addressed without it being punished or judged by men or other womyn. I want to believe straight folks can deal with how they feel about their own sexuality without putting their fears and anger on queer folks. I want to believe we can act as a whole without becoming or pretending to be monolithic.

I want to believe we can celebrate our difference without always being so fuckin' suspicious of each other's motives and give and take each other at face value. If we don't have hope and faith that we can change, how the fuck do we expect to change anything and anyone else? How do we talk about freedom when we do not try to experience it? I am not a victim, though I have been victimized, and I do not belong to a culture of victims, nor do I want to. I don't want to define myself or people around me by how hurt they are or how our people have been hurt. I want to live free, I want to be able to meet somebody new and not react to them as if they are the last few people (or the system) that hurt me. And that's exactly what I see with here. COIN-TELPRO worked so well that right now, baby, they don't need to send no agents in to disrupt "the work." We do a fine job of forgettin' the personal is political (it's not just a slogan) and that sometimes means struggling through our contradictions. We should be able to do better then icing each other out, gossiping and judging each other. But we don't, so where is the new world? Where is the safe place? Where is the revolution? We are mirroring the ugliest of what we are tryin' to change. We need to stop hiding behind our oppressed victim roles that keep us scared and at each others' throats.

For now, my love, I'm out. Back home in the world without talk of revolution is safer for me. And even though I'm leaving you I still have hope; that's why I'm still writing here. Still hoping you hear me, feel me, and forgive me for being wrong, for being insecure and jealous for not knowing what I'm doing and doing the wrong things at the right times. Mostly, forgive me for judging you. I forgive you, for being hurt, for being damaged and not knowing what to do. I forgive you for judging me, and prioritizing foundation outcomes, over time for your-self or time with me.

We need to live as revolutionaries, guided, as Che Guevara said, "by great feelings of love." And reserve judgment for how best to go about living free. I could be safe here if, when you feel hurt by me, you could tell me rather then letting me hear how much shit you talkin' thru so many other people. I could be safe here if you could give me a chance to tell you when you are fucking up. I could feel safe here if folks would try to help mediate a problem rather than taking sides and amping beef up. Maybe we could all feel safe here if we took prisons and exile and ice and shade out of our vocabulary for dealin' with beef and con-tradictions. Then maybe we could learn and teach and unlearn how to really deal with each other when we are hurt, when we feel betrayed, maybe we could take the time to really find out why we feel like that before we add to the sores that cover our bodies. Maybe then I would feel safe enuff to work within the movement again and love it again. You have lost more than just me to all the bullshit, so maybe if the movement cleaned its house and worked through its problems and contradictions a lot of other people could come back too. Till then.

In hope,
Nilda

A Letter to the Beautiful People Holding Hands on the Day Nothing Went Down in a Big Way,

I saw you there on the Great Lawn of Central Park, after the Big Day of protest against the Republican National Convention, the "RNC" to those of us in the know. There was a group of you, holding hands. You were white, like me; from the middle class, like me. You were celebrating. I was there trying to ruin the mood. I remember hearing you chant: "We are beautiful! We are beautiful!"

It was a calm and comfortable night. The park was full of revelers, with hardly a cop in sight. The towers of Manhattan stood in dignified repose along the skyline, police helicopters hovering on guard between them. Somewhere to the south, Republican Party delegates arrived at hotels, restaurants, clubs, escort services—apparently you and all the other protestors who had gathered to celebrate had forgotten them already. We never spoke, but I remember you well, because your professions of beauty, frankly, made me sick. You were not unique; on the contrary, I found you memorable because of how well you exemplified a general trend in our ineffective yet self-congratulatory portion of the movement.

After the RNC, we weren't any closer to building accountable and sustaining relationships with other communities in resistance; we hadn't challenged ourselves or confronted our sense of privilege within the movement; we didn't win ground or empower anybody in any meaningful sense; we didn't illustrate the necessity for struggle, or define the struggle as being against anything larger than the Republican Party; we didn't improve our tactical competence vis-à-vis the police (and didn't even injure that many of them); and George W. Bush was still in power—undefeated, neither dethroned nor defenestrated. Other than joining the rough statistic that tomorrow's newspapers would interpret and characterize in whatever way they chose to, exactly what did we accomplish? The RNC protest, and the long line of mass mobilizations to which it is heir, was just voting in the streets.

Admittedly, protesting is a lot more fun than voting. Maybe that's why you were there. To tell the truth, that's why I went to my first protest. That and a healthy but inarticulate desire to see shit go up in flames. It is this desire that we white, middle-class wannabe revolutionaries need to understand and utilize. We do not become active to survive, to soften the crushing weight of oppression, to liberate ourselves from slavery. As privileged people we are on the other side of those societal forces. Rather, I think we see that the privileges being offered to us are poison. Perhaps our entrance into this world coincided with our parents achieving the American Dream, yet the nightmare we awoke to included, for ourselves or our friends, being raped and abused, seeing our fathers beat our mothers, starving ourselves to conform, getting beaten as "faggots" if we didn't fit in, becoming addicted to a hollow televised culture that filled us with insecurities, getting forced into a narrow range of unfulfilling career tracks so we could reenact the hypocrisies of our parents. The nightmare did not include healthy communication and loving relationships, a sense of home or identity stronger than real estate markets or advertising schemes, the freedom to develop our minds and explore our world in the way we see fit, or a community to sustain us.

Our rejection, as wannabe revolutionaries, of the moral depravity of our society's Haves accompanied a growing awareness of the deprivations suffered by the Have-Nots—people of color, poor people, and the colonized peoples of the world. Eventually we made the connection that the wealth and power of the privileged was stolen from the oppressed. Roughly at this point, we became activists working toward revolution. But we can't leave our pasts behind so easily, especially when the conditions of that past continue unobstructed into the present.

Imagine for a moment that activists from privileged backgrounds weren't actually interested in destroying the system that gives them privilege, but simply wanted to amend it (to make the privileges more enjoyable); or at best they sincerely wanted to tear the whole fucking thing down, but had never taken the time to consider what sacrifices would then be required of them. What would these people look like? They would vocalize their activism without ever backing words up with actions, they would isolate themselves in subcultures to create the appearance that they had rejected their privileges, they would be sure to maintain a privileged sense of comfort in all their activist spaces, and throughout the whole process they would congratulate themselves on their moral superiority. In short, I think they would look like you. Not very beautiful at all, is it?

Maybe now you can better understand my revulsion. Set the scene: the government is pushing ahead with a genocidal war in Iraq, providing continued support for the bloody occupation in Palestine, intervening in Colombia, Haiti, Korea, and a hundred other countries. The normal functioning of our economy utilizes starvation, disease, and genocide as market pressures; calls ecocide productivity; and consigns everyone on the planet to varying degrees of subjugation. White supremacy on the home front flourishes in the form of income gaps, impoverished ghettos, police violence, insatiable prisons, and coopted cultures. The Religious Right and Hollywood are coming from different sides to bolster patriarchal social relationships that play out in pervasive sexual and domestic violence. Enter the activists. The confrontation billed by the white, middle-class portion of the movement as the big event of the summer ends in a large turnout, political capital to be misused by the Democratic Party, and no measurable headway against any of the aforementioned problems. This is cause for celebration?

For me, it's cause for scrutiny. I think activists from privileged backgrounds need to start asking ourselves some critical questions.

What are we doing to build relationships of integrity across barriers of race, class, and cultural background?

How are we owning up to the problems within our own communities?

How will our actions contribute to changing society in a way
that destroys oppression and authority?
What level of commitment is required to be in true solidarity
with oppressed peoples?

These four questions are important, to me at least, for a number of
reasons. I think it's our responsibility, as middle-class white people, to
find out why so many of us are missing from the frontlines of the
struggle. There aren't enough of us volunteering at AIDS clinics, organizing fundraisers for battered women's shelters, bombing banks,
redistributing stolen groceries in poor communities, tutoring disad-
vantaged students, enlisting in the military to shoot our officers and
encourage mutiny. Instead we gather in the streets every few months
in response to the symbolic meeting of some powerful institution, and
ask "why is our movement so white?" When we do engage in real organizing, it is typically on our own terms, in organizations we control. We
expect oppressed peoples to come to us and follow our lead. How can
we expect to even notice all the racism and privilege we have internalized if we never step outside our white, middle-class bubbles? Too
many of us who want to change the world can't even leave our comfort
zones and build relationships with people from different backgrounds.

A strong movement, if it's not going to be built on party ideologies
or institutional hierarchies, has to be built on strong personal relationships, and I don't think we've been very successful on this front.
There is too much dishonesty, too much ego, ultimately too much insecurity. Often, activist spaces feel like high school all over again, with
everyone trying to get in the cool crowd. It's even hard to talk about
these problems, and it certainly doesn't help if we think we have to
exemplify beauty and righteousness. I don't think it's beautiful that
we're recreating traditional gender roles of domination and control in
our activist spaces, or that people who criticize this are characterized
as "oversensitive." I don't think it's beautiful that activist men are still
raping other activists, and we don't even talk about it that much. With

this level of distrust and alienation, the government doesn't even need to sic some COINTELPRO on us. We will be self-defeating.

Our idea of action reflects this alienation, along with a fear of giving up our comfort. I don't see many of us white, middle-class activists seriously attempting to either build autonomous social relationships or destroy the existing power structures. Instead, it's protest, protest, protest, and eventually "the people" will rise up, or the state will crumble, or something like that. I guess we're not used to thinking strategically about how to get from Point A to revolution because a real revolution means we lose our comfort. So protesting becomes an end in its own right, and we keep waiting for that magical day when everybody comes out to protest, the cops all quit their jobs, and Bush and Kerry have to admit that they're wrong, apologize, and give up their power. Often, such questions of strategy are circumvented with a moral insistence on nonviolence. But what is violence? Is paying taxes or driving a car really nonviolent? How about demanding rigid adherence to an ethical code that makes us avoid numerous opportunities to stop the war machine? Isn't it a good deal easier to appear nonviolent when we're not the ones facing bombs or billy clubs?

This idea that we can claim solidarity with people who are losing everything, without risking anything ourselves, is what bothers me so much. On college campuses, at vigils, in radical bookstores, during safe and entertaining protests, I see proclamations of solidarity with the Zapatistas, the Iraqis, and others fighting imperialism. How can we actually fool ourselves into thinking that we are aiding people engaged in armed struggle—people faced with bombings, genocide, and occupation—with moments of silence or colorful placards? How can we claim to oppose imperialism when our number one priority is quite clearly to remain safe, as we fail to bring the war home or even admit the existence of the war being waged against people of color and poor people in this country? We will have upheld solidarity with the occupied and colonized people of the world when we've reduced the Pentagon to rubble, when Halliburton is sabotaged into bankruptcy,

and when white people incur real risks in the fight against global oppression.

As long as these problems go unaddressed, I think self-congratulation is premature. These are not egotistic comparisons made to suggest I'm the better activist. What I really want is to see us do our part in building a strong, accountable movement—one that fights to win. As a good friend of mine says, "We need to take ourselves less seriously, and our activism more seriously." Given what we're up against, I have a lot to ask of you. I hope you can ask the same of me.

Stumbling in love and rage toward a solidarity worthy of the name,
Peter Gelderloos

Dear friends,

Somewhere in this process of trying to be better people, we got worse. With all the glory and gore of our ancestors, we dedicated our lives to what we thought was the best solution to undo the racism they brought to and perfected in the United States. And we trained. Like Olympic hopefuls, we trained and as soon as we got trained, we were out training more and more white people committed to be better, for better or worse. I have to give it to us for pure dedication, hard work, and persistence. But if a good work ethic were all it took to eradicate white supremacy, patriarchy, and the class hierarchy, then Protestant Texas farmers would be revolutionary heroes.

So here's the deal—I think we've got some damn fine theory. We have built on the strengths and weaknesses of previous movements. We have, with help from others, developed language around

antioppression. We have created study groups. We have listened to (and sometimes heard) critiques from people of color, friends and colleagues. And we've walked across the room so many times, in a particularly popular exercise, that the carpet is striped.

We work to make our theory and educational methods tight, but our practice stinks. This is not to say that we don't throw a great workshop now and again; however, we fail to connect our theory to solid, sustainable practice. In our impatient, overeager—dare I say, white—ways, we have ignored vision. We do not articulate clear goals, specific connection to ongoing work, or long-term vision for the struggle against white supremacy.

Neglecting vision leads to at least three detrimental effects that we must examine to move forward in more productive ways. One effect is that in our well-intentioned efforts to dismantle our racism, we play dangerous status games that tear apart communities and diminish our compassion for people. Antiracist work is not an identity. It is a set of principles to which we should hold ourselves accountable, not add-on trophies that only rebels and freaks get to wear. White folks committed to this work should be expected to integrate antioppression principles and practices into their work whether they be teachers, organizers, health care workers, or mothers. Another effect of our short-sightedness is that liberals have adopted the language of antioppression. Our goals include shifting folks from a personal analysis to an institutional critique, but "politically correct" and overtly un-political trainings sweep the nation and undermine the work we do. Finally, we spend an inordinate amount of time mobilizing and falling apart, mobilizing and falling apart. We need that time, energy, and talent to create real strategies that target white supremacy in meaningful ways. We stand at a significant crossroads where we can integrate antiracist and anti oppression work into a broader movement for justice, or we can continue to spin in circles until the principles themselves become overused and, ultimately, dismissed. Eliminating ego competition, developing clear goals and vision, and putting ourselves to work beyond the trainings is essential to stay true to the principles and analysis we have bravely put forward.

When I say "we," I am talking about progressive white folks who hold the principles of antiracism and antioppression central to our work. I speak, specifically, from my experience in white queer communities of predominantly twenty-to-thirty-something folks. If pressed, we articulate our politics as anti-capitalist, and we work in a wide variety of issues for the radical transformation of the existing systems. Our work includes organizing against the prison industrial complex and international solidarity work with Palestine and Latin America. We work as teachers on the inside and organizers on the outside of the education system. We have experienced the good, bad, and ugly of the global justice movement. We have organized in affinity group structures and experienced a glimpse of powerful direct democracy and direct action. And we have challenged the lack of reflection and evaluation in antiglobalization efforts, sometimes at the expense of our participation. We work on gender issues from the perspective of the emerging transgender movement. We work as community-based organizers, we stand in solidarity with people of color—led economic and social justice formations, and we struggle with what our role should be within our communities and the movement.

I am talking to folks who appreciate and use the antioppression framework but who feel stuck and don't know what to do next. I am talking to white folks who take this work seriously and want to find ways to do our work better. I've made all the mistakes I mention, and this letter offers some ideas about why we got to this moment in order to see and work our way to a new one.

The kind of questions that I kick around with coworkers, colleagues, and white caucus facilitators: Have you ever felt like you're not antiracist enough? Have you ever patted yourself on the back for being the best antiracist in the room? Have you ever kicked someone out of a group for not speaking the right language about racism? Have you ever judged someone as "fucked up" and let everyone know it—maybe even before you've met the person?

Status games do not dismantle racism. They do, however, alienate potential allies and discourage people who are working to understand complicated positions in the world. These dangerous dynamics emerge because our practice has not caught up with our theories. At the trainings, we say the work doesn't end here. We say we need to be flexible and meet people where they're at. But then we walk around like we wear some badge that separates us from whites who haven't gone through the right training. We'd like to believe that if we distance ourselves from white people who don't know the deal, we'll shed a bit of our skin as our contribution to the movement. Judging each other and hoping to win a medal from an auditorium of people of color advisors is just a different kind of racism that keeps white people at the center of debate and action.

We dismantle our power at the same time as we dismantle our racism. We organize ourselves into working groups, affinity clusters, and align ourselves loosely to networks and coalitions. These alliances and formations often fall apart, for many reasons, one being that we are not building organizations with purposes, constituencies, and visions. We are not building for community power. The formations come together to figure out how to be allies but our privilege allows us to be flippant, mobile, and temporary. We allow internal conflict to dominate because we don't rely on strategy to move the group forward. I've been part of this dynamic and have seen it play out numerous times in different parts of the country. If it's not an isolated event, then let's examine the process, call out the flaws, and change the model. If we don't know how to build long-term power or organize our communities, let's admit our shortcomings and ask for help. If we join together solely on the basis of being antiracist white people, we will falter unless there is a specific organizing effort that connects to our analysis.

We've substituted workshops for work. We did not anticipate the liberal co-opting of antiracist work, and we created a pattern that does not address the roots of the issues. We started community work-shops as a form of damage control. Our groups got called out by com-munities of color, we got called out by friends or colleagues, or racist comments were made in large group settings. And so a pattern is born: if there's a problem, organize a workshop.

We know we can't solve the problem with a workshop, but we don't often lay out the following steps. That's an easy pattern to duplicate. Having trouble in your office? Racism rearing its predictable head in the panel choices of your conference? Hire a workshop where the "melting pot" metaphor is enthusiastically replaced with the "tossed salad" approach and be done with it. This is not what we intended, but this is what has happened. When folks with broader notions of systemic change don't articulate our goals, then simpler goals dominate. The terrain is set for conference organizers to include antiracism trainings like they have to include snacks at eleven. Damage control, often only the whispered prayer that people of color will not call us out this time, is the beginning and end of a lot of work that is labeled antiracism. We're facing the unintended consequences of antiracist curriculum that has become more about personal healing than identifying and removing the institutional and societal tumor. We've got to develop new curriculum that inherently connects to ongoing work and stimu-lates innovative solutions.

Here in Atlanta, I had the honor of hearing Anne Braden, a Southern white woman who has worked for racial justice since the 1940s, give a short lecture. In her deceptively sweet Kentucky accent, she stated, "Racial justice remains a priority for our movement. However, I do not see an effective counteroffensive against white supremacy in this country." I was ready to be challenged, but I was not prepared to get run over. Counteroffensive? Who talks like that? In all the conversa-tions I've had about racism and white supremacy, we have never framed the discussion in terms of real action campaigns targeting specific power holders and forcing them to loosen their grips on the mechanisms of that power. We often stand in solidarity with struggles that affect people of color, as does Ms. Braden. But she is calling for a kind of action that is deliberate and strategic. I hear a challenge to organize against institutions and structures of oppression rather than merely responding to oppressive behavior.

I don't think Anne Braden would be that impressed with our razor sharp ability to call people out in meetings. I think she is more interested in the content and focus of the meeting and what we do in between and after them. Is our organizing effort addressing the root causes of white supremacy? Are we building organizations to confront institutions and transform the current patterns? The runaway workshop train is not getting us where we want to go. In the next breath, I must add that we don't know where we want to go. Here's where vision comes in.

Let's imagine tangible work where our position is clear and we are not in constant conflict about whether or not we should be there. We've got to think bigger than we have. Listening and talking to white folks who have struggled in the movement for many years shines a bright light on the limitations of our thinking. All who struggle for liberation face the difficulty of strategy and tactics. Our identities and privileges shape how and where and why we struggle, but it does not confine white people to some dungeon of antioppression trainings for eternity.

Vision work is difficult. The primary questions are: Why are we doing this? What will the world look like in ten years as a result of the work we are doing today? Not like answering a question for a grant application, but real heart-wrenching conversations that unearth the true intentions and concrete realities we are working to create. In my work at Project South, a movement-building organization in Atlanta that uses popular education to strengthen organizing and leadership, we ask people these questions all the time. Project South does not put forward a specific vision, just like I don't have a clear vision to put forward here. I trust us to do this work in groups, to discuss and clarify our ideas and dreams. Letting go of our egos or the need to be the one who came up with the best proposal is a piece of antiracist work. There are models of work that hold antiracism as a guiding principle and confront white supremacy head on. Let's learn from what we've done and what others are doing in order to forge our own solid paths.

Let's put aside the guilt, paralysis, and policing games and discuss our next steps. Let's create spaces for people to have these larger, comprehensive discussions of purpose, vision and active solidarity. Let's build on our work and our analysis rather than repeat the same ideas over and over. It's about stepping up to leadership and getting out of the way at the same time, so that people of color have the space to lead without additional obstacles. The challenge is to put our principles into practice—we have to toss around a lot of ideas, try a lot of things before we discover tight models that build on the momentum of the current moment. So, let's get started.

I want us to be excited about our work. I have a hunch that all the back-stabbing and social patrolling comes from a deep sense of insecurity that we know that something's wrong and we're not doing the right things to handle it. I think digging a little deeper, listening to all generations, defining a coherent and tangible vision of what we're fighting for, and building long-haul organizations rooted in the community will allow our creativity, passion, and skills to support a broader movement for real justice.

I write this letter because I believe in us. I write because we are a part of the emerging leadership of our generation, and we stand on the edge of a critical moment. Let's be frank and honest, discuss and expose the conflicts within our political perspectives, challenge each other compassionately, and create a stronger, more lasting framework to match our commitment and imagination.

Love,

Stephanie Guilloud

7

LETTERS ON THE WAR ON TERRORISM

Matan Kaminer
"Open Detention"
Tel Hashomer Camp, Israel

August 12, 2003

Dear Stephen,

Is this what they call "globalization"? We live half a world from each other, we have led quite different lives, and yet we are both in the same situation: conscientious objectors to imperial war and occupation, we are both standing military trial this summer. Reading your statement, I couldn't help but smile at the basic sameness of military logic around the world, including its inability to understand how anybody could be enough against a war to resist going to kill and die in it.

In case you aren't familiar with my situation, let me fill you in briefly. I was slated for induction into the Israeli army in December 2002. After a year of volunteer work in a Jewish-Arab youth movement, I had made up my mind to refuse to enlist. Together with other young people in my situation, I signed the High School Seniors' Letter to PM Sharon, and to make myself absolutely clear I sent a personal letter to the military authorities notifying them that I was going to refuse.

They let me know they weren't about to let me go: the army only exempts pacifists (at least that's what it claims), and I didn't meet their definition of a pacifist. So, in December I was sentenced by "Disciplinary Proceedings" (do they have this ridiculous institution in the Marines, too?) to twenty-eight days in military prison three consecutive times. After my third time in jail, I asked to join my friend Haggai Matar, who was being court martialed, and within a few weeks three of our friends also joined us in prison.

Now we are on trial and stand to get up to three years in prison for refusing the order to enlist. Sounds familiar? But it's not just what they're doing to us that's similar, it's what they're doing to others: occupying a foreign land and oppressing another people in the name of preventing terror.

People like you and me know that's just an excuse for furthering economic and political interests of the ruling elite. But it's not the elite that pays the price.

The people who pay the price are in Jenin and Fallujah, in Ramallah and Baghdad, in Tikrit and in Hebron. They are the Iraqi and Palestinian children, hogtied facedown on the floor or shot at on the way to school. But they are also the Israeli and American soldiers, treated as cannon fodder by generals in air-conditioned offices, whose only way to deal with their situation is dehumanization first of the strange-looking foreigners who want them dead, next of themselves. You can ask your Vietnam veterans or our own.

Stephen, people our age should be out learning, working, and transforming the world. People our age should be going to parties and protests, meeting people, falling in love, and arguing about what our world should look like. People our age should not be moving targets, denied their human and civil rights; they should not be military grunts, exposed to harm in mind and body, lugging around M-16s and guilty consciences; they should not be thrown behind bars for not wanting to kill and die.

Your trial is set to begin soon. Mine has already begun so maybe I can give you a few pointers. Look the judges in the eyes. Use every opportunity you have to explain why you stand there. They are human just like you, but they try to deny it to themselves. Don't let them. War is shit and they know it. They should let you go and they know it.

It's likely that we'll both get thrown in prison when this all ends. There will be dark moments in prison, moments when it seems that the outside world has forgotten all about us, that what we did and refused to do was in vain. Well, I know what I'll do in those moments: I'll think of you, Stephen, and I'll know that nothing we do for humanity's sake is ever in vain.

With greatest solidarity,
Matan Kaminer

Matan Kaminer (signature)

Stephen Funk
Camp Lejeune Base Brig
North Carolina, USA

January 1, 2004

Dear Matan,

I am writing this letter knowing that you will never receive it. The policy of the United States military prevents me from sending or receiving mail from other prisoners be they military, civilian, or foreign national. But in spirit I wanted the first letter I wrote this New Year addressed to you.

The letter you wrote me just before my court martial really meant a lot to me and helped me get through the final weeks leading up to the trial. Your letter gave me so much hope and encouragement. Most of all, your letter reminded me that we are all on this planet together and that we all must contribute however we can in the struggle for a healthy and peaceful world. That can be easy to lose sight of when one is facing persecution, sometimes it was too easy to get distracted in my own personal problems and forget the big picture.

You and I are imprisoned because war is wrong, and we refused to believe otherwise. Because we spoke up and refused to step down. We were able to garner international attention to our personal trials and deflect the spotlight toward the antiwar movement. I am so proud of these achievements, and I hope you are as well. What you said: nothing we do for humanity's sake is ever in vain. I wish never to forget that.

If I may offer any advice to you it is to be grateful for it all. You and I have so much to be thankful for. We were given the opportunity to stand up for what we believe in and given the courage to do so in face of persecution. Not many people can claim that.

What I am so eternally grateful for through all this is the support that I received and continue to receive from the international peace community. When I struggled with my conflict of conscience they opened an ear to listen. When I decided to speak out they offered a platform to stand on. When I needed access to legal advice and the media, they showed the way. When I needed resources to help spread my message they gave what they could. When I struggled they offered strength. Now that I am isolated in prison they let me know that I am not alone.

This journey has taught me of the profound similarities existing in all people. We are all the same and have no reason to fear one another. Those propagating this war seek to perpetuate the "Us vs. Them" mentality, refusing to empathize with anyone whose opinions differ from their own even if just slightly. For them the world is only black or white, good or evil. I feel sorry for them and hope they can someday realize how limited their worldview is, that they don't even have sight of the real world.

We can be thankful that we have stood with right in opposition to the powerful governments we come from.

Even our time in prison is something to be grateful for. I joke with people who write that I was in desperate need of a vacation and received it in form of a jail sentence. The time in rest and solitude has been good for me. Since I joined the Marine Corps two years ago my life has been in turmoil, first in boot camp and further trainings, then in the personal struggle of duty and conviction, then in standing up against the war and coming out publicly, traveling the country, and dealing with the media and my trial. I have learned that my capture has been my release in so many ways. While life in prison is no walk in the park, it is a rare opportunity to catch my breath, gather my thoughts, and reflect on this experience. I hope you see it this way as well, letting an unjust sentence brew hate, desperation, and resentment is not only unproductive but can damage your health and your soul.

In the end the time spent in prison is nothing compared to experiencing the horrors of war and undermining one's beliefs, dignity, and purpose. I hope the best in your future endeavors and for your quick release. You will receive a hero's welcome.

In Respect and Brotherhood,

Stephen Funk

Dear Cousin,

It was great to get a chance to see you again, hear about your experiences visiting home in Iraq, and most importantly, see that you made it back safely. I've been thinking quite a bit about your descriptions of daily life in Iraq: the constant threats and humiliations, the complete absence of any economic means for survival, and above all, the indignity of foreign occupation. These are the strange fruit of what is banally referred to as the "War on Terror," and it has struck me how this war not only swallows foreign countries and peoples whole but also lays waste to the domestic freedoms and means of resistance which are left to those of us, like myself, who find ourselves living in the heart of empire. The fact that these two impulses exist side by side should be no surprise to either you or me, but what is surprising to me is how interlinked and interdependent our experiences are. The roots of these two "fronts" run deep and as such our personal struggles are not only unified in spirit but in actuality.

When reading the notes you kept while traveling throughout occupied Iraq, I could not help recalling my experiences in occupied Palestine. The near destruction of your nephew's school with the students inside, the frequent and deliberate murder of civilians at checkpoints under the justification of fighting "insurgents," the daily shell fire destroying your neighbor's house—these are the realities of America's "new front" and any one of them occurs daily in Bethlehem just as in Baghdad. I suppose it is only fitting that the U.S. government borrowed its laughable title for these human rights violations, "the War on Terror," from an inseparable ally committing the exact same crimes only a few hundred miles away.

I can almost hear the anger and indignation in your voice as you write about these scenes, and while I can't possibly feel the depth of your resentment, I share the sense of hopelessness you convey. I was surprised to hear how many of the Iraqis you spoke to admitted an initial willingness to believe that some good could come from U.S. intervention, despite deep reservations about the war and the occupation that would follow. It was no surprise, however, that the inability of the Coalition Provisional Authority to restore even basic utilities in the nearly two years since the invasion (let alone some semblance of a functional economy), has let that tepid optimism give way to a puzzled rage. Why would the most powerful nation on earth invade another country without any reasonable cause and then fail to build even the appearance of improved conditions? This seems to be the question on every Iraqi's lips, and I doubt very much that the touted Iraqi elections have dislodged it. We should not forget that during the U.S. occupation of Vietnam, the elections for the Saigon government supposedly drew an 80 percent turnout—far outdoing the paltry 56 percent now cited in Iraq. If history is any lesson, I trust that those who went to the polls on January 30 went for the same reason that you and I did not: to bring a swift end to the occupation.

After reading your account of a few days in Iraq, I began to consider my experiences over the past four years in the U.S., the experiences of an Arab-American activist born and raised in the United States but unwilling to accept American global hegemony. My heart is with the people of Palestine and Iraq but my feet are firmly grounded here, and while I try to help resist from within, effective methods of dissent have become limited and elusive. I live in a democracy where protestors are corralled into self-serve prisons euphemistically called "free speech zones." All Arabs and Muslims are immediately under suspicion—American citizen or not. When I was an undergraduate at Yale and the law school was bombed late one night, other Arabs and I were the ones to receive calls from the FBI the next morning. Deception is not simply the tool of the corrupt or desperate politician; it is the *modus operandi* for "good" government. Have you revisited the speech that former Secretary of State Colin Powell gave before the UN to justify the imminent invasion of Iraq? From the faked Niger uranium documents to the satellite photos of harmless aluminum tubing, every point reeks of deliberate misinformation. In all the times I've heard the neoconservative punditry compare American global hegemony to the heyday of Roman Empire, not once have they mentioned the simple fact that the Roman Empire ended the Roman Republic. This is my struggle in this war, and like the war as a whole its victims are anyone who resists the march of American empire.

The environment of fear and eroding civil liberties created by the U.S. government certainly provides them with many practical advantages. Without the constant presence of that "mushroom cloud over New York" eclipsing even the most basic truths, I doubt that the American public would have so fully supported an invasion against a country that posed no threat to them. A long-term strategic plan pushed by the neoconservatives which only ten years ago was too radical for the American political mainstream has managed to become official American policy, and Mr. Bush and his cronies have used and twisted 9/11 to their own ends. Even the reelection (or should I say simply election) of Mr. Bush owes much to the daily terror that Americans believe they face. Despite the immediate conclusions splayed across the American mediascape that moral values played a singularly decisive role in a tremendously close election, more nuanced work since then has revealed the crucial role played by "terrorism" in framing the American public's votes. Just as cultivating domestic fears gave the neocons a free hand in the world at large, they use the frequent attacks on U.S. soldiers in Iraq to enhance the narrative of Americans as victims of terror and clamp down at home. "You see how they hate freedom!" they shriek as another American military convoy is destroyed—all the while unraveling the Constitution behind our backs.

But I don't think these practical advantages are the end of the story. At the heart of the neoconservative movement lies an ideological core that brings both of our experiences into focus. As ludicrous as this may sound, I truly think that Mr. Bush and his advisors passionately believe in democracy—just not the type of democracy you or I consider when we hear the word. The democracy they strive for is a hollow shell where citizens are only *mostly* enfranchised but constantly deceived and manipulated. Minority rights are treated as a mere formality to be ignored as necessity dictates. Their ideal world is one where, at best, the people elect their dictators or, at worst, the people only appear to. For all his folksy populist imagery, Mr. Bush and Co.

deeply distrust the people. Why else would they continuously lie to them about everything from the war, to health care reform, to basic facts about the environment? This attitude is no different when Mr. Bush talks about his dreams of bringing "democracy" to the Middle East. A "democratic Middle East" means little more then replacing government after government with a leadership willing to bow to American political and economic interests. If the peoples of these nations must be involved symbolically in order to give this modern imperialism legitimacy, so be it.

For all of this, you and I have good reason to feel helpless, but we must catch ourselves if only by the knowledge that helplessness among the oppressed amounts to victory for oppressor. Ultimately we must take solace in the belief that injustice against a people who will not accept it cannot continue forever—whether they be in Iraq, Palestine, or the United States. If we look around both of us there are reasons for hope: Only two years after the invasion of Iraq there exists a well coordinated Iraqi resistance that can only hasten an end to the occupation. In the U.S., there is a small but growing movement to demand democracy—real democracy—for ourselves in spite of a Democratic Party that has flatly refused to accept its role as a true opposition party. Years or even decades may pass during which our challenges will only multiply, but eventually all things must change, and, if we continue to organize, they will change for the better.

With love and solidarity,
Badr

Badr

A Letter to Political Prisoners of Racist and Sexist Sexual Politics:
To Our Iraqi Sisters at Abu Ghraib

Dear Sisters whose spirits soar high above prison walls,

Though I cannot imagine the hell that you experienced while imprisoned at Abu Ghraib (and I hear are still suffering there and at other
sites of torture at the hands of imperialist occupiers in Iraq), I wish to
extend my hand through prison bars to let you know that I am aware of
what has been and is happening to you. I want no one to ever deny that
these atrocities occur(red). Yet, in the spirit of true sisterhood, I am
also aware that I need to speak carefully about what has and is happening to you. For I have learned that the mere mention of your rape
and torture may result in your death. I hope you find in this letter my
sincerest attempt to remain accountable and build a bridge of solidarity that might allow us to call ourselves sisters. It is my prayer that
one day we will be able to build the most defiant act of protest, a new
world, that would never tolerate these acts or the unconscionable
silence that is left hovering in the air when they are committed.

   As our hands touch, I want to take a brief moment to share a particular story of my sisters of African descent. This is not my attempt to
equalize or compare our experiences. Our respective pain and oppression are not things that we should use to defend our right to speak,
silence others, or forge false alliances. I just want to tell you of the specific pain that I experienced when I heard of what happened to you at
Abu Ghraib. As an African American woman, I am a member of a race of
women who for centuries has been considered "unrapeable." By
unrapeable, I mean that racist and sexist portrayals of Black women as
sexually insatiable has meant that for centuries, Black women could
not legally be raped. For over five hundred years, all Black women
brought into the slave economy in North America, South America, and
the Caribbean were castigated as prostitutes and insatiable sexual
savages in order to justify our rape and sexual exploitation, and such

labeling was critical to the historical maintenance of the institution of slavery and to current white supremacist global capitalism. Whether addressing the way President Thomas Jefferson's rape of his slave Sally Hemmings is treated as an "affair" by historians and Hollywood films like *Jefferson in Paris*, or continuing public debates about the usefulness of forcibly sterilizing "welfare recipients," our bodies continue to be objects to abuse, rape, torture, and commodify to serve the interests of the same imperialists who defile you.

Though our histories and present day experiences as Arab women and women of African descent—particularly those living in America—differ greatly, when the racist and sexist global media decided to treat your rape and torture at Abu Ghraib as a non-incident they created an intersection in our histories. The way in which the media chose to make visible and sexually exploit the Arab female body and at the same time make invisible the degradation of it, is an abuse women of African descent know all too well. Our respective "non-rapes" and the way the global media uses our bodies to advance a white supremacist, patriarchal, imperialist world order is part of a reoccurring narrative that has global implications for deciding who is human and who is not. The global media plays an important role in establishing who is non-human and therefore expendable.

Viacom, Time Warner, and other global media conglomerates transmit misogynistic images of African American women and women of African descent every day across the globe. Images of the hip-hop "video ho," the welfare queen, or the poor African woman straining the national or global economy with unchecked sexual and reproductive propensities function to strip us of our humanity. African American author Patricia Hill Collins, in her book *Black Sexual Politics*, calls mass media and popular culture the conduits of the new racism that works to maintain old and create new racist and sexist gender ideologies about African American women. Too many of the rapes, tortures, and killings of Black women within the United States, both in and outside of the prison industrial complex, are ignored because of the primary perception that the Black woman is a sexual savage devoid of humanity.

I would like to tell you about the case of Joan Little, who was charged with first-degree murder for resisting rape by a white prison guard in 1974. In the article "Joan Little: The Dialectics of Rape," Angela Davis lays out the racist and sexist premise of Joan Little's murder charge and the attempts of the media to reinforce the notion of the Black "prostitute" to assert that Joan Little could not possibly be a rape victim. Davis explains that the state of North Carolina tried Joan Little under the same nineteenth-century laws that said "no white man could be convicted of fornication with a slave woman." Throughout the trial, Davis states, the media reported unfounded stories that she was a prostitute and had engaged in sex acts with jailers. The Black or woman of color as prostitute is an essential racist and sexist construction used historically and presently to justify the oppression and exploitation of women of color.

The racist and sexist imagery of the woman of color prostitute or sex worker is recycled by neo-imperialists and their media outlets to further subjugate brown women, particularly South East Asian, Middle Eastern, and other women of color from the so-called "Global South." In 1998, reports emerged about the United Nations International Labor Organization (ILO) and international development NGOs conspiring to legitimize the global sexual exploitation of women of color by attempting to acknowledge "sex work" or prostitution as an overlooked economic sector (that poor women of color willingly choose to enter) that could boost the gross domestic product (GDP) of developing countries. Neo-imperialists seek to legitimize the racist and sexist image of the woman of color as the willing and perpetual prostitute to enable them to disregard calls for third world debt cancellation, ensure the unjust distribution of resources, and continue imperialist militarism onto the exploited bodies of women of color (all components of a political economy that force women of color into the "sex industry"). Their solution to global poverty is to condone sexual exploitation and make third world women responsible for revitalizing their countries' GDP. We can see the effects of this racist and sexist gender ideology of the brown woman prostitute most recently in the media's treatment of the atrocities committed against you in the Abu Ghraib prison.

In general, the media's treatment of your rape and torture reinforced the notion that all women of color, particularly brown women who resemble the global media image of the "sex worker," cannot be raped. First, the scarce coverage of your abuse and torture sent a message that your persecution as women of color is definitely not newsworthy, virtually making it invisible. On the rare occasions when the media did cover the story, the images of your torture and abuse were used like pornography. In May of 2004, when CBS Worldwide Inc. weekly TV news show *60 Minutes II* released photos of the abuse and torture of male and female prisoners at Abu Ghraib online, captions were inserted under the images of men being abused as torture. No captions were presented to name the abuse of women featured in the photos. When the media exhibited pictures of your abuse without labeling them as criminal acts of rape and torture, the result rendered you mere pornographic props that simply gave additional shock value to the primary story of the torture of the male detainees.

Based on media coverage of Abu Ghraib, it appears as if the only atrocities that occurred happened to men. The word "rape" was used by the media to describe the sexual violence that was perpetrated against the male prisoners. Graphic details of the sodomy of male prisoners with stick ends treated with toxic chemicals were reported on, yet the rape of women went unmentioned. According to global media sources it seems as if the sexual violation of the male body is rape, while the sexual violation of the female body, particularly female bodies of color, is just "inappropriate" sex. While it is critical to acknowledge that men are also victims of rape, particularly Black and Latino men subjected to rape and torture within the prison industrial complex, it should never be done at the expense of women. It seems as if another coconspirator in the sexist omission of the violence perpetrated against women prisoners is homophobia. Patriarchy's abhorrence of male-on-male sex results in media coverage which focuses on the horrible sex acts were performed on the bodies of men by other men.

When I searched the news sources for truthful accounts of what had occurred at Abu Ghraib, I did not find the rape and torture of the Iraqi women actually named as such. In the sources that I examined, which included: CBS Worldwide Inc.'s initial release of the photos and captions, the *New Yorker, Time, Newsweek, The Nation* and the release of Major General Taguba's report on Abu Ghraib, the media did not once refer to the torture and rape of the women prisoners as rape. The typical language that was being used to describe the abuse against women was retold as accounts of "soldiers having sex with female detainees" (Johanna McGeary, "The Scandal's Growing Stain," *Time*, May 17, 2004). Just as Sally Hemmings was detained via the system of chattel slavery, and Joan Little via the U.S. prison system, none of you can be realistically referred to as "having sex" with anyone whose job it is to enslave or detain you.

According to the media's interpretation, the rape of women did not occur, only inappropriate (but not forced) sex between soldiers and female prisoners. As a woman of African descent who comes from a people who lived and continue to live under an oppressive white supremacist regime in America, the sexist and racist media accounts of "sex, but not rape," that occurred between solider and female prisoner at Abu Ghraib, sounded eerily familiar to the accounts of "sex, but not rape," that occurred between White slave master and Black female slave, White male employer and Black female domestic, and White male jailer and Black female inmate. The context for the silence of the rape of women like Sally Hemmings, Carrie Butler (the servant of Strom Thurmond whom it was recently revealed had a child fathered by the senator), and Joan Little is best explained in sections of the "Black Codes" in acts passed at the First Legislature of the Territory of New Orleans. These provisions stated no Louisiana law makes rape of a Black woman, slave or free, a crime. Under Louisiana law, only a white woman could be the victim of a rape. Our rape as women of color—whether under slavery or imperialist occupation—does not exist, in order to hide the atrocities of white supremacy's exploitation of people of color.

Both the institutions of slavery and the current war and occupation of Iraq had to hide their atrocities to justify their missions. The War in Iraq: "Operation Iraqi Freedom," like slavery, has to present itself as a moral endeavor which seeks to bring "civilization" to a primitive people. It is the attempt of an imperialist regime trying to hide war crimes to suggest that sexual contact taking place during war between occupiers and the occupied of any gender, particularly women, could be anything but rape. As women know, rape is pervasive, if not institutionalized, in times of war. In order to maintain the system of white supremacy and continue the war on the Iraqi people, white men (the primary perpetrators of the rapes and other sadistic acts of torture) can never be depicted as the rapist or sexual deviant. Staying true to the white supremacist narrative, the role of sexual deviant is reserved solely for people of color. Women of color function as the whore, men of color as the rapist. Preserving the image of the white male as liberator and civilizer is as critical for the United States at this moment in history as it was during slavery.

Living in this particular moment in history, I understand more and more how high the stakes are if we let them diminish our humanity. If the notion of the "unrapeable" Iraqi women persists, it will allow the sadistic, misogynistic soldiers to escape true justice and will effectively obscure the issue of white supremacist imperialism's institutionalization of rape against women. As the racist and sexist ideology of the "unrape-able" woman of color suppresses the systematic rape of Iraqi women, it also camouflages U.S. motivations for the war on Iraq: the unabashed rape and killing of human spirits and bodies to exploit the human and natural resources of the Iraqi people.

More and more, I come to understand how my specific thread of history of oppression as a woman of African descent may share an intersection with your thread of history of oppression as an Iraqi woman. To highlight our particular interwoven threads in no way seeks to disregard those other threads that may be more tightly woven to yours, or those that even entwine to make a more culturally palpable and relevant pattern. The recognition of the intersection simply strengthens my commitment and resolve as a woman of African descent to combat the racist and sexist idea of the "unrapeable" Black woman and all women of color.

Seeking Solidarity,
Tiffany Lethabo J. King

Tiffany Lethabo King

Dear members of the activist community, those who are seeking change because their souls and spirits demand it,

I write to you to share an internal letter, a letter among family that I have decided to extend to others.

This is a letter whose source is The Brotherhood/Sister Sol, an organization based in Harlem, New York. Entering our tenth year of operation, we are an organization that is devoutly committed and dedicated to providing support, guidance, and love to Black and Latino youth. We provide comprehensive services to two hundred Black and Latino young people, who range in age from six to twenty-one. Our full-time staff of thirteen provides the essential support, guidance, and resources that all youth need. We are seeking to help young people not only survive the oppressive conditions facing our communities, but to excel, for we must raise the bar.

After the 2004 presidential election many members voiced outrage and confusion at the state of America. They questioned why and how such events could come to pass. This is the letter that I wrote to them.

Harlem, New York

January 2005

Dear members of The Brotherhood/Sister Sol Family,

When the 2004 presidential election concluded, two members of The Brotherhood/Sister Sol, powerful, insightful, young Black men, founding members of the organization, wrote passionate and angry emails filled with hopelessness. One stated: "They are stealing our country right in front of our eyes." Another asked: "These men are evil, in every sense of the world. Why aren't people more enraged? We have to do something."

As the Bush presidency begins its second term, many in progressive movements, many who struggle for change on a daily basis, have echoed this sense of despair, questioning of whether there is in fact any possibility of success. Some have stated that they want to leave a country that contains so many who would vote for a political ideology fundamentally based on prejudice, exclusion, and war. In response to the sentiments expressed by our members I offer these words.

This is not a time for hopelessness and despair; on the contrary, it is time to fight.

Know that we will win because our numbers are growing and theirs are not. We will win because lies cannot continue to evade the light of day. We will win because in the long line of history, this is a mere evening in time. We will win because no matter how intimidating those now in power believe themselves to be, they pale in the face of enemies we have overcome and defeated. They, too, shall fall.

We will win because we used to be enslaved. We will win because it used to be illegal for us to read. We will win because it was only recently that we could not even testify in their courts of so-called law. We will win because they used to hang our bodies from trees. We will win because it used to be that Black women's hands were only expected to clean floors. We will win because Black bodies were carried to these

shores inside ships whose existence brought into question the trans-
porter's very humanity. We will win because they used hoses and attack
dogs on our bodies, but our spirits remained intact. We will win
because there has been a concerted effort since 1619 to destroy us—
and yet we have survived.

And we are joined in the historic struggle. We will win because no
woman could vote until 1920. We will win because they used to have
laws on their books that kept out the Chinese except as laborers to
be worked until their death. We will win because it used to be that
those who merely believed in socialism could be incarcerated. We will
win because they interned Japanese Americans as a supposed precau-
tion against internal enemies of the state, yet let German Americans
and Italian Americans walk free. We will win because they used to enter
people's bedrooms and declare their consenting sexual acts to be
illegal, never mind their own twisted voyeurism. We will win because
they sought to deny human and civil rights to Mexicans in California,
while expecting them to work land that once was their own. We will win
because there was a concerted attempt made to slaughter every single
Native person in the land, and they still stand. We will win because
Puerto Ricans have being fighting for full citizenship or freedom for a
century. We will win because progressive whites join us in rejecting the
lies that led to war, rejecting a dangerous silencing of political discourse, in demanding more jobs and opportunity, in decrying a complete void of political leadership.

We will win because their vision of America is narrow and ours is
broad. We will win because they seek to keep out fellow Americans, and
we seek to include them. Their policies are in direct contradiction to
the interests of the majority of Americans: they stand against the right
of all children to an equal education, against a more peaceful world,
against support services for the economically poor, against protection
of the environment and nature's resources, and against full health
care for all the residents of this, the wealthiest nation on earth. They
believe the rich are better and more deserving than the economically

poor and middle class; they ensure their wealthy base receives tax cuts and insider deals while others, lacking in clothes and necessities and opportunities, struggle to merely survive. We will win because the schools are in shambles and people have no health care and anger is brewing. We will win because they fight for domination and excess and elitism, and we fight for equality and schools and sustenance. They fight for mass incarceration and war around the world; we fight for giving our children a true opportunity and for peace.

We will win because, and mark my words: they do not, in fact, have any god on their side. No one has a monopoly on concepts of god and if some group did, this crew would most assuredly not be the one holding god's ear. They claim to follow the teachings of Christ yet they violate each of his teachings: they war, they condemn, they oppress, they deny rights, they kill. They speak with hubris of knowing god's will, and then they seek vengeance and death. They are cold of heart and ungracious of spirit. This is not a conflict between people of good faith and differing minds, not a time for accommodation and unity—these people have a deeply corrupt, violent, degrading, oppressive, elitist, and brutal view of how the world should be. They claim to do god's will, to be "pro-life," railing against a woman's right to choose, to decide what goes on in her own very body. Yet these same hypocrites serve as zealots for the death penalty. They are "pro-life" and pro-death. They cannot support state sanctioned death and then call themselves "pro-life." They cannot kill thousands of innocent civilians in Iraq in a fundamentally illegal war, whatever the ills of the despot they deposed, and then call themselves "pro-life." To do so mocks the very religion they claim to serve. We will win because we are consistent and they lie.

We will win because we believe in the ideals found in the written tenets of America and they do not. If they did—if they believed in plurality, diversity, freedom, equality, and democracy—then they would not pursue such oppressive and silencing policies. We know that America has never lived up to these ideals, but we fight daily for a little more justice, a little more equality, a little more freedom. Knowing its horrific history and continued reality of injustice, we still believe in what America can one day be, otherwise we would not be engaged in the struggles in which we are engaged—we would have given up long ago and moved from this soiled land. So it is not they, but we who are the patriots. We do not believe in a view of America as expressed by the so called "founding fathers," for these were men, who, all save one, owned human beings, bartered in the flesh of children, believing that our kind, our color, belonged not to the human family, but instead to the line of livestock and cattle, deeming us three-fifths of a human being. These were sins determinative of their very nature. We believe in an America that we express, that we envision, that we will create.

We will win because America's only hope is for it to be what we are and who we want it to be. America's death is certain if it remains the unachieved dream and becomes the land that they represent. We will win because we have struggled for too long, and too hard; won too many battles; achieved too much; changed this land for the better in too many ways; demanded too successfully that this land alter its course and begin living up to its creeds, to give up now. We will win because we have no other choice.

Sharpen your swords, your pens, your missions, your words, your actions—there is work to be done.

Khary Lazarre-White
Co-Founder and Co-Director
The Brotherhood/Sister Sol

8

LETTERS ON THE INTERNATIONAL QUALITY OF THE MOVEMENT

Pittsfield, Massachusetts

Caracas, January, 2005

Dear Abigail,

It's hot and it's raining. I'm on the terrace watching a vertical river on three sides. Beyond the river stretches a mass of misguided seventies-era concrete and glass, buried under forty years of soot and smog, every surface greasy to the touch, preserved like a twisted twentieth-century Pompeii.

I miss our conversations, our debates, and sitting here waiting for the rain to stop I have time to think. Though letters are no longer as fashionable as they once were, it seems to be the next best medium for us to continue our discussions *in absentia*.

If capitalism isn't the future, what is? How could socialism possibly work, when we in the North have been inoculated with capitalist logic for so long? How can we imagine another form of government, or a way to get there? I doubt you've ever asked me this in quite these words.

Generally, you have a way of writing orally, and the question doesn't trip over itself. *Capitalism is no good*. That much we agree on. Private property, the role of religion, possible futures: these are a different story. "From each according to his ability, to each according to his need," I'll tell you. *Do you really believe that? Do you really think it's possible to convince people to work merely for the good of society? With no personal incentive, no individual risk?* you respond. And I think you may have quoted Ayn Rand's "morality of rational self-interest."

It's a tough question. I usually get around it by arguing that answering that question involves not only details of a society that has yet to exist, but most importantly the elaboration of the transformation necessary to get there. I don't mean to say that engaging the question is somehow disingenuous or unimportant. But it's gradually occurred to me that I've been coming at this from the wrong direction. I'm skipping a step, which is what initially aroused your skepticism: if you assume, for the moment, that another world *is* possible (no small assumption), the question is not "is socialism possible," but rather, "can we even imagine socialism?"

With the World Social Forum opening next week in Porto Alegre, Brazil, this question is perhaps a bit less abstract than it may seem. I should go to Brazil, but I need to stay in Caracas to find us an apartment and to write a hundred things that must be finished by February. And as hard as it is to miss the fifty or one hundred thousand people gathering in Brazil to assert that another world can be made, in Venezuela there is a movement of several million asserting that another world *will* be made. That's a tough context to abandon, even for a week.

With its evaporating historical ties to Porto Alegre—now that participatory budgeting is out the window—next year's WSF will be held in Venezuela. It's strange that the move didn't happen sooner, but it's less strange when you consider many activists' distrust of state power. I understand, as I'm sure you do (what with your small-government tendencies), this distrust. The history of the Left is a history of real possibilities for change corrupted by power. The tendency today is to reject our parents' obsession with political parties, in favor of social movements. As an embryonic new New Left that is building on 1998, as well as 1968, we've replaced the quest for power with the quest for democracy; the dictatorship of the proletariat is not our rallying cry. And in so doing, we've managed to redefine the term to replace the emptiness of representation with the revolutionary energy of participation. Once we have real democracy, once people govern by participatory budgets, local councils, and through fully accountable representatives, so the argument goes, we'll be able to control state power. Taking it for ourselves would be redundant—a mere symbolic gesture.

But how do you get to that point without power? How do you mobilize people to that point without the state's help? Brazil's landless workers' movement would seem to be the ultimate proof of that. For twenty years the landless workers' movement in Brazil has been one of the most progressive, inventive, and dynamic social movements anywhere, as well as the largest. The changes they've brought about in twenty years are incredible. But they were forced to fight the government every step of the way, and the human cost—measured in lives lost—would test the commitment of the most die-hard activist.

In six years under Hugo Chávez in Venezuela, the balance of positive reforms to violent repercussions has left Brazil far behind. With the government leading the struggle, allied to embryonic social movements and community organizations, they have (so far) squared off successfully against the traditional elite and their U.S. backers. Historically, Venezuela has had a social movement deficit, yet perhaps it is not so far from an organic, radical social movement after all. There is a fundamental uniqueness to *Chavistas* as a mobilizing force on a scale never before seen in the nation's history.

I came down here a wide-eyed, do-gooder. I was lucky and got published—and all of a sudden I'm a journalist, because no one else is down here writing about what is really going on. But, to be honest, I'm not that interested in a career in journalism. What I am interested in, and the reason I came to Venezuela in the first place, is in participating in a struggle against U.S. imperialism and neoliberalism (not just "globalization"), in the only capacity in which I am able: writing, spreading the word. There is a genuine battle to be won in the U.S. media with respect to Venezuela. What is especially daunting about this task is that not even the "Left" press is yet on side.

If you were here right now you'd be kicking me. *You're not at the lectern. Give me ideas, not big words.* Ok: *here* is where it's happening. Venezuela is the future. Bolivia is the future. Argentina is the future. Brazil is the future. We as North Americans are so far from engendering the kinds of changes so many of us know are necessary. And that's the North American perversion. It's twisted: we *know*—even those of us who aren't "active"—what is wrong with our societies, or at least some of what is wrong. But to go from there to conceiving of a plan of action is a big step, and there's a lot of emptiness in between. To the South, where the structures of imperialism are more visible, a vibrant culture of resistance has survived. Its 500-year history is something you trip over. Somehow these people are making the jump. Something is happening, people are moving—more than anywhere else, in Venezuela, where massive popular mobilization is buttressed by state power. The give and take of progressive government and politicized mass movement has meant that Venezuela is in a position to effect structural change in our lifetimes. In six years education programs have brought free education to the 70 percent of the country living in poverty, from literacy to university. Free health care is available in the most remote *barrios*, alongside community organizations facilitating the urban and rural land reform. A process of capacity-building is drawing more and more Venezuelans into direct contact with their neighbors, helping to create a culture centered on solidarity and community, rather than introversion and personal gain.

In 1964 a freshman at Oberlin College participating in a "freedom school" in Mileston, Mississippi, wrote in a letter to a classmate, "As a white northerner I can get involved whenever I feel like it and run home whenever I get bored or frustrated or scared." For me the frontier of activism is political journalism in Venezuela, but it presents me with the same political/moral contradiction—that razor wire we walk between political activism and political apathy, between opportunity and introversion. The trick is to know when it's time to go home and bring the Venezuelan experience to bear on the North.

Rain is splashing off the rail, soaking me. I need you with me now. You need to see what is happening here, the incredible changes that have already occurred. This is something for us to experience together; when we return to the North we will be closer to imagining a society that depends less fanatically on individualism, for as the British historian E. H. Carr once said, "Suicide is the only perfectly free act open to individual man . . ."

Love,
Jonah

To anyone who will listen,

I will never forget the tension in their backs. Massaging the backs of the nine- and ten- year-old kids living in Palestine felt like massaging my grandmother. Perhaps it had something to do with having their homes consistently raided by the army, or seeing their family members and neighbors killed. Maybe it also had to do with having their land confiscated, crops destroyed, and villages erased. After being there for two weeks I was already starting to feel tension building in my own back; it is impossible for me to imagine what a lifetime living under occupation would do.

I took a trip in July of 2004 that had a profound effect on how I view my role as an activist. I went with a group of Jewish women to the occupied territories in the West Bank to support the Palestinian resistance to the Israeli occupation. I had the opportunity to go past the media, beyond anyone else's word, and witness with my own five senses the reality of life under occupation. It is a reality neither the Israeli government nor the U.S. government wants you to see. The trip showed me what it means to be an ally to a foreign social justice movement.

I went to work with the International Solidarity Movement (ISM), which is one of several non-governmental organizations working with the Palestinian-led *Nonviolent* resistance movement. ISM was founded in 1996 during the second *Intifada*, or popular uprising in response to severe military invasions of Palestinian cities led by the Israeli army. I went with the ISM because I believe that nonviolent resistance is the only viable solution to ending the occupation. I went just in time for the launch of their summer campaign titled "Freedom Summer." Similar to the "Freedom Summer" in the United States in 1964, which was a direct action, community organizing, and voter registration campaign to focus national attention on racism in the south, "Freedom Summer" in Palestine was a series of direct actions to focus *international* attention on the construction of the Wall.

Literally speaking, the Wall is a twenty-five-foot massive concrete block that separates two pieces of land: Israel proper and the occupied territories in the West Bank, known to some as Palestine. The Israeli government has stated that they must build the Wall to separate themselves from the Palestinians and thus protect themselves from suicide bombings. The construction of the Wall, however, has been deemed illegal by the International Court of Justice, mainly because it is not being built on the Israeli side of the Green line (the border that was agreed upon at the end of the 1967 Six Day War), but instead in the West Bank as well, thereby placing some Palestinian communities on the Israeli side of the Wall. It only seems fair to wonder about the real motivation behind the construction of the Wall, which effectively serves to separate Palestinians from other Palestinians, their jobs, schools, other important institutions, valuable resources such as pipelines and water, and finally, to give Israel more land.

The Wall adds further difficulty to an already difficult daily life under occupation. (The Israeli occupation of Palestine is illegal under international law.) Three main elements define this occupation: checkpoints, curfews, and roadblocks:

All along the Wall and throughout the West Bank Palestinians must pass through small openings known as checkpoints. These checkpoints are extremely dehumanizing in nature: they are monitored by armed guards and they can open and close at will—this means that a Palestinian may cross in one direction and not be able to get back home. Oftentimes Palestinians are made to wait at checkpoints for indefinite periods of time in the hot sun; in order to pass they must show ID, and they are subjected to being searched. The only way to avoid checkpoints is to find an "illegal passageway." I witnessed hoards of people—children and commercial goods in hand—maneuvering around the ledge of a roof in an attempt to avoid an extended five-mile detour to move approximately three feet.

Curfew under occupation is like house arrest for a whole city, nobody moves for twenty-four hours for days on end. There is nothing in the street, all stores are closed, and nobody can leave their house. Kids do not go to school and nobody goes to work. Ambulances and fire trucks can move but are subject to being searched on departure and arrival. Usually doctors treat patients by going to their house in the ambulance because bringing them to the hospital is too difficult. Every few days the curfew is lifted for a few hours so people can shop.

Roadblocks are actual boulders or blockades that are placed in the middle of Palestinian roads by either the army or Israelis who are living in nearby settlements so that Palestinians cannot drive freely in and out of their village. They are impossible to remove without a bulldozer and they severely impact transportation to and from the village. Oftentimes Palestinians must engage in what are referred to as roadblock removals where the whole town gets together, to physically remove the dirt and boulders from the roads. Unfortunately the roadblocks are often put back within twenty-four hours of their removal.

On a practical level my presence in the West Bank served to do several things: First, to deter the use of live ammunition against unarmed nonviolent protesters during actions. (The army will rarely fire live ammunition if internationals are seen or perceived to be in the crowd). Second, to attract media attention, as both a means of protecting protesters from extreme violence and a way of alerting the international community about the nonviolent resistance movement opposing the Wall. And finally, to bear witness to a military occupation with all its horrors and to bring that message back home.

In addition, going to Palestine was an opportunity to make an overt distinction between the policies of the U.S. government and my own beliefs. Whenever I spoke to Palestinians about the United States and its foreign policy, the distinction was often made: The government is not its people. They are able to have this impression precisely because they have stood, literally, in solidarity with people from all over the world. Together Israelis, Palestinians, and internationals opposed the occupation and the construction of the Wall. Together we raised a critical voice in opposition to an Israel/U.S. alliance that is out to pursue its own agenda at the expense of enforcing international law.

As U.S. activists, we must recognize that along with our privilege comes a responsibility to confront our government and to hold our elected officials accountable. We are, so to speak, in the belly of the beast. Ironically, I went all the way to Palestine to oppose an enemy that exists right here at home. Our government is greatly responsible, if not solely responsible, for the ongoing occupation of Palestine. Billions of dollars are pumped into Israel every year, and that money comes from our tax dollars! If we don't voice our opposition and demand that we cease funding the occupation, who will?

Spreading the seeds of awareness is always a first step in building an international movement. We need to know the truth about the conditions in other parts of the world in order to be able to respond appropriately. Aside from the brave children who continue to resist the occupation with their mere presence in the West Bank, I met with Palestinians who were old, young, male, female, poor, middle-class, highly educated, non-educated, employed, unemployed, students, urban dwellers, rural dwellers, and everything in between. All of them had the same message: "Tell our story." From their perspective the most valuable thing that I could do is to tell anyone who will listen the truth about the conditions under which they live.

Sincerely,
Joya Colon-Berezin

February 2005

Santo Domingo, República Dominicana

To curious friends new and old,

Sometimes I stop and ask myself why I am here.

The simple answer is that I have been hired as an "activist professional," the Caribbean Region Coordinator of the Agua Buena Human Rights Association. Agua Buena is a small Costa Rican NGO advocating for universal access to treatment for people living with AIDS in Latin America.

I met Richard Stern and Guillermo Murillo of Agua Buena, both long-time AIDS activists, in October 2003 while at an HIV/AIDS conference in Panama. The two were instrumental in creating pressure and a legal petition that convinced the Costa Rican Supreme Court to require that health authorities provide antiretroviral (ARV) medicines to all who needed them, back in 1998. In Panama, I was particularly impressed by the quality of their research and demands, and by the unique confrontational style of Agua Buena.

What struck them about me, I believe, was that I had sat on a bus almost four days in order to come to the conference in Panama all the way from Tegucigalpa, Honduras. I was in Honduras to research access to rapid HIV testing and ARVs as part of a Fulbright Scholarship. Since Honduras has been the country hardest hit by AIDS in Central America, and Costa Rica has long had universal access to antiretroviral treatment, Agua Buena was especially interested in communicating with me about what was going on in Honduras. We began exchanging a series of e-mails between Tegucigalpa and San Jose, Costa Rica, and one thing led to another.

But prior to this my interests in Latin America had been growing for many years. In college I spent a year as an exchange student at the Universidad de Chile in Santiago. One day in Chile still stands out among others. I was completing health and socioeconomic surveys in the shacks of some of Santiago's poorest residents, or *pobladores*. I felt the intensity of their poverty, but also, more importantly, I experienced the human strength and spirit of just about everybody we spoke with that day. I learned that the land beneath the shantytown we visited, like many others in Santiago, was obtained over forty years ago during a series of heroic struggles. I also learned that the conditions of the poor in Chile, now one of the most prosperous countries in Latin America, demonstrate the need for more sustained and radical social and economic change. Even with Chile's rapidly growing economy, the health, education, and wages of the poor have shown no significant signs of improvement.

I also remember the first time I entered a small, hot, public hospital room filled with gaunt, coughing, bedridden, people living with AIDS in Tegucigalpa, the capital of Honduras. The Instituto Nacional del Tórax was the first of many poorly funded public hospitals and clinics I visited in Central America. Many of these provided useful data for my research project, but more importantly these visits aroused indignation about what was lacking in these centers and what could and should be provided to prevent and control avoidable sickness and disease.

In Kingston, Jamaica, I accompanied several friends, mostly poor HIV+ women, to the hospital. They showed me the wards where they struggled for life and their friends died because they lacked ARV medicines and other pills. These medicines would have cost the Jamaican government less than a dollar a day. I felt especially privileged as an activist when afterward they offered to ride the crowded public bus with me back into the city showing me the way to my guest house so I need not take a taxi, even more proud than when I had been invited to speak about my work on a popular university radio show earlier that same day.

I have met many people who are alive today simply because they were able to start ARVs. Guillermo Murillo, assistant director of Agua Buena, is one of these. Another is one of those gaunt patients with AIDS I met that first day in the hospital in Tegucigalpa. Seeing the same man who I had presumed would likely die, alive and well seven months later with his family on the beach reminded me yet again how important it is to get these medicines to those in need. In AIDS activism, small victories can make a big difference.

As an activist who is used to making demands, I realize that consciousness, knowledge, and commitment to social change also must be nourished. I thought about this as I sat in an Evangelical church and listened to a support group of people living with AIDS in La Romana, a small city in the eastern coast of the Dominican Republic. La Romana, coincidentally, is home to Casa del Campo, probably the most famous hotel resort in the Caribbean. Ironically, I saw firsthand how despite the extraordinary opulence of the nearby resort and villas, few if any of the HIV+ women in the audience at the church had decent paying work, access to affordable health care, education, or adequate housing.

How could this be? How do tourism, the sex trade, poverty, the free trade zones, and migration from Haiti related to the sugar industry combine to cause the area of La Romana to report some of the highest rates of HIV in the Dominican Republic and the Western Hemisphere? Instead of placing value on the quality of poor people's lives, our society worships expensive shiny metal jewelry, plastic cell phones, enormous cars, and guns. But the majority of Dominicans barely have access to electricity for a few hours each day.

In the Dominican Republic the privately owned textile processing and exporting zones, immense soft drink and alcohol production, distribution and storage networks, and four multinational cell phone consortiums compete for customers and make millions of pesos and dollars. Yet it still remains difficult, if not impossible, to get a one dollar rapid HIV test, a ten-cent condom, or pills to keep many thousands of Dominicans with AIDS alive for a cost of less than a dollar a day.

Buses, motorcycles, and hundreds of thousands of big and small luxury cars have made their way to this island, the poorest in the Americas. The cars come all the way from factories and ports in Germany, France, Japan, New York City, Detroit, Korea, England, Brazil, Miami, China, and other corners of the globe. At the same time thousands die every year because a sufficient quantity of medicines, which could fit in a couple of shipping containers or an airplane cargo hold, cannot arrive and affordably and efficiently be administered to those who need them. Worse still, despite the increasing abundance of expensive four-wheel drive vehicles, many people can barely afford the costs of public transport to get to the clinic.

We see that HIV/AIDS can be treated in places as different as Costa Rica, Chile, Cuba, or Chicago when relatively more resources are invested in providing public health care for the poor. It seems evident now, twenty-five years into the epidemic, that HIV/AIDS and other diseases that primarily affect the poor, thrive in conditions of extreme poverty and inequity. Of course, infectious microbes and viruses are blind to social class. When a shirtless migrant Haitian construction worker from a region where malaria is endemic happens to be building or landscaping a new hotel in the resort area of Punta Cana in the Dominican Republic, and he is bitten by a mosquito which in turns goes on to bite a tourist sitting at a nearby hotel, the problems of the poor become everyone's problem.

I consider myself lucky not to have had to sit in a bank, work for the military, the CIA, a multinational cosmetics company, a corporate law firm, selling luxury cars, importing textiles, stamping documents, or work as a cashier like some friends. Similarly I haven't had to work in an office for an elitist, stifling, wasteful, bureaucratic, perhaps powerful and well-paying institution like PAHO, UNAIDS, USAID, or the World Bank. This has been a real blessing in terms of my intellectual freedom and activism. I even sometimes feel privileged to be here when I find myself crammed in with three other large adults in the backseat of a battered and rusty old public car powered by propane gas chugging along with the windows down and radio blaring merengue in the sweltering and traffic clogged avenues of Santo Domingo.

My experiences have helped to connect Latin American history and politics to real life struggles and have helped define who I am today. My interest in health, human rights, and HIV/AIDS cannot really be separated from a passion for Latin American history and culture. This passion in itself is sparked and motivated by an intense sense of injustice about the inequality, racism, oppression, and war in and between the United States, Latin America, the Caribbean, and beyond. I hope, in addition, that by writing this letter, I have given some voice to the many people I have met in Latin America over the last four years, who have taught me very much and who continue to inspire me.

In Solidarity,
Eugene Schiff

9

LETTERS ON LEADERSHIP

Dear feminists (radical and closeted alike),

I woke up this morning feeling inexplicably bad-ass. I thought about catching a bus down to Alabama—that remarkable state where it's legal to buy a handgun but not a sex toy—and risking the $10,000 fine for a wild romp with my pink bootleg Pocket Rocket. Then I contemplated sneaking into the main dining hall here at Yale, calmly hijacking the prominent portrait of George Bush Sr., and replacing it with a more agreeable painting of Emma Goldman in her wide-brimmed hat and I'm-gonna-kick-your-capitalist-ass bifocals.

For almost twenty minutes after that, I daydreamed about becoming a Stereotypical Crazy Feminist: one of those wiry spinsters who could bring Pat Robinson to his knees with my hairy armpits and schemes to wreak havoc on the patriarchal military-prison-pharmaceutical-petrochemical-industrial-complex. But I soon concluded that I'd prefer to do all of this with a friend—or two, or ten, or ten thousand. So I sat down to write you this invitation.

Wouldn't you agree that our world is in dire need of more frequent feminist fantasy sessions, particularly ones that culminate in irreverent political action? I ask because I'm sick of feeling hesitant to fully claim the f-word—no disclaimers, no implicit question marks—and I wouldn't be surprised if you are too.

Sure, I harbor the standard fear of being taken for a bitchy, humorless Feminazi who's out to castrate your boyfriend, sue your brother for sexual harassment, and smack your local minister over the head with a copy of *Our Bodies, Ourselves*. But a million times more central to my reluctance, I'm uncomfortable with what it means to embrace feminism on the terms of the "Third Wave"—the very movement that, according to unofficial spokeswomen Amy Richards and Jennifer Baumgardner, aims to represent every possible incarnation of modern feminist, whether "you're sexy, a wallflower, you shop at Calvin Klein, you are a stay-at-home mom, a big Hollywood producer, a beautiful bride all in white, an ex-wife raising three kids, or you shave, pluck, *and* wax."

I say fuck that: what ever happened to fiery old-school diatribes against industries like Hollywood and practices like plucking? Or to a critique of the fact that Calvin Klein thongs are sewn by young women in Puebla, Mexico's *maquiladoras*—many of whom are regularly cheated of their (already paltry) wages, subjected to compulsory pregnancy tests and sexual harassment, and fired for attempting to unionize? You won't find me toasting to designer sweatshop panties or Martha Stewart weddings any time soon, nor will I be joining Richards and Baumgardner in saluting female cadets at the Virginia Military Institute and the Citadel as champions of gender equality.

My intellect and imagination demand so much more than the Third Wave's convenient brand of "be whoever you are" feminism delivers. As a white woman at an Ivy League institution, I want—no, *need*—to begin untangling myself from the subtle webs of power that implicate me in the domination and dehumanization of others; when my fashion preferences fuel young women's exploitation in the global garment factory, for example, why should this fly under my feminist radar screen? I also want to confront my own internalized oppression, instead of rushing to greet the voices telling me I'm long overdue for a cleavage boost, a gardenia-scented douche, a tan, a man, a trendy bisexual tryst, a glossy guide to giving unforgettable head, or all six of these at once. If our generation's feminist movements say nothing of the need for self-confrontation and soul searching, at what costs does this omission take place?

In efforts to ditch the perceived ideological straightjackets of our feminist foremothers, too many prominent figures of the Third Wave have chosen to celebrate ideas and icons that leave sexism's deepest foundations uncontested. Remember the whole Girl Power trip that gave us *Buffy the Vampire Slayer* and the Spice Girls? While it was fun bopping around to girls-on-top innuendo and cheering on Ally McBeal in the courtroom/boardroom/bedroom, reveling in our newfound "lipstick liberation" quickly proved a crappy replacement for breaking a sweat through genuine political action. As commentator Jennifer Pozner pointed out, "It's probably a fair assumption to say that 'zigazig-ha' is not Spice shorthand for 'subvert the dominant paradigm.'"

What lessons can we draw from the fact that shopping-and-fucking feminism hasn't made so much as a crick in patriarchy's Omnipotent Dick? In an age when feminist rhetoric is co-opted to peddle just about everything—from glittery eye shadow to *Sex and the City* DVDs—and to justify almost anything—from breast implants to the wars on Afghanistan and Iraq—we need to choose our bedfellows carefully. Feminism can't always be flirty and fun; more often than not, it's transformative precisely because it's scary and cumbersome. If we want the Third Wave to look more like a tsunami than a cutesy little cultural ripple, we must stick to the notion that "the personal is political" while resuscitating the equally subversive conviction that "the political is personal."

It's not as if we have any shortage of crises to tackle. No shit, women have already won the right to vote, get legal abortions (if and where we can afford them), and play professional basketball. But only models and porn stars earn higher salaries than men, given that the wage gaps still hovers around seventy-five cents to the dollar. And only when playing *Street Fighter 2* can we hope to throw flaming Dragon Punches at those who relentlessly threaten us with physical and sexual violence.

Have you ever noticed that the talking heads who constantly trumpet the dawn of the postfeminist era seem oblivious to the fact that some twenty million women still lack health insurance here in the world's wealthiest nation? Do you think they missed the update that teenage girls now comprise America's fastest growing prison population, along with the equally alarming news that the number of women incarcerated for petty drug offenses—mostly mothers and women of color—rose a mind-boggling 500 percent from 1986 to 2002?

If they didn't get the news flash, I can't say I blame them; the mainstream media makes it ten times easier to learn about Britney Spears's latest battle with butt fungus than to ascertain any substantive information about the real issues facing young women in America. Stupid white men—to cop an infinitely useful phrase from Michael Moore—still control the vast majority of our country's television stations, newspapers, and other media outlets, not to mention the lion's share of political, legal, economic, and social institutions.

These kinds of glaring inequalities are only magnified in the international arena, where young women of the Global South increasingly bear the burdens of corporate globalization while reaping few of its promised rewards. Sex trafficking, sweatshop labor, and precarious service sector jobs have become staples of the borderless economy, thanks in part to neoliberal economic policies that exacerbate—in the name of human freedom, of course—the very structural inequities from which such industries arise.

If one thing is clear, it's this: the time is not yet ripe for feminists in the Global North to fold our tents and go back to the Goddess-worshiping, baby-killing lesbian coven from whence we supposedly came. Our local women's shelters need us. Our schools and cities need us. *Our world really fuckin' needs us.*

One simple way we can meet this rallying call is to start showing up when and where it matters. Think back to the legendary Battle of Seattle in 1999 that marked the beginning of the union between "the Teamsters and the Turtles." Why don't we remember it as "the Teamsters, and Turtles, and the Third Wave"? Is it just because the latter sounds too clunky? Or is it because the bulk of us stayed at home that week, failing to recognize the rise of unfettered corporate power as a pressing feminist issue? Or—perhaps the most likely explanation—is it because thousands of us attended, marched, chanted, built puppets, staged guerrilla theater, smashed windows, and built activist networks, but neglected to proclaim a feminist critique of corporate globalization as one of our primary reasons for doing so? The same line of inquiry holds for the 2003 fight against the Free Trade Area of the Americas in Miami, the 2005 mobilization against the World Bank and IMF in Washington, D.C. . . . And the list goes on.

Our generation's feminist movements must learn the language of the global justice activists, and vice versa. Beyond our right to wield vibrators, miniskirts, and sex positivity—the Third Wave's implicit holy trinity—young feminists must fight to ensure that women (and girls, and men, and transgender folks) everywhere have access to economic and political self-determination. We must move beyond naïve and essentialist discourses about "global sisterhood" to recognize and resist the various oppressions that crosscut feminist constituencies.

And to top it all off, we must reacquaint ourselves with the lost art of the feminist fantasy session: that inspired practice in which we let our activist imaginations wander all the way from the ceilings of our bedrooms to the trenches of Baghdad to the fenced-in sneaker factories of Jakarta, then back around to the contours of our urban streets and lovers' backs, eventually winding up in that maligned-but-sublime space between our very own legs (where else?). In so doing, we have to suspend our disbelief long enough to envision new directions for globalization—ones in which women's rights are valued over copyrights—and alternative futures for gender relations—ones that shatter the gender binary and the related confines of traditional femininity and masculinity. This kind of radical daydreaming can help us connect the dots between sexism, racism, heterosexism, imperialism, and other symbiotic forms of oppression. But it's not an end unto itself; to the contrary, it's a means of discovering an action-oriented feminist roadmap, as well as the confidence to carry it out.

How's that for an invitation? If you're feeling overwhelmed, it's always cool to start small, with minor attempts at what Inga Muscio calls "the transformation of destructive, negative crap-ola into constructive, positive brilliantiana." Maybe you could write your own letter outlining your goals for re-politicizing feminism, then plaster it to your mirror and the bathroom stalls inside your local Hooters chain. Next, you could tell a few friends to do the same. Meanwhile, I promise to follow up on my end of the bargain by working on my watercolor homage to Emma Goldman, which you'll soon find—if all goes as planned—hanging in the Yale dining hall where Papa Bush once reigned supreme.

Of course, neither of us will stop there; together, I have a hunch we'll become a force to reckon with. We'll have fun, but our mission will remain a profoundly serious one: to reclaim our collective freedom from patriarchy and other systems of oppression currently at work in our schools, prisons, governments, factories, families, and selves.

I think we'll make one hell of a Fourth Wave.

Much love and courage,
Sarah

To The Left,

When John Kerry conceded the 2004 presidential election, people around me were in a deep funk. One friend told me it was like being punched in the stomach; another said she was living through her worst nightmare. The Left put so much hope and energy into the election—unprecedented voter turnout efforts, massive outreach to youth and communities of color, traveling across the country to protect voting rights in Ohio, Florida, and elsewhere—it was hard not to feel crushed after the Republicans won. The election was an incredible crisis for the Left, and it seemed the most urgent and accomplishable task was to defeat George Bush. In the end, however, we were the ones who lost.

We didn't lose just because George Bush was reelected. We lost because we didn't take advantage of an opportunity to promote Left-wing politics; to project our commitment to substantive equality; to state clearly the need to eliminate white supremacy, patriarchy, heterosexism, and even capitalism. We will continue to lose in this way until we develop our own political organization, independent of both the Democrats and Republicans. We need to plan long-term to develop a national, multi-issue political alliance or party that is grounded in our social movements and will emphasize the centrality of fighting for our demands in the streets. Such an organization should have the capacity to project a Leftist agenda in the media, but also in the political process. This organization would prioritize the platforms of social movements and integrate them into the electoral strategy, rather than vice versa. Joining or aligning with the Republican Party is obviously out of the question, but the Democratic Party has proven that it will also never suit the needs of the Left.

The Democratic Party doesn't share our understandings, like our belief that all forms of oppression and exploitation are inextricably interconnected, or our common understanding that powerful, inclusive social movements are crucial to winning long-lasting, substantive change. Could you picture the Democratic Party ever acknowledging white supremacy and actively working to end it? What about subordinating itself to a radical social movement or program, such as ending the prison industrial complex? Will the Democratic Party ever move away from an elite leadership of white personalities—of the ruling class and supported by other members of it—with a few token people of color, to a more mass-based, democratically responsive one? Because my answer to these questions is a resounding "No!" that is, we will never move the party enough to reflect my vision for the world—I believe we have to start with our common goal of ending all forms of oppression and build from there, never compromising on our goals.

The Democrats have hindered the expression of Leftist ideas and positions, not just because of their platform, but because we on the Left have put so much time and energy into using the Democrats as an electoral expression.

Take, for example, how detrimental the presidential elections were for the antiwar movement. By the time you read this letter, the antiwar movement might be back on its feet, clearly demanding withdrawal from Iraq and Afghanistan. But leading up to the 2004 election, the antiwar movement fizzled out, muddling into various Democratic electoral projects. Even though the antiwar movement hasn't built organizations that do much beyond putting on protests, at least there was a sense of urgency and unity around an issue. All the energy the Left once had—for example, the massive, worldwide demonstrations before the war hit—was sucked into the black hole of the ballot box. Kerry's message on the war was equivocal and defuse; it certainly was not in line with the antiwar movement's message. The collapse of the movement into the Democratic Party was far less productive than if we had continued to critique and build it. At this point, no one seems to remember any of what happened before the war or feel the same urgency. People even forget that everything the antiwar movement claimed about the war is true. There are no weapons of mass destruction in Iraq; Iraq and 9/11 aren't related; the invasion has led only to chaos and instability—*not* to stability and security.

We should be proud of what the antiwar movement accomplished and the potential that it still has. But we should also realize that there was no visible antiwar message in the presidential elections. We need to think about how we change the options available to us, so that year after year we're not stuck in this same position on such an important issue.

If we built independent, strong social movements with sustainable organizations, they would be able to both demand reforms in the streets and win gains in elections, while training new generations of leaders and building long-term power. But we stunt the very growth of such movements when we weed out messages that might be too radical or contrary because we're worried about how the Democrats might do, come election time. And when we project the idea that the best option is to support the Democrats, we don't put any effort into supporting our own views, signaling that they're not worth building on. This isn't to say that I put great faith in electoral strategies—in themselves, they will never be sufficient to achieve the kind of change I want to see—but absent a more radical alternative, individuals on the Left will be drawn into the Democratic Party, which will be inevitably and perpetually compromising.

I want to pose the challenge of creating a new organization or alliance to people of my generation in particular. I'm thinking of all the activists and organizers radicalized by campus activism around sweatshops, efforts to abolish the prison industrial complex, living wage campaigns, massive global justice protests, environmental justice fights, and more. They're anti-imperialist people of color, direct action anarchists, community and union organizers, socialists, nonprofit employees, as well as Left-liberals. We should feel confident enough to formulate and act on our own visions of how the Left should be organized, at the same time that we listen to what those around us have to say and try to understand the experiences and insights of those who came before us.

There are very real obstacles to doing this. Envisioning and building this kind of organization requires patience and vision; it will be years before we ever get there. The scope of such an undertaking is enormous, and we will be starting with a small nucleus of committed people. We will have to openly confront much of the racism, sexism, heterosexism, and national chauvinism that exists within the Left. But the task is important—the Left needs leadership that is a part of and listens to our social movements, and that can be an electoral expression of our values, refusing to compromise on them. I've only been old enough to vote in two presidential elections. But I have a hard time being excited about the prospect of the rest of my life, every four years, being told to hold my nose when I go to cast my vote. I like to think that at a certain age, you get too old to accept that as democracy. I'm urging the Left to be bold and act with hope, so that in the future we don't have to compromise ourselves or our movements, and maybe we can start winning again.

In Solidarity,
Arthur Liou

Dear Movement,

Last night, after more than a few glasses of wine, I found myself yet again lying in bed staring at the ceiling and thinking about you. The sheets were all tangled up with my legs and the blankets felt too heavy and hot. Rain knifed in the cracked window and prickled my face. I was tired, and I wanted to be asleep. But as usual, I couldn't get you off my mind. For years now we've been close, intimate even. We've stayed up all night dreaming, drinking coffee, and smoking cigarettes back when I was too young to worry about emphysema. We've shared endless bus trips to demonstrations against more wars than I care to count. We've run from cops and challenged cops and painted banners and sweated and froze and huddled around barrel fires. You never laugh at me when politics lay me low, when I cry watching the news. You've comforted me after so many elections and defeats and heartbreaks. You've given me hope, reminded me time and again that I am not alone, that we are many and that we may well be winning.

But lately, more and more, I have to wonder if I even know you at all. Maybe I've been too willing to see only what I want to see, to make you what I wish you were. I thought you had our future figured out, or that you had some sort of plan for how we were going to get to the more just world that I know we both so desperately seek. Now it seems like that was all show. You're so into being against things. What are you for—not generally, but exactly? You get so hung up on the superficial things sometimes. It makes me crazy—we have better things to worry about than who's wearing Nikes and who eats meat.

Sometimes when we get together, you just gripe about who has "good politics." Why do you assume I know what that means, or that we agree on what "good politics" are? It's like when you talk about how we want "social change"—fascists want social change, but not the kind that I do. We need a vision of social change, one that we can articulate with specificity. "Fuck the man" doesn't quite do it for me anymore, although I will admit I thought it was hot and radical back when we first met. But that was a long time ago, and we're both different now, and older. Whether we're any wiser remains to be seen.

Remember back in college when we saw that movie, *Fire from the Mountain*, about the Sandinistas and their dreams of overthrowing Somoza? One part of it stuck with me very clearly. One of the Sandinistas, maybe Omar Cabezas, is describing the moment in 1979 when they finally won their guerilla war against the government. He talks about coming down from the hills where the Sandinista fighters had been hiding for years, streaming triumphant through the streets of Managua, and taking over the capital building. And he says that they all looked at each other, and their hearts sank. They had no plan for picking up the trash, for repairing the roads or the sewers, for managing the infrastructure of the country. They realized that in all the planning for battle they had not planned for the peace. Sound familiar?

Look, I know. I can hear you shaking your head and sputtering your protest. I'm not saying we're the same as the Sandinistas, or that we're totally without a vision for the future. And I'm certainly not comparing our planning for the future with the mess Bush and his crew have made of the "peace" in and "rebuilding" of Iraq. But we have to stop thinking only in opposition and talking only about how much things suck. How, how exactly, will we do it better?

We need to be brave in new ways. I know you're not into capital "L" leaders, and you have your reasons. You learned a lot from the sixties, when enemies and disillusioned allies both managed to discredit our prominent leaders. They were murdered. They were incarcerated. They were under too much pressure and burnt out or got into drugs or got tired. So now you eschew hierarchical structures of organizing. You try to create within our groups the kinds of relationships we'd like to see in the larger world: structures based on consensus, on equal participation. All that is good. I'm glad that us ladies don't just have to run off mimeographs and serve oatmeal at the breakfast program.

But I worry that you're throwing the baby out with the bathwater. We can have leadership that isn't top down. In fact, I think we need leadership to give us some direction; maybe not one leader, but many. We can have a multitude of voices articulating visions for social change. We can have new models of leadership that are participatory, leadership that has humor and flexibility. And we can back up those people who do stand up and take a leadership role, and make sure that we don't leave them and ourselves vulnerable to the machinations of whatever federal agencies the administration decides to rain down on us.

Maybe getting knocked on your ass during this presidential election will teach you a thing or two. I mean, I think you did some great stuff, despite the fact that the Democrats lost again. Seeing so many young people fired up about politics was so exciting to me, and it wasn't just the presidential election they were talking about. Even the mainstream media couldn't ignore the mobilization. But don't you think that if we had had some charismatic leaders spearheading the push for change, along with a more specific articulation of our vision, we might have pulled out a win? I'm not talking about Michael Moore, or celebrity-activists like Springsteen or the ubiquitous Ben Affleck. And I don't mean johnny-come-latelys like P. Diddy. And while I appreciate all the money that was poured into 527 groups, I don't really think million-aires are going to hand out the kind of social change I'd like to see. The thing is, if we don't develop and support leaders from within our own ranks in the Movement, we're going to be stuck with people like Puffy or the lesser half of Bennifer leading the charge.

I know it can be scary to take a stand and put yourself out there as a capital "L" leader. With the infighting in our movement, leaders will get plenty of shit from our allies, let alone our many enemies. I suspect it's something more than fear of the limelight that is holding you back, though. Sometimes I think you've read too much Foucault and Derrida. Lord knows you bored me to tears talking about them in college when you went all postmodernist and drank too much espresso. I'm down with the idea that everything is relative, that nothing is certain, that there are no absolutes. But look, there comes a time when it's not useful anymore for everything to be relative, when you have to say "I don't know about everything. I haven't got all the answers or all the details, but these things I know for sure. Can you stand up and be counted behind this idea?" I think we agree on the basics, that everyone should be able to live with dignity and decency, with clean water and air, with shelter and food and health care and green space. Without bombs or depleted uranium. If we're dreaming, a world without dog shit on the sidewalks or Spam, of both the e-mail and canned kinds. But how are we going to pick up the garbage and fix the roads in this new world you keep telling me is possible?

Ah, who knows? Maybe it's me, maybe I'm getting older and more impatient for change. Maybe I should start smoking again and staying up all night, maybe that would loosen me up. At least I'm still drinking, and I do go out and party sometimes, honest. And I'm really, really glad that you've loosened up a little, too, bringing more cultural activists and hip-hop artists and painters and partiers into your organizing, taking them seriously as equal contributors to the struggle for social justice. There are things that give me hope, that make me proud to be so involved with you. But I look at my boyfriend's daughter, and I fear for the world that she might grow into. We don't have time to be fucking around here. Life is short, and with global warming and this second Bush administration it might be shorter than we think. Did you see that Israel has been beset by a plague of locusts? Maybe all the evangelicals are right, and this is the end of days.

Dear Movement, my hope and my frustration. I'm sorry to ramble. It's late. I always thought we'd spend the rest of our lives together. I still want to get old with you. You've been good to me, and I like to think that I've supported you. I'm still idealistic, I promise. But the next time we get together, can we start to translate our dreaming into something concrete? Words are pretty, but I need a little something real to hang my hat on.

We both know that in some ways this is all just words. You know I won't leave you. Where would I go? All of us who love you, who struggle and celebrate with you, you're all we've got. So I can't force you to change—abandonment is an empty threat. You have to change because it's the right thing to do. Change because you love me, because you love the world. Change because you still believe that someday we will reach the end of this long road to justice. And when we get there, I want to know how we'll take out the trash. Let's have some coffee and figure it out. Just don't offer me a cigarette, I'm trying really hard to quit.

Love,
Kat

FUTURE:
LETTERS TO THE NEXT
GENERATIONS

Recognizing that we will all, ultimately, cease to be young, the authors in this section dialogue with those who will come after us. Those writing here are high school students and farmworkers, teachers and travelers, graduate students and parents. All of the letters, however, capture the passion we have today as we look toward tomorrow. In chapter 10, we engage tomorrow's youth, cautioning against political skepticism or narrow-mindedness. The letters here serve as warnings: about racism in the academy as well as the perils of consumption. Above all, we challenge future generations to take a strong stand against injustice. Recognizing that many people in the future will already be activists, the letters in chapter 11 pass on lessons from the streets of global justice protests to the agricultural fields of Florida to the rural towns housing many of our country's prisons. Just as today's young activists have the history of the 1960s/1970s, the struggles we engage in today will serve as the backdrop for those of future activists. The book ends with a rhetorical conversation with our future selves. The letters in chapter 12 function as a time capsule, written for us to read in a few years or in a few decades. All of the letters in this chapter discuss what politics mean to us now, whether it involves parenting or prison, teaching or family. As we move forward in life, we all make difficult decisions and compromises. We struggle to live our lives in a way that is consistent with our values. Here, we present messages that we want to ensure our future selves remember, as we throw ourselves into the world to come.

10

LETTERS TO THE YOUTH OF TOMORROW

Dear Doubter,

Ever since we formally met, I've remembered your words with perfect clarity. I remember telling you about an event that was being organized to support the Sudanese people in the midst of the internal genocide. Our group was attempting to teach others about the human rights abuses within Sudan's borders. We explained the basics that we understood at the time: the rebel groups had risen up against the government, the Janjaweed Arab militia had struck back by targeting black African communities, resulting in fifty thousand dead and two hundred thousand refugees. We began to talk about our event again, when you politely interrupted, "Fort Wayne's not the type of city for that."

I must admit that I was shocked by your reaction. You suggested that *activism* was a "vague concept" that existed in large cities like New York or Los Angeles—not Fort Wayne, Indiana. Activism certainly wasn't something that people did, and if it was, it was done in those metropolitan places populated with drug-loving hippies. According to you, such an outrageous idea as human rights couldn't possibly survive in a conservative Midwestern town. Fort Wayne's two hundred thousand residents had more important concerns that did not revolve around the plight of others in a foreign nation. You contended that any issue outside of the continental United States was too far removed for Midwesterners to care about. Even if we did, how could it help anything? I've heard your narrow-minded voice throughout my life, but this was the most pronounced instance of your doubt, your lack of faith in the ability of citizens to change themselves and others to make an impact on a community.

Surroundings, of course, affect people—political climates do differ from region to region. But the idea that individuals could only care about others that they personally knew, or had at least seen portrayed in movies and television, was bizarre. I wouldn't wish harm on an innocent stranger any more than I would wish harm on my family and friends. I don't know the persecuted individuals in any of the cases that I work on, but I have always known that I would want the help of strangers should I find myself in danger. Human rights are supposed to be universal; while the world does not yet uphold them universally, it seems to me that everyone should support their fellow humans. I understand that each citizen cannot fly around the world to help others, or regularly dedicate hours of work to a cause, but I had always assumed that nobody would deny the importance of supporting others. But you *did*.

You have often told me that people can't change the world. I have to admit, for a while I believed you. Even when many people support change, it seems as though today's world is so full of devices and technicalities to keep the powerful in power and the status quo, as undesirable as it may be, intact. Paperwork must be exactly right for an ordinary citizen to make a suggestion to the government; one must use the correct form, and give the appropriate amount of money to the correct charitable organization. Many times, it is who supports an idea that gives it merit, rather than the quality of the idea. I wasn't sure exactly *who* set the guidelines, but I knew that I didn't. At first, the thought that I could not impact my community was a depressing one, but I don't believe that I was alone in thinking that my actions toward change would be in vain. Once I had made the decision that I was helpless, I felt absolved of responsibility. In some ways, I liked it; the feeling was comforting. While I don't believe that ignorance is bliss, ignorance does have some blissful qualities—namely, not seeing the pain and suffering in the world.

History pulled me back from apathy. I realized that ignoring pain and suffering only allowed it to persist, and that change was indeed a possibility. New technologies and ideas didn't just "poof!" into existence. Somebody was behind them. Somebody *did* change the world. Some*bodies*, to be exact.

Your opinion presents a striking contradiction to me. It is not that people are apathetic. I've been to rallies and fundraisers for human diseases of all kinds; medical foundation fundraisers are a staple of Fort Wayne. We have great hospitals, and it makes sense to support research. These events—like walk-a-thons, duck races, and bicycle tours—you maintain, unlike others, "belong" in a community such as ours. Without introducing any controversy, they demonstrate what has often been labeled "community strength." But why does support for fellow humans stop there? "It's not their fault," you've said, "if one is diagnosed with some sort of disease; it is not because they have done something wrong or have in some way 'asked for it.'" Yet the cancers of society are not limited to medicine.

Does anyone ever truly ask to be a victim of domestic violence? Have prisoners of conscience longed for the day that they will be imprisoned for expressing their viewpoints? Have I ever consented to having my civil liberties taken away? I challenge you, doubter, to look into the eyes of a mother who has lost her daughter in a wave of government-ordained disappearances and inquire why she has asked for the murder of her child. Perhaps then you will understand why I cannot understand your narrow-minded point of view.

It is easier to wear a ribbon in a fight against a disease that won't speak back. Nobody is going to argue with a cancer fundraiser, and

rightly so. It is much harder for a person to condemn the corrupt practices of another group, individual, or government—especially in the cases
in which one's society may still support the corrupt body for economic
or political reasons. It is harder to see the truth through conflicting
messages, even if one is looking for it. It is also scarier to think that
individuals and institutions cause such horrendous problems. But in
some ways, it's reassuring. Unlike diseases, we know for a fact that
human-made institutions can be undone and redone. We may have to
wait for a cure for breast cancer, but we can *be* the cure for ignorance,
persecution, and hopelessness. We shouldn't limit ourselves to helping
those of a certain skin color, religion, or political association. Help
should be extended to all who need it. As soon as we stop deciding *who*
to help and begin targeting *how* to help, humanity will bloom.

In the midst of everything, you make activism especially frustrating
sometimes. Even though my beliefs are strong, it's easy to lose sight of
a goal when faced with criticism. There's always at least one of you
piping up every time a new idea arises, at every event, or even simply
at the adjoining table in a local restaurant. You seem to doubt
activism as strongly as activists support it. It's more than mere inac-
tion on your part; it's opposition. Maybe it's apathy, but maybe the
opposition stems from racism, sexism, and homophobia. Maybe you do
not care about others because they are not you. The work of activists,
however, lies in believing that if this is the case, we will be able to pull
you from your hateful isolation and show you the importance of caring
for others.

If I thought that all others truly didn't care, the work of activists
around the world would be in vain. Nobody would even attempt to support a cause. I don't believe you can change a nonexistent opinion. You
are very entrenched in your condemnation of activists by demeaning
everything we try to do. In the face of this, we will continue working,
whether our actions are small or large. Activists believe that you, too,
care about the same basic things. We may not change *your* mind, but
we will change minds like yours. New societies and philosophies are not

built overnight; rather, individuals need to have faith that in time, they will make a difference. And come that time, you'll stop, Doubter, and remember *my* words, stated strongly and clearly. You'll know that *every* city, mine included, is ready to care about the world.

Yours faithfully,
Andrea Listenberger

Andrea Listenberger

Dear concerned citizen,

Last summer I participated in a summit to coffee farms in the rural mountainsides of Nicaragua with the United Students for Fair Trade (USFT). USFT is an inter-school network of students that, on both a regional and national scale, works to connect various student groups into a web of fair trade resources and a larger collective potential. We descended upon this small, Central American nation to gain more empirical knowledge about the coffee industry and Fair Trade's effects on small-scale coffee farmers. As an independent, third party monitoring and certification system, Fair Trade certification guarantees that those who cultivate the agricultural products we need for nourishment, such as coffee, are paid a livable wage for these commodities they grow.

In these forested mountainsides I met longtime coffee farmer Don Carmelo. He told us that he has farmed coffee since he was eleven years old and, though today he is fifty-seven, he still struggles as much today as he did in his youth. Carmelo is an older, thin, dark-skinned man with deep-set eyes and inverted sloped cheeks. His smile reveals a number of missing teeth, and the dry coarse palm he offers as a greeting testifies to the strain he has endured maintaining a living as a coffee farmer.

As a composing member of the Global North, who has seen the causality and lack of care with which coffee patrons purchase their espressos or simple drip-brewed coffee drinks; and then having seen the tremendous hardships these farmers must endure to cultivate the beans eventually utilized in coffee beverages—only for the mere pleasure or part of a trivial routine for us in the Global North—I've come to witness firsthand the injustice inherent in our valuing of labor and the hideous nature of our international trade agreements.

I've learned that not only must you and I work to effect progressive change in our local communities, but also we must become cognizant to the burden our consumption routines bear upon those in the so-called "developing" nations of the Global South. Everyday our modes of consumption trap peoples from the Global South into unjust neoliberal free-trade agreements. Onto peoples from lands suffering from long histories of exploitation, we saddle with burden their governments, and therefore, their working poor, with debt. We, as patrons to corporations of concentrated wealth, knowingly or unknowingly contribute to this despotism with our mere participation in this vicious cycle of exploitation.

For benefit of the fruits and vegetables we enjoy throughout the year at reasonably cheap prices, farmers in the Global South must work long hours in treacherous agricultural fields under grueling conditions. We may rouse ourselves to protest for animal rights, environmental health, or even to demonstrate against policy makers that engage our society in war on questionable circumstances for illogical reasons. But how often do we raise dissent against the more relevant authoritarian regimes we daily encounter, the large-scale corporations that dictate these policies onto our elected representatives for benefit of their increased wealth? Everyday, as we purchase produce from large-scale supermarkets, or buy clothing from retail giants, we not only participate in a supply chain that burdens the already too troubled peoples of the world, but we also help to encourage this sick system of capitalist repression.

Dear concerned citizen; we must hold ourselves, those with unearned but inherited wealth, be it societal or individual, to higher ethical standards in our dealings with peoples from distant lands or peoples with dissimilar advantage. As activists in this nation we have a duty to work for justice on an international plane, for our compliance to capitalism solidifies other's suffering.

We, the economically privileged in the Global North with disposable income and free time must be the driving force to implement a redistribution of wealth that adequately rewards the efforts of those who toil for hours through dust and dirt to grow the agricultural products we use to nourish our bodies. We must work to grant those who assemble our clothing in subhuman conditions a return that better reflects the woe they have endured for benefit of one of our most basic human needs. Not only is it our duty as common citizens of the world, but it is also our moral obligation as benefactors of such undervalued labor.

Alternative trade exists. There are means of people-to-people connections, between communities and cultures that do not involve repression, exploitation, and dominance. Through networks formed by activists, people of faith, and producers weary of "first world" cruelty, supply chains act to improve the livelihoods of artisans, crafters, and farmers all too often forced to sacrifice their welfare for the benefit of their various nations' preexisting elite.

Through consumer action, we can quickly make positive changes in the lives of those we are dependent upon for our most essential goods. In our local groceries, convenient stores, and coffee houses, we can demand that these businesses sell only Fair Trade certified goods when possible (e.g., coffee, tea, fruit). There is no rational or moral justification for continued economic repression when well-established and verifiable alternative networks like Fair Trade exists.

In the spring semester of 2004, a handful of us attending the Albuquerque Technical Vocational Institute (TVI) based in Albuquerque,

New Mexico, campaigned to convert our brewed coffee offerings from Starbucks to a locally based roaster and distributor that would serve only Fair Trade certified coffee. We understood the economic inequality sustained in our school's simple choice of a coffee distributor, so we worked to replace this injustice with Fair Trade. We formed around principles of Marxism and created in our activism the Student Socialist Coalition. With this we were able to attract excited new energy, link with USFT and we effectively convinced our school's food service provider to switch from selling Starbucks to Albuquerque-roasted Fair Trade certified coffee through Red Rock Roasters.

Ultimately, although there are many ways we can engage ourselves to work for progressive change, in order for us to affect the international quality of our larger, broader, more advanced movement, we need to realize the nature of our relationship with the rest of the world as consumers. An important mode in realizing such goals is through consumer action, since much of the exploitation plaguing the rest of the world is built on the dominative relationships between the Global North and the Global South established through commodity networks. It is therefore our responsibility as not only activists but also as consumers to see a just revolution made in the very character of our consumer bond with the producers of the commodities we consume.

When asked about Fair Trade, Don Carmello said: "To me, Fair Trade is something where people come together and they determine what are the [coffee] prices. It's adjusting the price that represents honor, and a general consciousness about where things are coming from. I think there has to be a conciseness, there has to be an understanding on how [coffee] is produced. Why do we call it shade grown? Why do we call it organic? When we talk about quality, we also have to be talking about the quality of our lives. This coffee, this coffee is our life and we depend on the work to sustain ourselves, and this has been our culture."

As residents of the Global North, but citizens of a larger, world community, we must challenge economic imperialism and work to organize ourselves as consumers to end this fundamental root cause of conflict throughout the world. It is high time that we exercise dissent in the nature of our economic being as well as expressing our political discontent.

Andrew Curley

Dear Mañana,

I write to you as a man indoctrinated like a child is to religion. On picket lines and in demonstrations uttering first words I received my foundation of beliefs: freedom the Father, equality the Son, peace the Holy Ghost—and injustice, well it was as vile as the devil. These convictions extend from my center yet I struggle to gain an understanding of issues far more complex then they were presented. Over years, grappling with their complexity has proved to be difficult work, at times overwhelming, frustrating, and confusing. These issues raise questions that are essential to reflect upon if we are truly committed to progress. In a time addicted to rapid change, it is vital to revisit these questions—our approach can become dated in a moment. With that in mind, here are a few that I ponder as I confront my day. I hope you find them useful as well.

WHY DO YOU BELIEVE WHAT YOU DO?
HAVE YOU MADE A CONSCIOUS DECISION TO BELIEVE THIS?

> *To repeat what others have said requires education,*
> *to challenge it requires brains.*
> —Mary Poole

Growing up I was given political arguments and anecdotes that I recited on the battleground of debate to anyone who would listen. I found myself more concerned with winning the debates than figuring out what was the best solution to the challenge we faced. As I have grown, I have attempted to take ownership of my beliefs by gaining an understanding, trying to explore them beyond the rhetoric. I have come to find both strengths and holes in my inherited beliefs. Lacking this understanding I was vulnerable to the easy routes of simplistic extremism and unrelenting criticism without realistic solutions. Do you know what underpins your beliefs—the history, the ideology on which they rest? Have you thought about what influenced you to follow them? Is there a difference between what you were taught and what you believe? Do you understand it? I have found that it is only with this understanding that insecure arrogance turns to open-minded confidence and we become receptive to dialogue. Instead of a road paved by events and reactions, this understanding allows us to walk a conscious and determined path. In other words, if we act with vision we are stronger than those who merely react.

WHY DO PEOPLE WHO THINK DIFFERENTLY THAN YOU BELIEVE WHAT THEY DO?

> *The truth is rarely pure and never simple.*
>   —Oscar Wilde

Finding the bit of truth in the ideas of our perceived opposition sometimes seems like searching for a flower in the desert—but usually it is not that hard. We must not forget that it is impossible to hold the truth in its entirety; there can be simultaneous truths. It is not my intention to enter an exploration of the meaning of truth, it is simply to say that *most* arguments have strengths and holes and *most* contain an idea worth considering. Often, entire arguments are dismissed as people are resistant to acknowledge that their "opponents" arguments have any merit. Seeking the partial truth in opposing views and incorporating it into your analysis and actions not only moves you closer to the truth but empowers you to bring people together. If you as an individual and we as a group fail to address the elements of truth in contradicting opinions, we will not achieve the objective at hand. Are you genuinely open to dialogue or is your mind already made up? If your mind is firmly decided, how do you expect someone else to be open to your thoughts?

HOW DO YOU THINK ABOUT TIME?

> *Patience has its limits, take it too far and it's cowardice.*
>
> —George Jackson

> *Life can only be understood backwards; but must be lived forwards.*
>
> —Søren Kierkegaard

There is no definitive answer to the question of time. Essentially all we can do is attempt to gain a perspective that seems to be found in the tension between the short- and long-term. There is no reason to believe that with time our society will inevitably progress. Rather, we must guide and push it forward. And as Martin Luther King Jr. said, "The time is always ripe to do right." But the present must be conceived along the long road from which it came, and acted upon with an outlook to what lies ahead. Although at times unthinkable in the face of injustice, patience, to a point, may best serve a cause. More often than not, movements that attempt to produce rapid change either fall short of their goals or descend into times worse than those they fought against. To consider time forces us to contemplate a larger perspective, giving us a better understanding of our challenges and time's relationship to progress. An assessment of time is essential to both construct a vision and to act effectively.

DOES YOUR LIFE REFLECT YOUR BELIEFS?

> *Be great in act, as you have been in thought.*
> —William Shakespeare

I have found living my life in a way that is consistent with my values to be the most challenging aspect of activism. Our everyday life. Time. Money. Energy. Classes. Groups we participate in. What we read. Clothes we wear. The food we eat.

All will not be perfect, and we are often forced to make trade-offs, but we must be aware of and consider every aspect of our life.

> *Whatever you do will be insignificant, but it is very important that you do it.*
> —Gandhi

Give your life to life, and the way will find you.

Soon.
Love.
Samuel Kass

Dear Young Africanist,

When we decide to approach our intellectual, our vocational, and our spiritual development from the perspective of an African or African descendant, we are confronted with a world we did not create. As we understand ourselves as African people, we see and feel structures and institutions we had no part in making, do not represent who we are, or how we would organize this world. World structures, imperialism, colonialism, globalization, and international "loan" agencies, all seem to share a similar logic, the dismissal and eradication of African life and thought.

Engaging this willful dismissal of African life, we face one of the most powerful and destructive ideas of our time, white supremacy. As Africanists, one of the ways to challenge the very foundations of white supremacy is realizing it is, at its core, a thought. If we accept that chauvinism is socially constructed, i.e., it is not natural, divine, or born outside of us, but how individuals with power conceive(d) of organizing the world, then white (male) supremacy is a human creation which first starts in the mind. As James Baldwin said, "ideas can only lead to action." The color of our bodies, therefore, does not necessitate participation or exclusion from partaking in white supremacist actions. If anything, the "minorities" within the current presidential cabinet highlight this core. Understanding white supremacy as a method of thinking about other people—essentially believing one is somehow closer to God than the next human being—engaging the world of ideas is an invaluable method of destroying the center.

The intentions here, then, are to offer markers and guideposts as to how white supremacy may emerge in your work as an Africanist, and influence the conceptual structures by which you deal with Africa and African people. I do not mean to dissuade your work for Africa; but rather, with certain guideposts marked and pitfalls uncovered, you will not only continue in your education to find new, fresh ways of undermining the erasure of African people and thought, but also see attacking white supremacy in the realm of knowledge production is a form of homage to our African ancestors. The unearthing and the fronting of the suppressed knowledge of Africa and African people have the capability to make the present world the place we envision.

From whatever angle you enter the life of Africa, as a political scientist, a creative writer, an historian, or a painter, there are certain material realities one faces in Africa's existence. At one point in history,

Greeks learned about the cosmos from Egyptian universities. By 1400, peoples of Zambia and Zimbabwe had gained techniques of farming, agriculture, mining, trading, and developed a complex socio-political system to mirror such developments. East Africans, broadly speaking, traveled and traded fine porcelains, spices, and cloth from today's Middle East, China, Indonesia, and India. However, the advent of the slave trade (which African nobility were complicit with but under a different cultural understanding of what "slavery" entailed), encapsulating movement toward colonialism and eventually to globalization, marked a fulcrum point of willful underdevelopment for Africa and the dehumanization of Africans. Today, Africa is getting poorer, with average income per head being lower than it was thirty years ago. The HIV/AIDS epidemic is killing Africans at a rate of four out of ten infections in some countries. Now more than ever, is the time for Africanists to make knowledge production, the development of new ideas, serve Africa's interests.

As American Africanists, the loneliness of this endeavor usually pushes us toward one of two options, and sometimes both: entering academia and/or working for nongovernmental organizations (NGOs). These two options, as the primary ways to be present in the life of Africa, are themselves representations of an oppressed people. Whereas those who feel comfortable within the structures of this world find a plethora of options in which to realize themselves, academia and NGOs are the two popular and predominant options we are presented with as Africanists in America. These two narrowly defined options, however, can carry serious limitations and contradictions.

Within academia, there are several points at which you may question the virtue of being an Africanist. First, the knowledge base of African thought and people, who are not translated into English, is not incorporated into texts or entire bodies of knowledge. Therefore, what we read is fundamentally biased against knowledge produced on the African continent. Second, academic language can become a tool of marginalization, especially for the young scholar from a low-income or first generation college, or first generation graduate-school background. You may suddenly develop a symphonist's ear for the number of syllables in a word; and then reason it could easily have been replaced with a simpler choice. Fundamentally, the particular vocabulary of a discipline, its jargon, emerges out of conversations between individuals to serve the purpose of the discipline. It is there for a reason. It will take time and may be unclear to decipher, but not only is academic language understandable, the knowledge of your experience, either as an individual or part of a group, can contribute something unique and perhaps revolutionary to the heated battle of ideas which influence our lives.

This may be a moment in which the Africanist is called upon to be an activist or an agent of change. Many universities lack courses on Africa. By organizing, petitioning, thinking and "reading" your university system, students have the power to determine the inclusion of more Africanist content. As shown by the Black Studies Movement of the 1970s, you have the power to determine university curriculum. The reliance on the bottom line, on which many universities must now depend, could be used in your favor. The university is many things, good and/or bad, but, fundamentally, it would not exist without students. In a sense, and part of the physical isolation of being an Africanist, your body, by its mere placement in the academy, has the capability to disrupt the norm, the quietude of the idea of white supremacy.

The lack of classes in the curriculum is also representative of a much bigger problem. There is a massive lacuna within white supremacist knowledge production about Africa. You may have entered African Studies in search of African knowledge, but you will primarily cite and reference white European or American thinkers on Africa. Much like NGOs use Western development paradigms, Europe will be the conceptual lens through which you view Africa. An example of this is V.Y. Mudimbe's *The Invention of Africa*. The text is a staple of African Studies reading, and rightly so, but it is heavily dependent on Michel

Foucault, a French philosopher. Whereas present European thinkers reference their European ancestors for intellectual grounding, African thinkers, in order to be taken seriously, must also reference European thinkers. The project becomes fundamentally flawed. This is one of the sites of knowledge creation by which African people face erasure. Through this reliance on European thinkers, you may question the importance or the authenticity of your work and search for Black thinkers and Black theorists. But after all, if you are in academia, Black theorists exist; but yes, you will have to be determined and creative in making the thought of Black peoples part of human history.

When you in turn start to write yourself into critical discussions in the world of ideas, the process may seem an overwhelming and disheartening challenge. This is for two reasons. Written texts seem like definitive, closed endings, when in fact they are open conversations. The process of writing can force you to question the value of your thought. You may ask yourself, Why am I here? What is the purpose of my reading and writing? I'm sitting in a coffee shop reading, how am I affecting the lives of Africans for the better? If you find yourself doubting the value of the written word, the writing process, and perhaps even education as a form of activism, we need only turn to Frederick Douglass's autobiography: "'Now,' said [Mr. Auld], 'if you teach that nigger . . . how to read, there would be no keeping him.' These words sank deep into my heart, stirred up sentiments within that lay slumbering, and called into existence an entirely new train of thought. . . . From that moment, I understood the pathway from slavery to freedom."

As Douglass demonstrates, the powerful have always known the power of the written word: In 1835, the slave revolt in Bahia, Brazil, was inspired by Islam and its emphasis on reading the Qu'ran. So worried were colonial authorities by learned slaves that those who were literate were sent back to West Africa. Only illiterate slaves remained, who were thought less likely to engage in struggle. As African descendants, the development of our intellect through reading and writing is an engagement with the aspect of white supremacy which seeks our avoidance in the world of knowledge creation. It goes straight to the mind of white supremacy.

With such a formidable task at hand, becoming an Africanist is marked by a mental and a physical isolation close to none other. Family, friends, and even strangers will not understand your involvement with Africa. Personal or social interactions may turn sour in an instant when you defend Africa against a tirade of lies and misinformation, which, strangely enough, also seem to resemble the same ideas said about the poor Black folks around the corner. More than likely, you will be outnumbered and become frustrated with your seeming inability to convince others of the validity of your knowledge, desire to represent Africa truthfully, and willingness to challenge mainstream white supremacist perceptions and distortions.

On another level, from your family, friends, and strangers, you will experience a double-standard to studying Africa. You will have to explain that Africa is a continent and not a country; that countries have hundreds of languages each; that Africans do not live in huts and chase lions; and yes, Egypt is part of Africa, too. When individuals ask such questions, and test our knowledge of Africa, we are placed under a burden of knowing the history of the entire continent as if it is a single country. Africa has not been detailed: in the Western imagination, simple people have simple lives. Our duty as Africanists is to detail African existence, to show the complexity of African life and thought. If you are a Southern Africanist, do not be afraid to admit ignorance of North African history, politics, and art. Although the distance between Mauritania and Djibouti is approximately that between New York and Portugal, would a historian of New York be expected to know the roots of Portugal's popular culture? In this sense, it is actually respectful to admit ignorance. As a mentor has said to me, "If you don't know, be quiet." Better that we are humble enough to admit our own ignorance than to promote wrong, banal, information about Africa.

When you decide to engage the world on behalf of Africa, many times you may question the authenticity of your endeavors and the worth of your work. Engagement with white supremacist knowledge is fraught with deep self-doubts and self-contradictions. The reason for this: You are not meant to exist in the realm of knowledge production; you are meant to let your thoughts perish with your body. Even if we find ourselves fumbling with doubt through processes of trial and error, we must always seek a sense of hope in the context of our time. Always, always, always remember the ancestors. The idea of ancestry is real and alive. As living African ancestors, it is our responsibility to envision, to imagine, and to dream into existence a world of equal humanity—on this earth.

Uhuru.
Cheers,
Kevin

11

LETTERS TO THE ACTIVISTS OF TOMORROW

11/30/04

Dearest young organizer of the future,

I am writing to you from the political ashes of 2004 on the anniversary of the mass direct action that shut down the World Trade Organization in Seattle. Five years ago, movements in the United States marched in step with global movements for justice, and I was drunk with hope and choking on tear gas.

I am one of the millions of so-called "echo-boomers," born from the boomers of the sixties. The marketer types say we are "boy scouts," prone to follow the leader and not "rock the boat." But I have seen us rocking this boat with all of our might—with stories and hip-hop poetry and organized resistance. I have already felt this boat quaking under my feet.

I imagine you have probably heard the stories about the big summits of the so-called global justice movement in the United States. It might seem from afar that we looked so confidant—setting up high-tech websites and flooding the cities where the architects of empire chose to host their gala charades . . . from the WTO in Seattle to the

Summit of the Americas in Quebec City to the Republican National Convention in New York.

Now we are fighting to end the occupation of Iraq, and we are working to define our place in history. We are working to build globalized, cross-cultural, queer-positive, equitable networks and movements. We are working to challenge oppression and domination in all of its forms. We are working locally in our neighborhoods, schools, and union shops, and we are mobilizing to flood the streets in big cities when the so-called rulers must be reminded that they are few, and we are many.

Today, U.S. forces are assaulting Fallujah and other "hotspots" where the so-called insurgents—the resistance fighters of Iraq—are fighting back. Thousands of immigrants and people of Arab, Muslim, and South Asian decent are incarcerated in detention centers, and the escalation of overt racism in the "post-9/11" United States is at a feverish pitch. Unprecedented hurricanes ravaged the South last summer, and there is more and more acceptance that the climate crisis has begun, even by analysts at the Pentagon.

After the election, the White House is crowing with emboldened declarations of a "mandate," and "spending political capital": sound bites that chill us to the bone with the foreshadowing of an unbridled Bush administration, spewing homophobic hate, racist repression, and an unending war of greed and violence at home and abroad.

We are facing the day-to-day ground war of brutality, occupation, debt, and ecological destruction. But the ground war is impossible without the increasingly sophisticated air war: the war of images, ideas, messages, and culture . . . the contests of meaning, and the battles for stories.

The seas of our times are raging with racism, injustice, and war. Now is indeed an important time to be an agent of change—organizing people power and telling our stories for deep, holistic, transformative democracy. In these turbulent days, courage is my Polaris, keeping me on course, and shining with hope.

Five years ago, I was a student activist with a lot of big dreams and ideas, and I was in Seattle with my affinity group to "shut down the World

Trade Organization." The solidarity, joy, and momentum were palpable as we paraded toward the Sheraton Hotel with music blasting and puppets dancing and cheering echoing in the early morning gray air.

We got word in the streets that the WTO had canceled their meeting, announced in a repeat-after-me ripple effect: "We have shut down the Millennial Round of the WTO."

Later that day, and on through the convergence, riot cops—the likes of which a rural girl like me had never seen—beat and arrested demonstrators young and old. We were gassed by the National Guard and chased out of the city center by a hail of rubber bullets and swinging nightsticks, our cameras rolling and hearts pounding.

This was just the beginning of a chapter of our story, unfolding in the streets of Washington, Melbourne, Prague, Quebec, and Genoa . . . echoing the cries for justice in Quito, San Salvador, Manila, and Seoul.

Over those next few years, I was busy, and learning a lot about orchestrating mass nonviolent direct action. I stepped forward as an organizer, agitator, and mobilizer—quickly diving into the pool of a life's worth of work for social change in between the mass mobilizations . . . galvanizing farmers, inciting students, training activists, telling stories.

Debates emerged about nonviolence and embracing a "diversity of tactics." But these mobilizations became in themselves just a tactic—episodic and isolated from a larger strategic framework. I found that in some cases there was an unstated assumption that a radical political analysis called for a universal application of militant street tactics. There were vocal tendencies valuing militancy over strategy; form over content; demonstrations over organizations.

The question on everyone's lips was the issue of "summit hopping." Who is (and who is not) at the leadership of the planning of these convergences? What are the costs to the local community, and what are the lasting achievements? How are these demonstrations adding power to locally based struggles and relating with mass-based organizations fighting for economic and racial justice? How is all of this mobilization building a movement for deep and transformative social change?

These elaborate convergences, although exhilarating, are resource intensive affairs that are exhausting for the host organizing team—who is often left holding the bag when the post-summit fallout comes in the form of legal battles, debt, wounded coalitions, and state repression on community organizers and local communities. Nonetheless, these mobilizations forged new alliances; gave activists training and experience; and confronted power-holders, raising the political costs for the elite to continue with their "free-trade" agendas and giving visibility to a resistance movement inside the United States.

After those planes hit those buildings in 2001, the political landscape was shifting faster than I could calculate at the time. The mobilizations at the fall meetings of the World Bank were canceled. Some of us wanted to mobilize for a pre-emptive peace march—and some of us did—but there was no consensus. Even among a few of my comrades in the global justice movement, some felt that "retaliation" by the United States was justified. That this war we were on the verge of was a "just war."

It took the ongoing escalation of the war at home, and the amplified drum beats for war on Iraq, to kick the peace movement back into drive. By February 15, 2003, millions were marching in the streets of New York, Chicago, Montreal, and all over the world. The *New York Times* referred to this peace movement as "the other superpower."

When "shock and awe"—and bombs and rockets—hit Baghdad on March 19, thousands of people flooded the streets of San Francisco to "uproot the system behind war." Direct Action to Stop the War (DASW) was an exciting and successful experiment that inspired the antiwar movement across the United States with a story about shutting down the war profiteers and mass non-cooperation with the Iraq invasion. Through sophisticated and savvy organizing, DASW forged deep alliances with community-based organizations; effectively broadcast their message through the mainstream media; and harnessed the "mass psychic break"—that moment when people realize that the system is out of alignment with their values—into acts of empowering civil disobedience by over twenty thousand people.

But the war went on, and the peace movement did, too, sometimes boisterously in the streets of Washington, New York, or San Francisco—but mostly quietly and locally, with gatherings, petitions, local resolutions, and vigils. By 2004 there were still no weapons of mass destruction found in Iraq, and the ruthless occupation was growing increasingly unpopular in the wake of the U.S. torture scandal at Abu Ghraib.

The antiwar movement's focus was squarely on New York for the Republican National Convention (RNC) at the end of August, and a rainbow of issues and voices emerged in a resounding "No to the Bush Agenda" five hundred thousand strong. "Still We Rise" brought the voices of racial and economic justice to the doorstep of Madison Square Garden. Civil disobedience erupted at Ground Zero, Halliburton, and the INS. The father of a solider disrupted the convention from the inside, pleading, "Bush lied, my son died!" All told, it was the largest demonstration at a political convention, ever.

Last autumn came with a continued climb of anti-Bush sentiment. The milestone of 1,000-plus U.S. troops dead in Iraq had come and gone, and Michael Moore's expose *Fahrenheit 9/11* was a box office smash. All kinds of radicals were working in the swing states and in their local communities to build progressive, youth voter blocs and turn people out to the polls. Like many others, I voted for the first time on November 2—and hit the streets on November 3.

Now the Left seems to have fallen into a stupor. For so many people activated by this election, hope is drowning in a sea of shock, rage, and fear. In this moment, the inadequacies of an electoral strategy are clear, and the injustices of the system are magnified.

We are soberly facing the urgent task of recognizing our own weaknesses, as well as those of our opponents. It is a time for forging new strategies that can advance on the vulnerabilities of an overextended empire, and build stronger, deeper movements wielding courage, hope, solidarity, and story. It is a time to expose the chimeras of the imperialist project, and challenge the assumptions that make their stories stand as truth.

The power-holders' stories are the bloody mythologies of "Manifest Destiny," of the "American Dream," and now of "The War on Terror." Their grip on public discourse is so tight, it is strangling the collective imagination to envision something different. Their framing is closing in on our ability to tell another story of the future. It is chipping away at the aptitude for hope.

So now we too must fight the ground war and the air war—integrating strategy and story with base building work—infusing our movements with a fresh dose of hope, creativity, and imagination. Organizing is a timeless craft that requires fortitude, humility, patience, and vision; our work of organizing is also the work of storytelling. It is shattering the assumptions that bind the status quo, making the new society visible, immediate, and irresistible.

Our work, as change agents, is not only in the streets—it is in the task of institution building, and it is in the arena of ideas and discourse. It is to tell the stories of democracy, self-determination, and a living planet. It is the project of building resilient organizations and strong networks of solidarity, and it is a battle for ideas. It is a battle for stories. It is a battle for the future—a battle for you.

Five years on from that fateful day in the streets of Seattle, when the whole world turned to see that young activists in the United States had the boat pitching and heaving, I offer you these stories—a window into these stunning and stormy times.

As this terrible war continues, we will heave and ho together to turn the ship around. As the empire lurches forward into the twenty-first century—redesigning geopolitics with the brutal instruments of greed and domination—we will be rocking and rowing for a revolution. Welcome aboard.

In hope and solidarity,
Doyle Canning

Doyle Canning

En route to Caracas

To The Young Activists of Tomorrow,

My name is Gerardo Reyes Chavez, and I am a member of the Coalition of Immokalee Workers (CIW), a farmworker organization based in Florida. On behalf of all the workers in Immokalee, I send this message to young people everywhere who are organizing tirelessly for the construction of a more just and compassionate world. This letter is also for those who, until now, have not been exposed to the raging current of past and present struggles. This letter is for those who are not aware of the countless others who gave everything they had—including their lives—to preserve a simple hope, a hope that we are determined to keep alive today through our actions. It is in this spirit that I share some of our story.

The Coalition of Immokalee Workers is a community organization comprised of workers mainly from Mexico, Guatemala, and Haiti who are now laboring in the agricultural fields of Florida. Many of the workers are young men—ranging in age from fifteen to twenty-five—who have left their families behind, hoping to someday be able to return home. I was twenty-two when I came to the United States from Mexico, and it didn't take long to find my way to Immokalee, a place well known for requiring a large supply of workers.

The vicious poverty in our countries often leaves us with no option but to abandon our formal education and seek out a better future for ourselves and for our families. In the aftermath of NAFTA, for example, Mexico was transformed from one of the largest exporters of corn in the hemisphere into one of the largest exporters of cheap labor. Thousands upon thousands of small farmers, unable to compete with cheap grain dumped on our markets by U.S. corporations, were forced off their land and thrown into a desperate search for income.

That desperate search for work brings many of us to the United States. We arrive in this country believing that if people work hard here, they can eventually become whatever they want to be. We arrive in this country believing in a lie. Many of us end up working in the fields. We pick the plump tomatoes that are sold in U.S. supermarkets and fast food restaurants. They may end up in your hamburgers at McDonald's or your chalupas at Taco Bell. Yet those of us who bring these vegetables to this country's tables are invisible to most people.

Our dreams of the United States are quickly shattered when we find ourselves working ten to fourteen hours a day, earning barely enough to feed ourselves and pay rent. Our day begins before sunrise and ends after sundown. In order to survive, we are often forced to live with strangers in overcrowded, run-down trailers without air-conditioning in the summer or heating in the winter. Sometimes our bosses refuse to pay us. Even after working with the same company for years, we still lie down each night not knowing if we'll be able to find work the next day. We work in isolated settings without basic protections that many take for granted, such as overtime pay, health benefits, or the right to organize a union. In order to make $50 in a day, a worker must quickly pick and haul two tons of tomatoes. Pesticides stain our hands; sweat stains our clothes. We go to bed, exhausted, only to repeat it all the next day. At the end of a year, we're lucky if we make $10,000.

Today, we are fighting for dignity as human beings and we are fighting to end more than twenty-five years of sub-poverty wages. In the most extreme situations, we are confronting the hideous reality of slavery in the twenty-first century: workers forced to labor against their will under death threats and, all too often, the actual use of violence. In the past five years, the CIW has helped liberate over one thousand captive workers. For years, we focused our efforts on opening dialogue with the growers, but these efforts were met with silence. So we asked ourselves, "Who profits from our sweat and blood?" We began to realize that large corporations—the multinational companies that demand cheap produce from the growers—are the ones benefiting the most from our misery.

Taco Bell and its parent company, Yum! Brands (which also owns Pizza Hut, KFC, Long John Silvers, and A&W Restaurants, making it the

largest restaurant corporation in the world), are one of the major pur-
chasers of tomatoes from all over the East Coast, including Florida.
The extreme situations in which we live are directly connected to Taco
Bell's profits. They benefit from our poverty when they use their enormous market power to demand cheap tomatoes without also
demanding fair treatment for farmworkers. In April 2001, after several
failed attempts at dialogue with Taco Bell about farm labor conditions
in their supply chain, we declared a national boycott against the fast
food giant.

After four years of intense grassroots organizing, we finally won in
March 2005, when Taco Bell agreed to meet all of our demands for
improving wages and working conditions for Florida tomato pickers.
This historic victory—where farmworkers and their allies prevailed over
a powerful multinational corporation—would have been difficult to
imagine just four years ago. As Tom Morello, former guitarist for Rage
Against the Machine, explained in a public statement, "The Immokalee
farmworkers struck a blow for dignity and human rights in the workplace and received the long overdue raise they have been fighting for.
This is a major victory for the workers and demonstrates that by
standing up and standing together, we can overturn any injustice. By
standing up and standing together, we can change the world."

Through our organizing, one of the most important lessons we've
learned is the necessity of building strong alliances. For many years,
we, the workers of Immokalee, were invisible to this country—lost in
the darkness that agribusiness has helped to create. Now we know that
we are not alone and will never be alone again. Today, thousands of
students and young people from all over the country know of our
struggle, and they have come to understand that this is their struggle
as well. As the multinational fast food corporation oppresses farmworkers with the tyranny of extreme poverty, they oppress the youth of
this country with their marketing based on the assumption that youth
are hedonistic and apathetic. But we know differently. Young people
across the country are taking the initiative to fight shoulder to

shoulder with us for a world in which all of us may be heard—a world in which if one of us shouts for justice, there will always be thousands of voices echoing that shout. We say there is a seed called "consciousness" that is rooted and grows within the human soul. We struggle so that this seed might germinate and reproduce. Every time someone protests against injustice after learning of the situation in which we live, we know that more seeds are being sown.

In the case of farmworkers, leaving school to start working in the fields did not mean an end to our education. On the contrary, when you take survival courses that are given by the University of Life, you learn that the outcome of every education should serve others. Nobody can consider their education complete—regardless of what theories and philosophies they have learned—if they forget about everyone else. We, the members of the CIW, are proud to know there are students who are committed to using their consciousness to confront the injustices of the world. We know this requires commitment and sacrifice in a world where being "normal" means dressing in sweatshop clothing, accepting advertising without question, and remaining silent and complicit in a society that is drowning in commercialism.

The future is the result of what we do today. The future comes after every breath we breathe and every minute we live; it comes after every action we take in pursuit of our dreams. For us in Immokalee, each day is a day of struggle, but it is also a day of celebration because new minds are seeing the horizon with an awakened awareness. It is our hope that today's farmworker movement will serve as one of many points on the horizon that inspires young people to believe in the possibility of a better world—a world where the struggles of workers are tied to the struggles for dignity for every human being, a world where seeds of justice germinate freely, a world where we all have space to realize our dreams.

In the years since we began our boycott of Taco Bell, we have learned many valuable lessons, lessons that are available to the young activists of tomorrow. They do not represent the only way of achieving social change; they are one path out of many possible paths. Quite literally, this is one chapter in a book. It's up to tomorrow's activists to study and write the next chapters.

For the consciousness of all,

Gerardo Reyes Chávez

Member of the Coalition of Immokalee Workers

Hamlin, Texas

December 19, 2004

To all activists now and in the future,

I woke up this morning in my grandmother's house in the middle of the farmlands of rural west Texas. I drove alone through miles of cotton fields and watched the men on John Deere tractors harvesting this year's crop. They carve intricate patterns in the red earth as they strip the white puffs of cotton. Miles of these fields surround the prison where my father is being held. He can see little else beyond the fences and concertina wire, so the planting and harvesting of the fields provide some of the only non-prison activity in view.

I spent every summer of my childhood playing in this red dirt. My mother grew up in this part of Texas, and now a prison stands in the middle of these fields that fed and supported a whole community of country farming families. People who went to high school with my mother now stand sentry over my father and the other incarcerated men who live each day in one of the seventy-five Texas state prisons. Many of these prisons are in rural areas, and all of them are known to their inhabitants as "farms." Most of the folks who went to school with my mother thought they would grow up to work the land the way their parents had before them. Instead big businesses bought out most of the farmland in the state and brought in machines to replace the majority of the farmers who once made a living off the land. Unemployment soared, and many people left to find jobs in the state's urban centers. Those who stayed soon could find jobs nowhere but in the many prisons being built throughout the rural areas of Texas. The prison industry is now the primary employer in many of these former farming communities, and local high schools have cut back on their agriculture curriculum in favor of courses and after school programs to train young people to become prison guards.

As a child, I never could have predicted that this drastic economic and cultural shift would occur in my mother's homeland or the fact that it would have such a profound impact on my family. I was nine when we began our battles with the courts and fifteen when my father first entered the prison system. Today I watch the children in the prison visiting room and wonder what their lives will be like twenty years from now. How many of these children will eventually lose all contact with their incarcerated parents? How many of these children will grow up to be prison guards? How many will pretend they never had a loved one in prison? How many will be activists? How many of these children will one day be incarcerated themselves?

When I tell someone that my father is in prison, usually they want to know why. People want to know what he did to get locked up and judge for themselves what kind of a person that makes him, and perhaps what kind of a person that makes me. I do not speak publicly of the charge against my father. Some people assume that my silence implies shame, but I have never been ashamed. I do not speak of the crime of which he was convicted because it does not define who my father is.

According to the Prison Activist Resource Center, the United States now has the highest per capita incarceration rate *in the history of the world*, imprisoning over two million people, which constitutes one out of every four of the world's prisoners. A government that locks up this many of its own people must suffer from deep, systemic flaws in its concepts of justice. The government, the media, and indeed the people of this nation are obsessed with crime. Speaking of crime and who deserves punishment frequently precludes any realistic discussion about the material conditions of prisoners' lives and the injustices occurring inside our prisons, or the logic of using incarceration as the sole solution to any and all kinds of crime. It overshadows everything human, familial, and familiar about prisoners. As a society, we have forgotten the fact that prisoners are still members of our communities, our neighborhoods, our nation. We have forgotten that the vast majority of prisoners will return to free society one day, and most of them will have few job skills, very little education, no family waiting for them, and no place to live. After years of being told when to sleep and when to wake, years of having no choice about what to wear or what to eat, many newly released prisoners experience great difficulty making even the most basic decisions. Most of these people will be angry about the way they have been treated, and rightly so. No person deserves to live in such conditions, regardless of their crime. We must revolutionize our system of punishment in this country, but in order to do that effectively, we must simultaneously revolutionize the ways in which we think about crime and punishment, prisons and prisoners, victims and perpetrators.

I need your help to change the system, as all the children of prisoners do. Just as it took so much and so many to bring about the grave malfunctioning of our criminal justice system, it will take a great many people, numerous years, and ongoing struggles to improve the quality of life for prisoners and their families as well as crime victims and their families and society at large in meaningful and lasting ways. According to U.S. Bureau of Justice statistics, prisoners with convictions for nonviolent offenses comprise more than half of the prison population nationwide. Prisons cultivate violence, and the vast majority of prisoners will one day return to free society. We must consider how our

systems of punishment define who we are as a society and seek practical and effective alternatives to prisons, such as restorative justice,
drug rehabilitation centers, and community service combined with
educational programs. Our goals should be to make society safe and to
ensure our civil and human rights, not to warehouse and degrade those
among us who we have deemed "criminal." We must also strive to sever
our economic ties to imprisonment and the labor of prisoners. Since
capitalism relies on a constant supply of flexible and cheap labor, we
face the distinct challenge of eliminating the economic exploitation of
the incarcerated while safeguarding against the possibility of shifting
this burden onto another oppressed population.

In order to succeed, we must form a cohesive network of activists.
We should focus on really listening to one another, never believing ourselves infallible or the authoritative voices in any struggle. We should
form coalitions with unlikely and genuine allies. Above all else, we
should never assume we know what is best for others. We must continually engage the people who we seek to represent and let the members
of the community tell us how we can best help them to help themselves. A prison reform movement should emanate from within prison
walls and operate in tandem with parolees and prisoners' families
organizing on the outside. This does not mean that those of us not
directly implicated in any particular struggle should ignore it or not
take part. We should all be willing to engage in a struggle when we
witness overwhelming oppression, but we must also never lose sight of
the interests, living conditions, and civil rights of the people most
affected by the struggle and most vulnerable to the oppression in
question.

If you are reading this letter long after I wrote it, you must know
that there is work yet to be done, but what is the call to action you face
as you read this? You must know so much that I long to know. Did the
state of Pennsylvania execute Mumia Abu-Jamal in spite of the strong
evidence of his innocence? Did the prisoners at Guantánamo Bay, held
for years without charges, ever get to see their day in court or to return

home to their families? Did U.S. Attorney General Alberto Gonzales effectively use his position to increase the practice of torture in our military and civilian prisons? Which of these events had a profound impact on our lives? Did we learn from any of our mistakes? You future readers must know the answers to my questions, and I hope that this knowledge empowers you and inspires you to continue the work that we and our activist predecessors have started. Look to the future, as we do now, and fight against the injustices of the present with the knowledge that future generations will learn from your successes and failures, as you learn from ours. Remember my father and the millions of incarcerated people like him. Remember all the families of prisoners who struggle on the other side of prison walls. We continue to fight for human rights for every person touched by the criminal justice system. We do this for your generation as much as we do it for ourselves. Join your works with ours, and do not rest until the last prisoner walks free.

Yours in solidarity,
Ashley Lucas

Ashley Lucas

To the descendants of the struggle,

> *Remember these stories and do not let these experiences be written in water.*

I grew up in the 1990s in the midst of de facto segregation while living and attending public school in a small town in Arkansas. Railroad tracks literally divided the Whites and Blacks and served as clear symbols not only of separation, but also of oppression. I watched Black people defer their dreams day after day; some buried themselves in liquor, some in self-doubt, but all slowly died as they stared at those tracks. My mother was one of those people who thought that her life had only one option: work hard in the cotton fields in the summer and at whatever work she could find in the winter. Once I asked my mother if she was happy. She said, "Life in the South is not always about happiness; people often have to accept what life has given them."

My story is not unique; there are many people who have struggles in this society. I have met many people who have shared their stories with me; passing on their knowledge and experience through the oral tradition, so common among many people in Africa. Storytelling often provides understanding in such a way that you are changed forever. I will now share some of these so that you can learn from them.

Imagine telling a twelve-year-old Black boy that he has a 28.5 percent chance of spending time in a federal prison. This is compared to 2.5 percent for a White man, 3.6 percent for a Black woman, and 0.5 percent for a White woman (*The Journal of Blacks in Higher Education*, 1997). Whether or not you ever know these statistics, you come to know the role society has for you. Many young boys understand that from birth, society expects them to end up in prison. Schools help reinforce this by teaching a curriculum that glorifies whiteness and makes blacks into savages. The Black boy begins to think that his life is a lost cause because of this message. Teachers, both Black and White, preach this message, and the student begins to wonder why he is in school when he is going to end up in prison anyway, so he stops attending. Or imagine having darker skin and people, both Black and White, call you ugly at a young age and you grow up without any self-love because you feel horribly disfigured.

Just pause and think about being a woman living in a country where one out of every six women will be the victim of a rape or an attempted rape in her lifetime. You are encouraged to work at Hooters and be on *Girls Gone Wild* videotapes, and not to read or learn. You are held to standards for beauty where society expects you to alter your genetic makeup through things like breast augmentation and other plastic surgeries. Society says paint your face, fry and dye your hair in order to be beautiful, and when you can not reach this idealistic Barbie standard then your self-esteem is crushed.

You are poor, and going hungry when you are only six years old, living in a small dirty house, full of rats and roaches, the electricity, water, and heat are off, and it is fifteen degrees outside. You then turn to your mother and see tears in her eyes as she tells you that all you can do is pray.

I tell these stories to you because I do not ever want you to forget the struggles oppressed people have had to endure. Take these stories, learn from them and let them inspire you. Never forget history and figures like Harriet Tubman, Sojourner Truth, Fredrick Douglass, who fought so hard to change the system. History is the undeniable truth of the situation that oppresses us, a true sequence of events not manipulated by individuals, but recorded by time. It is a journey that shapes your self-identity, because it challenges social norms and values. History is the motivation and focus of the struggle; it is up to you not to repeat the mistakes of the past and to design a new path for future generations. This can be hard because the United States often does not truly acknowledge the injustices of past or present. James Baldwin wrote that, "American soil is full of the corpses of my ancestors, through 400 years and at least three wars. Why is my freedom, my citizenship, in question now? What one begs American people to do, for everyone's sake, is simply to accept our history."

Americans have never truly accepted their history. For if we had, we would be forced to make changes in the direction of equality. And change does not occur in Congress. Making a change starts when you stand up for a cause or a person, when you say that there is racial and gender stratification in the public schools, and even when you spend quality time with your child, so that he or she does not grow up insecure and lacking self-love. If your parents did not instill in you that sense of self-love, you should always believe in yourself and never let anyone tell you that you are worthless. You know that there may be times that you fail, but those times are just a part of life, and if you hang in there, you will grow from these experiences. Do not ever succumb to the pressure of conforming or giving in. Question the people in power and the policies they make. Do not be scared to admit your own shortcomings, and yet stand firm in your convictions. Understand that most factors are against you succeeding, and even though you are, as the title of a Walter Mosley novel states, *Always Outnumbered, Always Outgunned*, you must continue on until your dreams become reality.

The old dream is dead. The time when people of color thought that this country would actually live up to its promise of equality is a mere echo in the wind. The time is yours, my future activists, my descendants. Though by the time you read this I may have joined the angelic train, carried away from this world, my spirit and the spirits of the others, who have come before you, linger in your passions. The creation of a new dream, one that does not have ingrained sexism, racism, classism, and biases against most religions, is your responsibility. This new dream must go beyond equality; it must reach appreciation, love and respect. This is a seemingly insurmountable task, but you should remember, as W. E. B. DuBois once noted, that "you come from a gifted people blessed with a second sight, and this veil of oppression cannot hold you."

Dare to dream and react accordingly. Always work together, do not let differences divide you. This poses a major threat, because there are always those who would do anything to destroy you. Dick Gregory once said, "The revolution is not Black against White, this is a revolution of right against wrong. And right has never lost." Look closely because this will be a light in times of doubt.

If you are going to be an activist, be an activist wholeheartedly; anything else only exploits the efforts of others. You must look inside yourself and begin to accept the truth; that police terrorize people of color, that women are still viewed as servants and sexual objects, and that this country refuses to acknowledge the injustices of the poor. It may hurt, but it is necessary to acknowledge these truths if things are ever going to change for the better. You must begin to seek the truth. Fight for your ancestors, your present and future. You must become a truth seeker.

I hope that the impact of your ancestors and those who currently fight for equality serve as a positive beacon in your life. I want to tell you to never stop searching for knowledge, never stop reading, and take a realistic view of society. We are all with you and we give you all of our power, conscience, and strength.

Always know that I will never leave you because we are like a chain—linked spiritually through time. Though we exist only one link at a time, the bond we share can never be broken. It is fused with the greatness of our ancestors.

Love,
Myron Strong

12

LETTERS TO OUR FUTURE SELVES

To my future self, fifty years from now, aged 73:

Well, there you are, rocking away in a creaky chair, wizened and possibly balding. (Women do bald.) Your cat Whiskers is dead now, as are your parents Ming-Shang and Hwa-Mei. Very likely you're diabetic, because it runs in the family, and because you never had patience for the gym anyway—the shirtless men and the multitude of mirrors frightened you. Low-carb diets are now passé, the too-chewy soy pasta long forsaken, your girth has expanded heartily. Possibly, a heart attack awaits you.

   And here I am, sprawled on my bed, clad in pink plaid pajamas, mildly hung over, my breath stinking of cheap merlot. Last thing I remember is scribbling a drunken haiku. My room, by the way, looks (and smells) like a wasteland. An earnestly annotated copy of *A Genealogy of Morality* lies on a coffee-stained carpet, a dirty sock's length from a frayed *Autobiography of Malcolm X*. From my wall, a cross-legged Gandhi observes quietly. Partly out of boredom, he has begun counting how many pairs of shoes I own.

   I'm itching to defend myself now. Isn't that what activists do best?

If I truly represent a generation of activists—and I hope to holy God that I don't—I can't blame you for shuddering. Here I am, a youthful twenty-three, sanctifying myself with that label "activist," despite the unmistakable marks of immaturity: intellectual vanity, nostalgia for these postered heroes, a predilection for knee-high leather boots, and generally speaking, an incapacity to do laundry more than once every month.

So there you have it, my cantankerous, hopefully not—excessively senile woman. It's your wisdom I seek now. My ideals are a cluttered extravaganza: I pick up what I trip over. One day it's Nietzsche, the next day Neruda. Sometimes, it's Jesus and the Corinthians chapter about love; other days, Zen and the fat Buddha. To which visionaries, which leaders should I tether myself? To what shall I moor my beliefs? Give me something illuminating, horrifying, beautiful. Package for me a coherent, severe program, replete with rules and consequences. Hand me a template for how to live.

At this point, you're supposed to pull out a book from your shelf, perhaps a religious text, and say: "Read this. The secret's here, just read it backwards." Or perhaps it's even simpler. You'll recall an epiphany from your life, or a fable that ends with a tidy lesson.

I turn to you because you have written your will. You have said good-bye to certain objects and material habits. You have outlived your parents, your brother, your college roommates. You have out-lived the homeless man who told you which subway stop boasts the sturdiest heating vents. You have outlived the Kenyan woman who explained to you exactly why she shot the man who beat her. And you have long outlived one of your first students, a kid who loved basket-ball and never saw seventeen.

Amid all these funerals, what have you lived for? As a teacher in the small town of Helena, Arkansas, I worry sometimes that what I am doing is very small. Do you wonder what happened to my more grandiose ideals of dismantling systemic problems? Do you regret never taking the routes I did not choose? At times, I envy my policy wonk friends in Washington, D.C., or the ones at the United Nations. Alternatively, I think I should launch an earth-shaking worldwide movement—about what, I'm not sure. I gaze at the glossy posters of Malcolm X and Gandhi in my classroom, and I consider the sacrifices they made, the visions that seized them.

Surely you must look at my life and speculate, somewhat indulgently, whether you could have done something larger. Indeed, my classroom is a compact space, and the town I teach in is anything but large—the population is eight thousand and decreasing. The county in which I now reside has an average household income of $4,956 and is listed as one of the ten poorest counties in the United States. *Harper's Magazine*'s index duly notes that we have a higher teenage birth rate than that of ninety-four developing countries. The majority of my sixty-four students at Stars Academy are labeled "behaviorally challenged." They are truants, flunkies, or delinquents who got into too many fights at the regular schools. Both formally and informally, they are the outcasts of a school district already known for languishing academically.

Despite their reputation as the "bad kids" of Helena, however, they are anything but stupid. Some are wise from their contact with poverty and violence, and they write honestly, exuberantly. In one assignment "James," sixteen, pens a passionate account of overcoming cocaine addiction. "My so-called friends," he notes "never came once to check up on me in rehab." Another student, fourteen, recalls her decision to have a baby instead of aborting, wondering whether she will ever again feel a sense of freedom.

In this classroom of students, I glimpsed activism in a way I had never before. You might find this strange, because on this particular day, the third class period contained but five students—a couple were skipping, another handful were suspended—and activism usually involves a few more people and a visible system or law to change. I'd marched with hundreds of people for a living wage and hundreds of thousands against the war in Iraq; I'd worked with women's rights activists in Nairobi and Beijing and affordable housing advocates in

Boston. But it was here, in this classroom, that I felt my most genuine understanding of activism—here, in the Mississippi Delta, where cotton fields and river valleys hide the Shakespeares and Roosevelts, the Michelangelos and Ellisons of America. Here is a place where slaves died dreaming to read and write, and now their great-grandchildren skip school. They hunger for something fresh and revelatory and new, yet they feel those pangs only dimly. "I dream of moving away from this small town," a student writes, "but what if it's the same there?"

Because they fear dreams, or perhaps because I do not recognize my own, I ask them to write frequently about their dreams. In bright green erasable marker, I scribble onto the whiteboard, "What do you want most in the world?"

Some write, of course, what you'd expect from anyone. Hot red Ferraris with 20-inch rims! Contracts with the NBA! Giant mansions, private islands! Then I chance upon the response of a young woman, fifteen, who, like many of my students, is often absent. This young woman can recite poems by Langston Hughes, even the fifty-line poem "The Negro Mother." She lives in a crowded house with aunts, grandmas, uncles, sisters, and brothers who are young and old and sick and overworked. On her paper, she has written, "I just want to go somewhere quiet, away from all this noise."

Now, old woman, everything makes sense. I don't need your answers. I've found it, the secret of all this activism stuff: it's right here, in near illegible scrawl, and poor spelling. I admire this notebook paper: three-holed, ruled, slightly crumpled. This is what you have lived for, and this is what we are all fighting for, policymakers in Washington, D.C., activists in New York. Yes, that is it. What we're really fighting for, when it all comes down to it, is this one girl gone crazy from all the racket of life and suffering, this one girl who just wants a little peace, a corner where she can hear her thoughts, and write them down. What we're fighting for is the possibility that my Langston Hughes—loving girl will become her generation's Langston Hughes.

At age seventy-three, you are smaller. Every object must seem magnified, strangely massive. Your wrists are sore from the weight of your book; when you peer at your picture frames, the people look larger. But it is not just that you are physically smaller. You feel smaller because of the people you have met, the extraordinary lives they have lived. You sensed it every place to which you traveled, especially at night, when the starlight favored you no more than the person sleeping on a park bench nearby. And this feeling of smallness must have been breathtaking. What a comforting thought—that, through gracing us with age, God will make us small, so that our vision will be vast.

What do you live for? I asked you before, but now to myself I must ask: What do I live for? I worry whether my own vision is vast enough. But then I pause, and think: smallness is underrated. So much—too much—is given undue largeness. Even that phrase of ours, "public service," has too much heft to it. For whom do we claim to serve? At times, I am startled by how scarcely I know the people I "serve," how boldly I abstract and sociologize. I must live for that glimpse of how vast a single person is.

Peace,
Michelle Kuo

Michelle Kuo

Dear Future Me,

Sometimes, when I'm home alone and bored, I go down to the study and look through our old pictures. I see my sisters and me as babies, my parents before they were even married, my grandparents, and great-grandparents. The pictures of Mom look nearly identical to those of me, at every stage of life, and I wonder if that will always be true. Though we have the same face, the similarities are so much deeper than appearances. Our personalities, our quirks, the ways in which we interact with the world are so similar there are moments when it scares me. Being the oldest child, it's not surprising that I am so much like my parents in so many ways, but it makes me wonder. If I am so much like her now, will I be like her in the future? In many ways, it's not such a terrible thing. She's not a normal, boring mother. I'm sure you would say that she still isn't. Much as I admire and respect her, there is a part of me that wants to find some way to rebel. Some way to be different. I wonder if I ever will.

At first glance our family is not so unusual. Minivan, nice house in the suburbs, three lovely girls, all of whom excel in school. Abba (Dad) works for the state, the obvious aspiration for any resident of a state capitol. Ima (Mom) is older than she looks and acts. She had me, her first born, when she was in her mid-thirties, and had her last child, Tali, in her early forties. She's five years older than her husband, who stayed at home and took care of us for several years. This is, of course, an increasingly normal situation. There is also their overeducation, with upper-level degrees from Ivy League schools, the amazing way they managed to incorporate something educational into every moment of the first decade and a half of my life. A model bourgeois family, so it seems. I think I started to notice how my family differed from others when I was in middle school—when everyone else started fighting with their parents, and I didn't. Sure, we had our little squabbles about cleaning my room, or not arguing so much with my sisters. But in general, we got along. My friends liked my mom and dad, some of them more than their own parents. They still do.

So while everyone else started to drift away from their parents, I became closer to mine. I got older and more mature, and began to be treated as an adult, an equal. Then I became more politically aware. I can't pinpoint the exact moment; it must have been in sixth or seventh grade, when I realized I cared about the world a whole lot more than most people I knew. I realized nobody else in my class had grown up going to peace rallies, or heard names like Marx around the dinner table, or had their parents sing *Le Internationale* to amuse them on long car rides. I had always felt different, and that feeling only deepened as I realized that it wasn't only me who was different. It was my family.

Then came the stunning revelation, the bombshell, the closest thing we have to a family secret. It was the morning after my bat mitzvah, surrounded by all of my closest relatives; I was officially a Jewish adult. And my grandfather, the one who cared most about the bat mitzvah, perhaps the one who is most proud of our Judaism, said one of the simplest and yet most profound things he ever has to me. He mentioned, ever so casually, his "friends" at the FBI. My grandparents, the sweet old people who like to feed me matzo ball soup and show me off to their friends and lecture me about marrying a nice Jewish man, were investigated by the FBI. He said it so subtly, like it was the simplest, most obvious fact of life, knowing I would be curious and ask, because that's just who I am. I knew they were progressive, ahead of their time, maybe even a bit unusual, but communists? I never even contemplated the fact. Every bit of information I obtained about the family fascinated me to no end. I loved hearing the story about FBI agents knocking on Ima's door as a child, how her middle name was Ethel—after Ethel Rosenberg. Over time more came out, and I found out my great-uncle was blacklisted from teaching, Zaydie (Grandpa) was the chauffeur for the chairman of the communist party, my grandparents lived underground for a few years and Ima was lucky not to be born under an assumed name. The entirety of my heritage grows even larger as I learn more about it, and realize how incredibly different it is from what most people can call a heritage.

I have a pretty oddball personal identity because of all of this. I define myself by how I'm different from others as opposed to how I am the same, for simple reason of convenience. Given where I live, it's not too difficult for me to find others who share my Jewish background. What really distinguishes me from the crowd of kids at synagogue with great-grandparents from Eastern Europe is the radicalism. It seeps into every aspect of my life, from household attitudes about allowance and chores to familial support of my scholastic rebellions to our political involvement. My life would be profoundly different were I not raised by ardent communal socialists. I can see it in the subtle ways I interact with others, sharing my food, offering help, and expecting the same in return when I need it. Individualism doesn't rule my world and that creates a noticeable difference. I see it in the way I view the world. I question what's presented to me in class, petition against bad substitutes, and refuse to blindly obey authority. Sometimes it makes me feel a little left out. Proud as I am of my upbringing, it is an alienating thing. My side of the story is frequently left out of history textbooks. Full disclosure to my friends about my family history many times just isn't possible. When we talk about post-college plans they say career, I say commune. My values, of community, sharing, equality, and non-consumerism, are so far off from the highly individualistic and material obsessed world my peers reside in. I am on a different path, I live in a different universe, I see an entirely different reality. I have ideals, I have dreams, and I have a legacy beyond family names but with a family history that I feel a need to continue.

And that family history is also a burden I carry. It is heavy and ever present, mostly because it is the legacy of unfulfilled destiny. Despite my grandparents' lives as subversives, I wasn't actually raised in a socialist community. To the contrary, the lifestyle I live, through my parents, is in conflict with all that I believe in. And despite my enormous respect and immeasurable love for Ima and Abba, I simply can't live as I do now. It's been a difficult realization to come to, understanding that I disapprove of some of the things my parents do. But I know that I cannot simply live a typical lifestyle—own a house by myself, drive a minivan, belong to a synagogue. None of these things, things that are part of my existence right now, fit into the life I need to lead to be a happy fulfilled person. I feel that I simply must be a living, breathing embodiment of all that I believe, that doing otherwise is not an option. Not because of self-righteousness or a sense of entitlement but because of a sense of duty to my own sanity. This does not make my life easy, but I cannot change whom I am, nor do I want to. I am committed and idealistic and youthful and energetic, and my upbringing has taught me a lesson. I have been shown firsthand why I can't be like everyone else.

So have you done it? Have you lived up to everything I yearn to be? I visited my friends last weekend, and we talked about how it's going to be hard. We gazed out into our future, the one we've planned together (are we still together, like we always say we will be?). We looked forward to the hardship, naïve and innocent and already fucked over by the world all at once. Has it been as hard as we thought? Are you discouraged? Do you ever wonder if you should just give up, let go, perhaps admit that a silly youthful dream is not worth devoting your life to? Please don't disappoint me. For once, the future looks bright and hopeful, and I see a way out of this life I live. You see, I only want the best for me. For you. For the world. So if you ever feel like giving up, just remember this feeling, the one I am having now, which I hope never fades. Remember what it's like to feel as if the fate of the world rests on your shoulders, as if every opportunity lies ahead of you, that the only doors closed are those you close yourself and that someday you will make things different. When, in your old age, you are absolutely sure you will look back and say that you are satisfied because you fought the good fight. You lived the answer. Because right now, I'm wondering how exactly I am going to fix the world. Don't let me down. Let me be my answer to myself.

Dara

To myself on the day I graduate medical school:

I remember being warned not to enter medical school. "It sucks your soul, and changes you for the worse," they preached. So, I hesitated and told myself that it couldn't be done. "It's impossible," I began to believe, "for someone like me to become a physician." So I put myself to sleep repeating the same stories that are still whispered behind your back: a high school dropout, juvenile hall detainee, young single mom, welfare recipient (in that order) cannot climb through the back windows into halls of power.

Slowly, I remembered that earlier the same people said I couldn't have a child *and* finish school. The same critics conceded that while I *might* be able to finish school, in order to raise a child properly, I *had* to be married to a manly jerk. They said that, in order to nourish the child with support from the government, I had to drop out of a four-year college and drop into the almighty low-paid (but productive!) service industry workforce.

They were wrong.

Girl, you did it. Phase One complete. Smile for the camera, and pick up your now ten-year-old boy-child.

For a while, yes, it was tough. All the coffee in the world wouldn't be enough to compete against seemingly perfect, childless students with their 4.0 GPAs and opportunistic volunteerism. And really, the whole school thing seemed inane after living in Chiapas and fighting for justice in my city's streets, in the squats, at road blockades, and tree-sits. So, was it worth it?

I don't want to constantly trade off my parenting, my activism, and my studies to be an amazing doctor. Both academics and activists present these false dichotomies: either I could be a good mom *or* a good student, a good student *or* a good activist. To me, providing women with access to reproductive health care is about all three: motherhood *and* revolution *and* learning.

There are many who exclude, and want to limit, my choices.

"Motherhood and school," the ecologists, anarchists, and activists alike dictate, "is for people who sell out of the revolution." Is becoming a physician selling out? Is it selling out to raise the next generation? If the answer to either of these questions is yes, we have already lost.

Many of the same revolutionaries that I went to jail with and laid down with are the ones who most failed to grasp the complexities of my life. The black-and-white revolutionary credo that spoke to me during my years of direct actions provide little clarity on the daily issues of my life as a mother. Activists continue to exclude women and children from the revolution by focusing on confrontational, media-sexxxy street battles instead of building supportive communities, forgetting that many women and kids struggle for basic safety.

By labeling family issues as irrelevant, will our generation of movements be as unsustainable as the counterculture movements of the sixties and seventies? Today, many of these radical voices dismiss their work as something that occurred outside of their normal life. Their revolution is waved off as "something I did when I was young and carefree."

It took having a child of my own to realize that "carefree" is a code word for "childfree."

When our Movement fails to include families and the daily complexity of caring for another person, we become isolated from our broader communities. In the United States, our revolution becomes incongruous with daily life.

As a new mom, I lost my voice—both in the Movement for social justice and in the larger society of the United States. The struggle for justice barely heard my voice as a young, poor single mom. Activist houses refused to open doors to families like mine claiming, "Children take energy away from the real revolution." At times, members of the activist community criticized me for utilizing the very few resources available (see also my favorite urban myth: "Accepting welfare is accepting the government"), while doing nothing to broaden these options. Too few created alternatives that were transformative and empowering for both parents and society as a whole. Being a mom is a foundation for radical organizing, because in order to survive we have to transform these limiting judgments into power.

Motherhood is continually soul stretching. As women, we aren't allowed to ask for help for ourselves, our voices are silenced. But for our children, our relations, and our neighbors, we will fight. For my sisters, I will become a physician.

I strongly acknowledge the work of previous generations to provide us the power to say yes. We draw from our mothers' fights for things we now take for granted: the social freedom to engage in sex out of marriage, medical birth control, the (limited) ability to obtain safe and legal abortion, quality childcare centers, entry into a workplace. "Yes" is a good beginning. But, in my learning, I see the impacts of what happens when the only word that is heard from women's mouths is "yes."

We have young mothers who cannot say "no" to abusive partners and abusive societies. So we leave our children to subpar childcare, in order to provide care to others. *Yes Sir, Want fries with that? Is your office sufficiently cleaned? Yes, I want to help you.* I see women anxious, depressed, and suffering. We are unhealthy. We need to define our space and existence in much more complex ways than "yes" and "no."

Today, I am tired of pretending there is a simple answer. Sure, I miss the simple glamor of the fights in the street, but I am building my own complex revolution. My revolution recognizes the gradations of sexuality and the power to engage in a dialogue of consent.

Deciding to enter medicine, like choosing to become a young single parent, was a battle. When I chose to be a parent at nineteen, they told me in hundreds of ways that my body was not mine. My decisions needed to encompass the wants and desires of everyone else. The space for acceptable sexuality and reproductive choices is continually limited, by society and by our allies in social justice movements. We are told that we stand alone, either in the choice to parent or in the choice to terminate a pregnancy. In this isolation, we grow afraid. Today I pray for you that as a physician you can provide community services—from supporting teen motherhood to providing young women the options to terminate an undesired pregnancy. It will not be a lucrative or easy track. As you stand there shaking the hand of a dean who charged $120,000 for the privilege of a medical diploma, have you sold out of these dreams?

It would be easy to sell out. It would be the downhill track. I have a heaping dish of privilege served to me daily. It is discomforting to address privilege. I am American, with access to information and power. I am white, and although I am blessed to have a multicultural extended family, my race delivers unfair external credibility and influence. In our racist world, I receive well beyond what I deserve. I was raised with more than enough. My parents cared about me, and created opportunities for me to grow. I am healthy. These factors, given to me by fortuitous birth alone, allow me to have (the perception of) a degree of freedom to direct my future.

Part of going to medical school is walking on this edge of privilege. Even though I moan and groan about it, the agony of medical school is a privilege. After being schooled for four more years on "professionalism," will you continue to address the disparities in the heart of this most privileged profession in the most privileged country?

Medical school teaches that individual physicians make the difference between life and death. Welfare schools me otherwise, reinforcing the structural nature of poverty; no matter how strong my bootstraps, I will never stand tall enough, move far enough. Individualism is a lie medical schools like to teach; poverty and motherhood are truths revolutionaries like to ignore. How will you rectify walking the line between my impending relative wealth of becoming a physician and my current reality of raising a child below the poverty line?

Yesterday, the director of a drop-in clinic said to me, as she scrawled medical notes across the chart of her homeless teenaged patient, "Medicine is a conservative institution, and we live in a conservative time. The only incentive to be a progressive physician is in us, as individuals." How can the movement for basic human rights like community health care ultimately rest on the continued commitment of a few altruistic physicians? More personally, only a year into the discipline of medicine, I know how it breaks you apart, piece by piece. Can we build a movement of battered, scattered individuals?

In the transition to physician, will you wield power and privilege as a weapon? Today, I carry privilege heavy on my back, like I carried my son as I scaled the walls of the ivory tower. I know I will win few accolades, few honors, and fewer elections. My job in women's health will not be extremely well-paying, if paid at all. But as a mom, I am used to it.

Study and Struggle,
Rebecca Trotzky-Sirr

December 31, 2004

To my future self,

Hello! I hope this letter finds you well. I wanted to write you, me, at age ninety-five so that you can reflect on life with the passion that now propels a twenty-three-year-old to dedicate his life to radical movements for social change. As you face the thought of being history yourself, it's time to consider the history that brought you to where you are. If you're ninety-five, I suppose that would make this the year 2076 (have our math skills improved in our twilight years?). Congratulations on making it to this ripe old age. Either the heart condition mom so worried about proved to be not that big a deal, or you actually have managed to keep on a regular exercise schedule. Of all the wonderful gifts bestowed on us by familial genes, I would have to say that con-genital heart problems is on top of the no-thanks list (followed shortly thereafter by flat feet and male pattern baldness). Despite those less-than-welcome gifts, however, both sides of the family have bequeathed us with the need for a strong sense of morality, the obligation to take life seriously, the value of good humor, and the importance of being studious. (And to think—my diapers weren't even red!) All these qualities seemed to have led me, almost inevitably, into the Movement—that hard-to-define space of active and dynamic opposition to forces of domination and subjugation.

A good friend told me several months ago that I've always been "going on fifty" (I imagine that takes on a different meaning from where you stand now). I suppose that's true of many of us young activists. I thought about the suffering of others as a young 'en, became an activist at fourteen, started my first political organization at age fifteen, and feel like a Movement veteran at the ripe old age of twenty-three. My experiences are my own, but I think they're similar to young activists across the country and throughout history: the endless meetings, late nights, Movement fights, family drama, personal trauma, good times, state harassment, car trips, long debates, coalition building, organizational conflict, skill sharing, and great people that comprise the Movement. I think that's just a defining feature of being an activist: feeling like the weight of the world rests on your shoulders, and taking seriously the commitment to be part of the millions making change. It's no small commitment. And for all its heartache, there is no place I'd rather be than in the Movement. (Even if it does mean that our obsession with consensus leads to hour-long debates over where to go for dinner.)

Unlike many of my comrades, I was not drawn to activism because my survival depended on it, but because I saw that there was injustice in the world and I had hope that I could be part of lessening it, maybe even eradicating it and installing something more humane in its place. But where does a kid born in 1981 find hope? After all, I was born when a reactionary B-rated movie actor was president, to be replaced by a reactionary ex-CIA director, to be replaced by a reactionary

Democrat passing himself off as a liberal long after that political identity ceased to have much meaning in U.S. electoral politics (outside of a
Right-wing bogeyman). For as long as I've been alive, then, the mainstream U.S. political climate has been one long succession of small-
scale wars, callous individualism, and blunted dreams—long before the
havoc of the current presidential administration unleashed itself on the
world. It has for quite some time been a rightward-moving environment
especially conducive to political cynicism and detachment. So it is little
surprise that many of the kids I went to school with are seemingly driven
by career and family concerns alone. And yet, beneath the surface lies
another reality, where young people regularly get politically inspired and
involved, and movements for fundamental progressive social change
continue to blossom. And with that opens the Pandora's box of hope.

Where do I find hope? Despite this question's surface-level sim-
plicity, the answer to it reveals the root of my organizing, so it's a
worthwhile query to engage. I find hope from my maternal grandmother, who survived Auschwitz and then lost everything again when
an authoritarian bureaucracy posing as revolution occupied first Hun-
gary and then Czechoslovakia, driving her from both places. As I write
this, my dear future self, she has been dead less than two weeks, yet
her legacy is what compels me to put pen to paper, to write for and
think toward the future. My grandmother, who showed by example that
no matter what happens to you, it is possible to live life with dignity
and principles. My grandmother, who taught me to know and love and
honor my family history and my culture—a lesson that, once imparted,
led me to study history more generally and genuinely, to uncover the
many hidden stories comprising people's history. To see that our
present realities and movements have deep roots. To see that resistance is as old as genocide—and that the underdog, the oppressed, the
marginalized can win. History, too, is a hopeful weapon, if you use it
right—which is why education has been central to freedom struggles
since time immemorial.

I draw inspiration from the political prisoners. From studying history, from friends' experiences with police, and from the constant talk of concentration camps that permeated Passover seders, I learned about incarceration as a strategy for social control—a weapon wielded against those deemed marginal, subhuman, or likely to revolt. Movement foot soldiers and strategists, leaders and thinkers, have all found themselves behind the gray prison walls—but they have been neither broken nor destroyed. From Ho Chi Minh to Emma Goldman, Phoolan Devi to Mumia Abu Jamal, Lolita Lebrón to Nelson Mandela, Bobby Sands to Assata Shakur, Mahatma Gandhi to Marcus Garvey, and on and on and on—prison is where so many have not only ended up, or passed through, but also where they have, if nothing else, redoubled their political dedication. All over the world, it is so often the prisoners who have remained hopeful and committed, long after others have given up. And that fact is sharper than any razor wire fence, more powerful than any prison bars could ever hope to be. Tell me, future self, do we still find hope from Kuwasi Balagoon's sentencing statement, where the former Black Panther confidently proclaimed that the system had a shelf life that wouldn't last through the twenty-first century? I don't know if he was right—was he, future self?—but I still take solace in his steadfast political commitment.

And I stay in the struggle because of the victories, the changes that have been won, even if incomplete and wrenched with great difficulty from and after bitter struggle with oppressive power structures. I wake up every day, distraught about all the terror facing our world and yet confident that all is not lost. Far from it, because today is another day to fight. Today, more people will begin to realize that occupation is *always* a barbarity, no matter its name or its cloak. Today, more people will start connecting the dots between the visible "isolated incidents" of oppression and the structures of society. Today, more people will attend their first political meeting or protest or rally or teach-in or speak-out. Today, more people will commit themselves to toppling white supremacy and eradicating patriarchy, to the redistribution of economic resources and the creation of directly democratic political structures. Today, more people will say "enough!" Today, we will win another victory. It's going to happen today, because it started yesterday and we're building for tomorrow. And so today, just like I did yesterday and will do again tomorrow, I recommit myself to the struggle.

Of course, we fight with hope that we will live long enough to enjoy our victories. But the Movement is not for the impatient; as the Spanish anarchists and antifascists of the 1930s said, we carry a new world in our hearts, even if it is a world that may not come to fruition in our lifetimes. We take these steps for the future as much as for us. We live our lives in the struggle because what we do now will have an impact on future generations. Truth be told, that wisdom is what keeps me up until all hours of the morning, operating regularly on just a few short hours of sleep. For as much coffee as I now drink, it's not the caffeine that propels me to stay up late into the night penning this radical screed or attending that meeting or doing any of the other projects occupying my time and mind. No, I could ditch the coffee tomorrow and not feel a thing—because in my prone-to-high-cholesterol heart, I know that people will always struggle, will always find ways to lift the boot off our collective necks. And that knowledge is something no coffee company can capitalize on, a drug politicians will always be unable to criminalize.

As you know, my dear self, we've never been good at predictions, so I won't attempt to guess the state of the world when you read this. Besides, such guessing would be fruitless, even if I did have a functioning crystal ball rather than just a yellowing collection of fortune cookie wisdom I seem incapable of throwing out. Crystal ball predictions are meaningless, because the future will be what we, the people, struggle to make it—from Afghanistan to Zimbabwe, Angola to Vietnam, Bali to Mali, the Congo to Venezuela, Argentina to the United States, and everywhere in between. Today the news says trouble in Iraq; tomorrow it may say in Iran or Syria or North Korea or who knows where else. But these plans of expanding empire will ultimately fail, sure as the frigid night air gives way to a warm day's sun. There is no force too powerful, no empire too strong, that it can overshadow the strength and determination of people, who have shown an incredible resiliency to keep moving toward freedom. After all, the sun has already risen and set on all empires before now, even if it took generations and generations of struggle to make it happen. That's a lesson learned from history, not from crystal balls.

Empires and oppressive systems have always fallen because enough people committed themselves to ushering in a better world. Even when it was clear that they would not live to see the fruits of their struggle, the enslaved have continued to resist in ways small and large. Women have always fought back against male attempts at denigration and domination. Colonized people have always taught their children to uphold and defend their culture and their land. Working people have always banded together to fight the bosses. Lesbian, gay, bisexual, and transgender people have always stood up to those who would confine or restrict sexual and gender expressions. In the end, empires fall because enough people stand on the side of humanity and live a life in dynamic opposition to systems of oppression with a vision of a better world.

Even under the most brutal regimes, there have always been people who refused to surrender or ascent to the backward march of the reactionaries. That's why activism feels more urgent now, more compelling, as an array of Right-wing agendas and brutal policies get enacted globally as well as domestically, all under farcical claims of liberation and democratization. Yet it is our refusal to collaborate and our embrace of alternatives that will, even now, help create a more just world. It doesn't mean we do everything right, of course, or that there aren't big stumbling blocks and obstacles and dangers on the perilous path ahead. It just means that, as the Vietnamese said during their centuries' long struggle for national liberation, "we will struggle from one generation to the next." They did and won a resounding, if incomplete, victory. And so we all struggle, from one generation to the next, working toward a better world for us all.

So what now, future self? From where I sit, another year is almost done. From where you sit, the end of the century approaches. Your youth is gone now, and surely your hair is as well. Yet I have no doubt that you woke up today with a smile on your face that carries you throughout your day, even if you do eat dinner hours earlier than I do now. So many fights behind us—and, I'm sure, so many more remain. Still, I know that every step—every meeting, protest, conference, newspaper, Web site, debate, civil disobedience, every action big and small—is an attempt to bring us all closer to being free of what feminist culture critic bell hooks calls the white supremacist capitalist patriarchy that has been dominating our lives for far too long. And I know that being free of *that* is worth the hardships that come from the risks taken in activism—because it *is* possible to create a better world. We didn't come this far to stop now.

In solidarity and struggle, from the beginning of the twenty-first century to the end.

With love,

Dan Berger

ABOUT THE EDITORS

Dan Berger is a writer, activist, and graduate student living in Philadelphia. Now 23, Berger has been involved in movements for social justice since the age of 14. He served as editor for two and a half years of *ONWARD*, an internationally distributed quarterly anarchist newspaper that emerged out of the global justice movement. The grandson of holocaust survivors, Berger has also been involved with organizing against white supremacy, sexism, and the prison industrial complex. He was a founding member of the Colors of Resistance collective, an antiracist group at the University of Florida and part of the Colours of Resistance network. He has also worked with Critical Resistance, the national prison abolition organization, and done support work for U.S. political prisoners.

Currently, he is a PhD student at the Annenberg School for Communication at the University of Pennsylvania, and a member of Resistance in Brooklyn. He is also the author of *Outlaws of America: The Weather Underground and the Politics of Solidarity* (AK Press). His writing has appeared in *Z, Socialism and Democracy*, and the *Philadelphia Inquirer*, among elsewhere.

Chesa Boudin is a 24-year-old itinerant activist, writer, and student. He recently finished his masters degree in refugee studies at Oxford University on a Rhodes Scholarship. In 2003 he graduated *summa cum laude* from Yale University. He is currently working in support of the revolutionary government in Venezuela and living in Caracas.

Chesa has used writing, campus and community organizing, and public speaking to advocate for social change through reforms in the criminal justice system and foreign policy. Chesa has also lectured widely on the impact of parental incarceration on young children. He was a leading member of the Yale Coalition for Peace. Chesa has participated in a range of community service projects in the U.S. and around the world.

Chesa has used his time abroad to learn Spanish and Portuguese. *Letters From Young Activists* is his first book. Some of his previous publications can be found online on salon.com, *The Nation*, and *Topic Magazine*.

Kenyon Farrow is a 30-year-old Black Gay man, writing and organizing in Brooklyn, New York. He recently served as the southern regional coordinator for Critical Resistance, a prison abolition organization, and continues to work in the New York City chapter. He has also served as an adult ally for FIERCE!, a queer youth of color community organizing project in New York City.

Kenyon has written several articles and essays, the most widely circulated of which have been "Is Gay Marriage Anti-Black?," "Connecting the Dots: Michael Moore, White Nationalism and the Multi-racial Left" with writer Kil Ja Kim, and most recently, "We Real Cool?: On Hip-Hop, Asian-Americans, Black Folks, and Appropriation." Kenyon has also appeared on radio including Pacifica stations in New York and Houston and Free Speech Radio, given many public lectures and served on many panels dealing with race and prison issues, and race and queer issues as well, including at Temple University, University of Wisconsin/Madison, and the University of New Orleans.

He is currently editing a publication on the prison system in the military, as part of a series sponsored by the Central Committee for Conscientious Objectors, and The National Youth and Militarism Program of the American Friends and Service Committee (AFSC). *Letters From Young Activists* is his first book.

ABOUT THE CONTRIBUTORS

Kat Aaron is a 26-year-old New Yorker who runs RYSE for Justice, a resource center for youth working for economic justice. Kat is also a media activist and journalist. She is a host and producer with *Rise Up Radio*, a youth show on WBAI 99.5 FM.

Badr Albanna, 22, is a graduate student currently living in Berkeley, California. Born to an Iraqi father and Palestinian mother, he grew up near Washington, D.C. As an undergraduate, he was active in the Students for Justice in Palestine as well as efforts to organize students of color.

Doyle Canning, 25, lives in Burlington, Vermont. She works in the core collective of the smartMeme strategy and training project (www.smartmeme.com; 1.866.763.5437), and co-coordinates the STORY youth training program. She is fourth generation Irish-American. When not off rabble rousing, she likes to daydream, share stories, and walk with her dog.

Gerardo Reyes Chávez—originally from Zacatecas, Mexico—is a 27-year-old farmworker living in southwest Florida and a member of the CIW. He has spoken at colleges, conferences, churches, and mass mobilizations across the country on farmworker issues, corporate globalization, and social change. He can be contacted at Gerardo@ciw-online.org.

Joya Colon-Berezin was born in 1980 in New York City. Joya graduated from Oberlin College in 2002, with a degree in sociology. She currently works as a grassroots organizer in the Northwest Bronx and she credits her meditation/spiritual practice for laying the foundation of her social and political activism.

Andy Cornell, 27, is an activist and writer attending graduate school in New York City. He has worked in labor, anti-prison, global justice, and other movements for more than a decade; he edits the zine *The Secret Files of Captain Sissy*. Contact him at: arc280@nyu.edu.

Andrew Curley, a Navajo student at Suffolk University in Boston, works with the United Students for Fair Trade, the Boston Fair Trade Coalition, and the Suffolk Students for Palestine. He co-founded in NM the Student Socialist Coalition, traveled to Nicaragua with USFT, and interned at Global Exchange.

Chris Dixon (chrisd@resist.ca) is 27, a white, middle-class, straight guy from Anchorage, Alaska, and an anarchist organizer and writer. He was deeply involved in the Seattle WTO protests, helped build the Colours of Resistance network, and is a graduate student in the History of Consciousness program at UC Santa Cruz.

Kaira Espinoza, 25, was born and raised in San Francisco, after her parents emigrated from El Salvador. Her passion for social justice blossomed in high school. A San Francisco State University graduate, she is pursuing her teaching credential so that she can make education relevant, interactive, and empowering for young people.

Kevin Etienne-Cummings, 27, was born in Victoria, Mahé, of the Seychelles Islands. He is currently a doctoral student in history at the University of Michigan, Ann Arbor. His work focuses on the southwest islands of the Indian Ocean.

Emma Fialka-Feldman is 16 years old and lives in Huntington Woods, Michigan. She facilitates Sibshops, a support program for children who have a sibling with disabilities, has published articles and is a contributor to *The Sibling Slam Book*. She loves to play soccer, the trumpet, laugh, and make the world a better place. (She can be reached at: EmSquaredA88@aol.com)

Jeffrey Frank, 26, lives in Gainesville, Florida, working as a massage therapist and teacher at the Florida Institute of Somatic Health. With a rich history in community organizing and political action, Jeffrey brings ideas of community, freedom, and peace into a nonhierarchal teaching environment, which fosters learning and individual development.

Stephen Funk enlisted in the military at 19, looking for a sense of purpose. Instead, he found it in the antiwar movement, becoming the first conscientious objector to the Iraq war and, subsequently, serving nine months in a military prison. He is now 22 and lives in San Francisco.

Peter Gelderloos is a 22-year-old anarchist organizing in Harrisonburg, Virginia. He focuses on anti-oppression work, prisoner support, and local groups like Harrisonburg Copwatch and Food Not Bombs. Peter is an editor for the online radical library, www.signalfire.org.

Jonah Gindin is a 24-year-old Canadian activist living and writing in Caracas, Venezuela. He writes regularly for www.venezuelanalysis.com. His articles have also appeared in

NACLA Report on the Americas, Canadian Dimension, Relay, and *Monthly Review,* among others. He can be reached at Jonah@venezuelanalysis.com.

Stephanie Guilloud, 27, is a white, middle-class queer from Houston. An organizer of the Seattle WTO shutdown, Stephanie edited an anthology of firsthand accounts. She also edited *Through the Eyes of the Judged,* incarcerated young men's autobiographies. She works as a popular educator and organizer with Project South in Atlanta.

Nell Hirschmann-Levy, 25, was born to politically active parents in New York City. Struggles for social justice have always been central to her life. She now lives and organizes in Oakland, California, with SEIU and is devoted to finding creative ways for us to support one another's efforts.

Walidah Imarisha, a 25-year-old Philly resident, is a spoken word sista and political poet. Part of the Human Rights Coalition, prisoners' families against the prison industrial complex, she helped found *AWOL* Magazine, the poetry duo Good Sista/Bad Sista, and hopes to help found an autonomous anti-state someday soon.

Chloe Joy is a 10-year-old activist in Gainesville, Florida. She publishes a zine called *Thomasina.* She quit public school in the second grade and is now a student of the Gainesville Street School. Jcjoy13@yahoo.com.

Matan Kaminer, 22, from Tel-Aviv, was one of the founders of the 2002 High School Students' refusal letter, and went to prison for his refusal to serve in the IDF in December 2002. Put on trial with four other refuseniks, he spent 21 months in confinement. He now lives in Jerusalem.

Samuel D. Kass, 24, Chicago, Ilinois. Member of NOWARIRAQ, resisting both wars against Iraq. Continuing work toward health and education for future activists.

Anna Rosario Kennedy, 19, is a sophomore at George Washington University in Washington, D.C. Anna attended Chapin and Riverdale Country School in NYC where she was president of the Amnesty International club and chaired a school-wide seminar on the death penalty. For her work she received the Zonta International Service Award.

Ismail Khalidi, 22, is a writer and actor currently completing his final year at Macalester College in St. Paul, Minnesota. Born to Palestinian parents in Beirut, Ismail grew up in Chicago. His work combines poetry, drama, music, photography, and film. He has written for the Electronic Intifada (electronicintifada.net) and Mizna.

Tiffany Lethabo King, 28, is an African American activist, educator, and writer living in Wilmington, Delaware. She is currently working with students in Wilmington's public vocational and technical high schools, doing organizing work with women in "public" and federally subsidized housing, and is the founder of Resistahs.

Michelle Kuo, 23, teaches high school English in Helena, Arkansas, for Teach for America. A Truman Scholar, Michelle graduated from Harvard College, where she directed a homeless shelter and edited *Diversity and Distinction* magazine. Michelle earned a masters at Cambridge and worked with anti–domestic violence groups in Kenya and China. mkuo@post.harvard.edu

Nilda Laguer, a 29-year-old Neurorican, grew up in BK and has been resisting ever since. She has been part of developing projects like Bronx PrYde in the Boogie down and Urban Mana in BK. She is a writer, poet, resister, hoper, prayer, and a magic bean buyer.

Khary Lazarre-White, 31, born and raised in New York City, co-founded The Brotherhood/Sister Sol (www.brotherhood-sistersol.org) in 1995. A comprehensive, holistic youth organization in Harlem, it provides rites-of-passage programs, after-school care, study in Africa and Latin America, activist training, summer camps, jobs, artistic development, and personal counseling to two hundred youth a year.

Dara Levy-Bernstein, 15, was born in Brooklyn, and moved to Albany, New York, when she was three years old. She spent her second- and third-grade years living in Jerusalem, Israel. She is a member of Hashomer Hatzair and will be attending Simon's Rock College of Bard in the fall.

Arthur Liou, 26, is a Chinese-American activist in Oakland, California. He is a former union organizer and a member of the socialist organization Solidarity. He is currently studying at the University of California at Berkeley's School of Law, Boalt Hall.

Andrea Listenberger, age 18, is a 2005 graduate of Canterbury High School, located in her hometown of Fort Wayne, Indiana. A human rights activist, she served as the Indiana student area coordinator for Amnesty International, working on issues including abolishing the death penalty and the crisis in Sudan.

Ashley Lucas is a 25-five-year-old activist, academic, playwright, and actor from El Paso, Texas. She does prison-related organizing with Families to Amend the California Three Strikes (FACTS) and All of Us or None, and she is an outside supporter of the Angola Human Relations Club.

Mervyn Marcano is a Blackfag working, living, and making art in Brooklyn. At 19, he has organized nationwide around issues of police brutality, gentrification, and public space. He is also co-founder of several art collectives. He is currently focusing on being a filmmaker and is working on his next piece.

Not4Prophet, a 27-year-old Nueva York native, is the voice of Puerto Punx political collective Ricanstruction, spoken noise experi-mental duo Renegades of Punk, and hip hop hybrids x-vandals. For years he has supported all aspects of people's struggle and is fond of throwing stones at corporate castles.

Sara Marie Ortiz, 22, is from Acoma Pueblo, resides in Santa Fe, and is a full-time student in creative writing at the Institute of American Indian Arts. The youngest daughter of Acoma Pueblo poet/laureate/professor Simon J. Ortiz, she would like to become the president of the Institute of American Indian Arts.

Laurel Paget-Seekins, 25, lives in Atlanta and volunteers at the Dekalb Rape Crisis Center. Involved in the movement to close the School of the Americas (by any name) for eight years, Laurel is a member of the Sexual Offense Prevention and Response Team and the Anti-Oppression and Accessibility Working Group.

Eboo Patel, 29, is the founder and executive director of the Interfaith Youth Core, which brings young people from diverse religious communities together in programs that build understanding and encourage cooperative service to others. He earned his doctorate in the sociology of religion from Oxford University on a Rhodes Scholarship.

Guadalupe Patricia Xochihuiztli Salcedo, a 24-year-old Xicana, is completing her masters degree in social welfare and lives in Los Angeles, California. She has worked with several immigrant and indigenous rights based non-profit organizations in California, Arizona, and Mexico, and will continue to struggle for social justice.

Najah Farley Samad, 24, is an African American Muslim woman. Najah grew up in the Cleveland area with her parents Khalid and Leslie Samad, where she participated in the National Movement for Urban Peace and Justice. She lives in Maryland and is involved with Blackout Arts Collective.

gabriel olga khougaz sayegh, 29, works to eliminate prisons and end the war on drugs. A queer Arab/European-American, gabriel grew up in the small farm town world of California's gorgeous central valley and now lives in Brooklyn, where the farm landscape has been traded for a brick and steel skyline. gabrielsayegh@gmail.com.

Eugene Schiff, 23, is from Chicago, and was educated in the city's public schools through high school. He studied history at Tufts University. In 2004 he completed a ten-month Fulbright research fellowship in Tegucigalpa, Honduras, and is currently the Caribbean region coordinator for the Agua Buena Human Rights Association.

Sarah Stillman, 21, enjoys rabble-rousing with groups like the Student Legal Action Movement, Critical Resistance, and the Yale Coalition for Peace. She edits *MANIFESTA*, a bi-annual feminist journal, and is writing a collection of essays about corporate globalization's consequences for young women worldwide. She has lots of glorious armpit hair. sarah.stillman@yale.edu.

Myron Strong, 28, is a PhD student at the University of North Texas studying sociology with an emphasis on race and gender. He has written an award-winning column in college that focused on social issues and systematic oppressions. He has dedicated his life to activism and to the struggle for equality.

Marian Yalini Thambynaygam, 27, a queer British-born, American-bred, Sri Lankan Tamil woman livin' in Brooklyn by way of Texas. She lives in borderlands where poetry is theater is love is movement is song is prayer is rebellion. She looks to reshape reality seeking peace through justice in lands of earth, psyche, spirit, and dream.

Rebecca Trotzky-Sirr (rebexxx@gmail.com) is 26 and lives in Minneapolis. She is a first year medical student, organizes and writes about reproductive freedom and family justice. Soon Rebecca will mend broken hearts and arms at your local free clinic. Her 6-year-old son wants her to work in a candy shop, instead.

Ella Turenne, 27, is an artist, activist, and educator. She is currently working on her second book, an anthology of short fiction by Haitian women. She is a member of the Blackout Arts Collective, the Movement of Independent Haitian for National Reconstruction, and co-founder of SistaPAC Productions. Visit www.blackwomyn.com for more information.

Jessica Vasquez, 21, born in Tulare, California, is a fourth year undergraduate at UC Berkeley and community activist with the grassroots organization TOJIL/XMC, Bay Area. Currently, she is a research assistant for Xicana activist, author, and educator Elizabeth Martinez. Concerned about youth's lives, she fasted twenty-six days to improve education.

Marc Washington, 31, is a husband and father to his 2-year-old daughter Mia. Marc's roots are in the Bronx and Queens, New York. His activism inspired ABC's *20/20* to produce a feature named "Street Miracles" chronicling the work that happens at Friends of Island Academy.

APPENDIX

LIST OF ACTIVIST ORGANIZATIONS AND WEB SITES OF INTEREST

21st Century Youth Leadership Movement
Pine Flat Road
Selma, AL 36701
Phone: 334.874.0065
youth421c@aol.com

American Friends & Service Committee (AFSC)
National Office
1501 Cherry Street
Philadelphia, PA 19102
Phone: 215.241.7000
www.afsc.org

American Indian Movement
www.aimovement.org

Anarchist People of Color
www.illegalvoices.org

The Angolite: The Prison Magazine
c/o Cashier's Office
Louisiana State Penitentiary
Angola, LA 70712

Asamblea Popular Revolucionaria
www.aporrea.org/

Association of Black Sociologists
4200 Wisconsin Avenue NW, PMB 106-257
Washington, D.C. 20016-2143
www.blacksociologists.org

The Audre Lorde Project
85 South Oxford Street
Brooklyn, NY 11217-1607
Phone: 718.596.0342
www.alp.org

Blackout Arts Collective
266 West 37th Street, 22nd Fl.
New York, NY 10018
Phone: 212.594.4482
www.blackoutartscollective.com

Black Radical Congress (National Office)
PO Box 24795
St. Louis, MO 63115
Phone: 314.307.3441
www.blackradicalcongress.org

**Catalyst Project: A Center for Political Education
and Movement Building**
4104 24th St.
PMB #669
San Francisco, CA 94114
www.collectiveliberation.org

Central Committee for Conscientious Objectors (CCCO)
1515 Cherry St.
Philadelphia, PA 19102
Phone: 215.563.8787
www.objector.org

CISPES: Committee in Solidarity with the People of El Salvador
PO Box 8560
New York, NY 10116
Phone: 212.465.8115
www.cispes.org

Citizens for a Quality Education (CQE)
PO Box 1023
Jackson, MS 39215
Phone: 662.834.0089
cqe@bellsouth.net

Coalition of Immokalee Workers
PO Box 603
Immokalee, FL 34143
Phone: 239.657.8311
www.ciw-online.org

Colours of Resistance
www.colours.mahost.org

Critical Resistance
1904 Franklin St., Suite 504
Oakland, CA 94612
Phone: 510.444.0484
www.criticalresistance.org

Electronic Intifada
www.electronicintifada.net

Electronic Iraq
MECCS/EI Project
1507 E. 53rd Street, #500
Chicago, IL 60615
www.electroniciraq.net

FIERCE!
437 W 16th St., Lower Level
New York, NY 10011
Phone: 646.336.6789
www.fiercenyc.org

Gainesville Street School
c/o the Civic Media Center
1021 W. University Ave.
Gainesville, FL 32601
street_school@hotmail.com

Good Sista/Bad Sista
www.poetryoffthepage.com

Gush Shalom
PO Box 3322
Tel Aviv 61033 ISRAEL
www.gush-shalom.org

Highlander Research and Education Center
1959 Highlander Way
New Market, TN 37820
Phone: 865.933.3443
www.highlandercenter.org

INICITE! Women of Color Against Violence
PO Box 23921
Oakland, CA 94623
Phone: 484.932.3166.
www.incite-national.org

Kensington Welfare Rights Union
2825 N. 5th St.
Philadelphia, PA 19132
Phone: 215.203.1945
kwru@kwru.org

Latino Union of Chicago
4174 N. Elston Ave.
Chicago, IL 60618
Phone: 312.491.9044
www.latinounion.org

The Los Angeles Indigenous People's Alliance
PO Box 42118
Los Angeles, CA 90042
Phone: 323.258.8003
www.laipa.net

Malcolm X Grassroots Movement
388 Atlantic Ave., 3rd Floor
Brooklyn, NY 11217
Phone: 718.254.8800
www.malcolmxgrassroots.org

Media Tank
100 S. Broad Street, Suite 1318
Philadelphia, PA 19110
Phone: 215.563.1100
www.mediatank.org

Medical Students For Choice
PO Box 70190
Oakland, CA 94612
Phone: 510.238.5210
www.ms4c.org

MIHRN: Movement of Independent Haitians for National Reconstruction
PO Box 2626
Wheaton, MA 20915
www.mihrn.org

National Coalition to Free the Angola 3
www.angola3.org

New Profile: Movement for the Civilization of Israeli Society
www.newprofile.org

New York State Black Gay Network
103 East 125th Street, Suite 503
New York, NY 10035
Phone: 212.828.9393
www.nysbgn.org

Prison Activist Resource Center
PO Box 339
Berkeley CA 94701
Phone: 510.893.4648
www.prisonactivist.org

Project South: Institute for the Elimination of Poverty and Genocide
9 Gammon Ave.
Atlanta, GA 30315
Phone: 404.622.0602
www.projectsouth.org

Real Reform NY: Reform the Rockefeller Drug Laws
70 West 36th St., 16th Floor
New York, NY 10018
Phone: 212.613.8048
www.realreformny.org

Resistahs
c/o Tiffany King
PO Box 7782
Wilmington, DE 19803

Ricanstruction
PO Box 205
New York, NY 10012
www.ricanstruction.net

Rise Up Radio
www.riseupradio.org

Signalfire
www.signalfire.org

Sista II Sista/ Hermana A Hermana
89 St. Nicholas Ave.
Brooklyn, NY 11237
Phone: 718.366.2450 ext. 0#
www.sistaiisista.org

SOA Watch Anti-Oppression and Accessibility Working Group
PO Box 4566
Washington, D.C. 20017
www.soaw.org/antiopp

Solidarity
7012 Michigan Ave.
Detroit, MI 48210-2872
Phone: 313.841.0160
www.solidarity-us.org

Southern Echo
PO Box 9306
Jackson, MS 39286
Phone: 601.982.6400
www.southernecho.org

Sylvia Rivera Law Project
322 8th Avenue, 3rd Floor
New York, NY 10001
212.337.8550
www.srlp.org

Talking Democracy Media
1238 Dean Street
Brooklyn, New York 11216
Phone: 718.953.1110
www.talkingdemocracy.org

United for Peace and Justice
PO Box 607
Times Square Station
New York, NY 10108
Phone: 212.868.5545
www.unitedforpeace.org

Urban Mana
89 Crystal St.
Brooklyn, NY, 11208
Phone: 718.827.5577

Xicana Moratorium Coalition/Fast4Education
PO Box 2772
Berkeley, CA 94702-0031
www.fast4education.org

Yesh Gvul
PO Box 6953
Jerusalem 91068, ISRAEL
Phone: 972 2 6250271
www.yeshgvul.org.il/english/about/